PENGUIN BOOKS

Outback Heroes

Evan McHugh's previous books include travel guides to Sydney and Australia, *The Rot Stuff* and *Pint-Sized Ireland*. He writes a weekly column, 'Dry Rot', in the *Sunday Telegraph* and *Sunday Mail* and has written for television and radio. He is married and lives in Sydney. More great Australian stories appear in Evan's *Shipwrecks: Australia's Greatest Maritime Disasters*.

Evan McHugh

Outback Heroes

Australia's Greatest Bush Stories

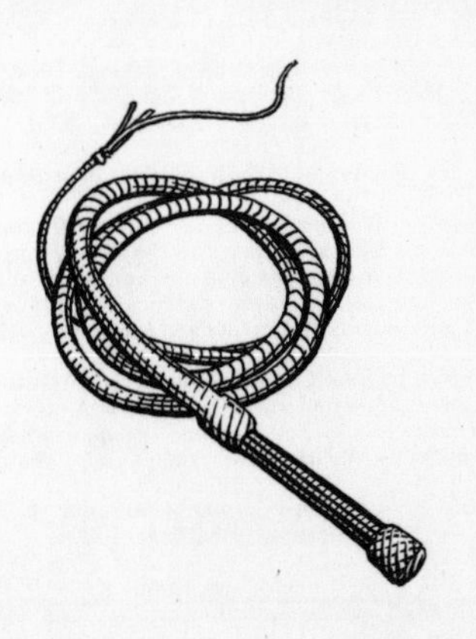

PENGUIN BOOKS

To the unsung heroes who also
built the legend of the outback

PENGUIN BOOKS

Published by the Penguin Group
Penguin Group (Australia)
250 Camberwell Road, Camberwell, Victoria 3124, Australia
(a division of Pearson Australia Group Pty Ltd)
Penguin Group (USA) Inc.
375 Hudson Street, New York, New York 10014, USA
Penguin Group (Canada)
90 Eglinton Avenue East, Suite 700, Toronto, ON M4P 2Y3, Canada
(a division of Pearson Penguin Canada Inc.)
Penguin Books Ltd
80 Strand, London WC2R 0RL, England
Penguin Ireland
25 St Stephen's Green, Dublin 2, Ireland
(a division of Penguin Books Ltd)
Penguin Books India Pvt Ltd
11, Community Centre, Panchsheel Park, New Delhi-110 017, India
Penguin Group (NZ)
Cnr Airborne and Rosedale Roads, Albany, Auckland, New Zealand
(a division of Pearson New Zealand Ltd)
Penguin Books (South Africa) (Pty) Ltd
24 Sturdee Avenue, Rosebank, Johannesburg 2196, South Africa

Penguin Books Ltd, Registered Offices: 80 Strand, London WC2R 0RL, England

First published by Penguin Group (Australia), a division of Pearson Australia Group Pty Ltd, 2004
This edition published by Penguin Group (Australia), a division of Pearson Australia Group Pty Ltd, 2005

1 3 5 7 9 10 8 6 4 2

Design by John Canty © Penguin Group (Australia)
Cover photograph by Chuck Fishman/Getty Images
Typeset in Centennial by Post Pre-press Group, Brisbane, Queensland
Printed in Australia by McPherson's Printing Group, Maryborough, Victoria

National Library of Australia
Cataloguing-in-Publication data:

McHugh, Evan.
Outback heroes: Australia's greatest bush stories.

Bibliography.
ISBN 0 14 300371 2.

1. Pioneers – Australia – History. 2. Australia – Rural conditions – History. 3. Frontier and pioneer life – Australia – History. I. Title.

994.0922

www.penguin.com.au

CONTENTS

INTRODUCTION

Throughout Australia's history, the outback has exerted an extraordinary influence on the character of its people. Its dry interior presents a vast, intimidating landscape of spinifex and red sand. Its forested mountain ranges are a dark and echoing labyrinth where the unwary can be lost forever. The outback is a place where death by thirst, hunger or exposure is an ever-present possibility. Even in an era of satellite navigation and emergency beacons, travellers who stray off the beaten track can still perish before help reaches them.

It isn't surprising then that the skills and knowledge of survival in the outback are still highly prized. And following in the footsteps of the greatest bushmen of all, the Aboriginal people, the history of Europeans' efforts to come to terms with the Australian outback is a fascinating journey, one where tales of courage, endurance and hardship abound.

Selecting a group of people who best illustrate the steps in that process was never going to be easy. It wasn't so much a question of who to include, as who to leave out. Throughout the research for this book, numerous worthy candidates for inclusion came up, enough to fill a second volume easily. Unfortunately, there was only so much space available, and while the final selection to some extent reflects my personal interests, all the choices have a great deal to recommend them.

William Buckley was certainly not the first convict absconder, but his story is one of the most extraordinary. From 1803 he lived around Port Phillip Bay, until that area was settled in 1835. Living with Aboriginal people for most of that time, he honed his bush skills to perfection, and could make an excellent claim to being Australia's first 'bush tucker man'.

Joseph Hawdon and his colleague Charles Bonney captured the spirit of adventure of young Englishmen, as well as being the first overlanders, taking cattle first from Sydney to Melbourne, then to Adelaide in 1838. Hawdon comes across as a bit of a toff, hunting roos with his horses and dogs while the practical Bonney got on with the business of droving. Yet they not only pioneered a new stock route, they developed the skills for moving cattle across often harsh country that have been utilised ever since.

The story behind the construction of the Overland Telegraph in the early 1870s ties together many threads of outback Australia – such as the development of communications and of barely explored regions, and the building of tenuous connections between the remote outposts of civilisation. The team that pioneered the route was led by John Ross, an experienced bushman, but the trip was documented by a young adventurer, Alfred Giles. When Ross outlined for Giles the immense difficulties involved in crossing the continent in search of a route for the line, Giles's reaction was a classic. 'How I thrilled!' he wrote.

For sheer audacity, you can't go past Harry Redford. More of a rogue than a hero, his feat of driving 1000 stolen cattle from near Longreach down Cooper Creek and on to the settled areas of South Australia had one immense consequence. It gave Western Queensland access to a market that has been of untold value ever since. His trial also makes one of the best bush yarns.

Jack Riley stands out as a great example of the ability of bush people to inspire. One of the leading candidates for the real life Man from Snowy River, the tales of his dashing exploits in the rugged Snowy Mountains make exciting reading, both in Banjo Paterson's poem and in the tales of the bushmen who knew him. The story of Riley's final ride, when his mates tried to get the dying horseman to a hospital, is one of the most moving episodes of the bush.

No selection of outback heroes would be complete without a swagman, and who better than the swagman of Paterson's other famous work, 'Waltzing Matilda'? Sam Hoffmeister was actually a unionist, but the events surrounding his death beside a Queensland billabong highlight one of the most sensational periods in Australia's history, and do much to explain the meaning of our much-loved national song.

Loved by some, hated by others, Sidney Kidman started his working life as a teenager trying to survive in the far outback of South Australia, Queensland and New South Wales. He eventually became known as the Cattle King, and made full use of the discoveries of men like Harry Redford and the work of men like John Ross. Yet he couldn't have built his empire without an intimate knowledge of the bush, gained from decades in the saddle.

If you read the official reports of Alfred Canning, who built the Western Australian stock route that bears his name, you wouldn't think it was so very hard. Yet read the accounts of his assistant, Hubert Trotman, and you'll discover the bush skills that saved their lives, and the sheer endurance that built the great stock route through some of the toughest country on earth.

As an illustration of women's selfless endurance amid the outback's difficult conditions and incredible loneliness, it would be hard to better Daisy Bates. For nearly half her life she camped among the Aboriginal people of Western Australia and South Australia, documenting their lives, and campaigning for their welfare. A controversial and somewhat enigmatic individual, her life exerts a fascination that persists to this day.

While all of the people in this volume exhibited great bush knowledge, many also grew to respect the environment in which they lived. Myles Dunphy epitomises that respect, a man whose love of wild places led him into the first battles to preserve pristine wilderness and made him one of the great conservationists of the twentieth century.

For sheer brilliance and bush skill, Bernard O'Reilly's search for the downed Stinson airliner in the wild mountain ranges on the New South Wales–Queensland border in 1937 remains unsurpassed. It's a gripping story of tragedy and courage, one that also galvanised an entire bush community to rescue the two survivors who lay injured for days in almost impenetrable rainforest.

Take a drive to the remotest locations in the outback, and there's a good chance you'll do so on a road built by Len Beadell in the 1950s. The roads of Australia's central deserts owe their genesis to Beadell and his team, but Beadell owes his fame as much to the fact that he was also one of the most likeable outback gentlemen one could ever hope to meet.

You may not know his name, but in the year 2000 bushie Steve Jefferys epitomised all the heroes of the outback when the eyes of the world turned to Australia. It was at the Opening Ceremony of the Sydney Olympics that Jefferys and his horse, Ammo, rode into the centre of the arena, reared up and cracked the whip that started the greatest show on earth. Getting there was an incredible story in itself.

In assembling this group of great Australians and telling their stories, invaluable help and encouragement has been given by a long list of people. The generosity of the people of the Australian bush is a legend of its own, and this book was an opportunity to experience it first-hand. Among many whose considerable assistance I am pleased to acknowledge are: Stewart Ross, Rachel Matthews, Professor Dexter Dunphy, Peter Meredith, Keith Muir and the Colong Foundation for Wilderness, Catherine O'Reilly and Rhelma Kenny (nee O'Reilly), Anne Beadell, Mark Shephard, Steve Jefferys, Mark Coombe, and the staff of the library at the Australian Stockman's Hall of Fame. The employees of many more organisations also provided prompt and professional assistance. Every effort has been made to locate the copyright holders of material, and the publisher welcomes hearing from anyone in this regard.

Writing this book has also been an absolute pleasure thanks to one of the most professional editorial and production teams one could ever hope to work with. Publishers Ali Watts, Kay Ronai and Clare Forster have been incredibly encouraging and supportive. Designer John Canty has taken the text to heart and perfectly captured the spirit of the book in his design. Most of all, editor Heather Cam (and subsequently Nicola Young) has combined the eye of a hawk with great patience and unflagging enthusiasm, and raised the standard to a level that is both challenging and immensely satisfying, making the finished product a thing to take pride in. The email exchanges have been great fun, too.

All of the people mentioned, and those outback heroes I've selected, have made writing this book a thoroughly entertaining journey. Sharing the adventures of my heroes, marvelling at their resourcefulness, laughing at their humour, has been a privilege and one that has inevitably changed my perspective on what it is to be Australian. We all share this extraordinary heritage, and in a world that is becoming increasingly homogenised, it is one of the things that still makes us unique. As I hope the remarkable people and amazing tales on the following pages show, when we set our minds to it, there aren't many things that Australians can't achieve.

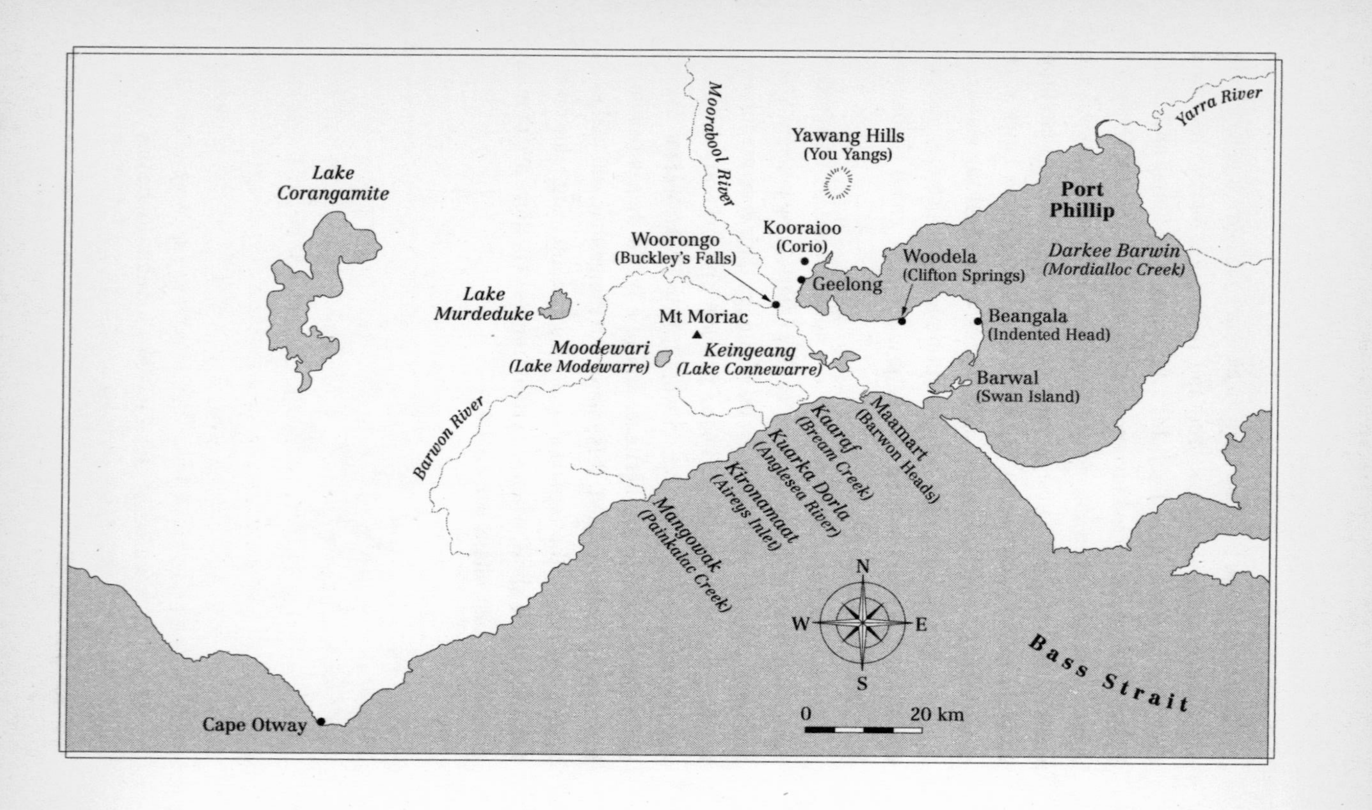
Lake
Corangamite
Mooraboal River
Yawang Hills
(You Yangs)
Yarra River
Port
Phillip
Kooraioo
(Corio)
Woorongo
(Buckley's Falls)
Geelong
Woodela
(Clifton Springs)
Darkee Barwin
(Mordialloc Creek)
Lake
Murdeduke
Mt Moriac
Beangala
(Indented Head)
Moodewari
(Lake Modewarre)
Keingeang
(Lake Connewarre)
Barwal
(Swan Island)
Barwon River
Maamart
(Barwon Heads)
Kaaraf
(Bream Creek)
Kuarka Dorla
(Anglesea River)
Kironamaat
(Aireys Inlet)
Mangowak
(Painkalac Creek)
N
W
E
S
Bass Strait
0
20 km
Cape Otway

William Buckley, frontispiece of John Morgan's *The Life And Adventures Of William Buckley*, 1852
(Mitchell Library, State Library of New South Wales)

I

THE WILD WHITE MAN, 1803–1835: William Buckley (1780–1856)

Even though they live in one of the world's most urbanised societies, Australians can still admire the special qualities of the bushie. A bushie can survive in situations where others would perish. They can laugh, even sing, in the face of adversity. They can transform whatever is at hand into what they need it to be. Most of all, they have a healthy respect for the land they inhabit, its beauty and its terror, and never take it for granted.

In doing so, Australia's bush heroes have helped to build a nation, and a national identity. For while most of us wouldn't last long in the harshest conditions Australia can throw at us, we all recognise the bushies' best qualities – common sense, good humour and resourcefulness – as national traits. In poetry and song, we celebrate them. And when it comes to defining who we are to the rest of the world, it's to the bushie we often turn.

It wasn't always so. The first Europeans to encounter the Australian bush, and so start to lay the foundations of Australia's national character, didn't do so by choice. The first of them, Jan Pelgrom and Wouter Loos, were abandoned on the West Australian coast for their part in the mutiny that followed the loss of the Dutch ship *Batavia* in 1629. More Dutch followed, in 1656, when the *Vergulde Draeck* (*Gilt Dragon*) was wrecked just north of Perth, leaving sixty-eight people marooned on the coast, while seven made it by boat to the Dutch East Indies. In 1712, the *Zuytdorp*, with 200 people aboard, struck the coast north of Geraldton. There is clear evidence that many survived, but like those marooned before them, they were swallowed up by the enormous island continent, their ultimate fate a lasting enigma.

Nothing had changed when, in 1788, Australia started being used as a British prison, with the establishment of a penal colony at Sydney Cove followed by others at Hobart Town, Moreton Bay, Perth and other locations. Once again, those who challenged the great unknowns of the Australian bush did so unwillingly. They were convicts, and it was the lives they knew (the dreaded lash, the grinding work of the chain gangs and the loss of liberty) that drove them forward. That and complete ignorance of what lay ahead. For as they stumbled away from settlements that were mere pinpricks on a continent that was vast, untamed and unforgiving, the convict absconders faced a struggle for survival that was beyond most of them. Some turned back and gave themselves up. Many perished, disappearing into the bush never to be seen again or to leave grim skeletal remains as a warning to those who followed. What those poor devils endured would be mere surmise today, but for the fact that at least one of them, one of Australia's first bushies, lived to tell the tale.

It was on a dark and stormy night at the end of 1803 that William Buckley and his fellow convicts made their dash for freedom, plunging deep into the Australian bush at Port Phillip Bay. It was the most desperate gamble that the Englishman had yet made in his twenty-three years. According to the *Hobart Town Almanack and Van Diemen's Land Annual*: 'This extraordinary man was born [in Marton] near Macclesfield in Cheshire [in England], about the year 1780.'

Buckley's most striking feature was his size. A later description of him included such details as: 'Height, without shoes, 6 feet 5 inches and seven-eights [1.98 metres]; Remarks: Well-proportioned, with an erect military gait; Mermaid on upper right arm. Sun, half moon, seven stars, monkey. W.B. on lower part of right arm.'

Initially trained as a bricklayer, he had entered the supplementary militia while still little more than a boy, then volunteered into the 4th or King's Own Regiment of Foot, seeing action in Holland under the command of the Duke of York, and gaining the good opinion of his officers. It was on his regiment's return to England that his life took a turn for the worse.

Around 1802, as Victorian settler George Langhorne's manuscript, *Reminiscences of William Buckley*, explains:

> One day when crossing the barrack-yard where our regiment was quartered, a woman, whom I did not know, requested me to carry a piece of cloth to a woman of the garrison to be made up. I was stopped with it in my possession. The property had been stolen. I was considered the thief, and though innocent was sentenced to transportation for life.

Drawing from the journal of the Rev. Robert Knopwood, chaplain and magistrate to the convict and free settlement that was established on the eastern side of Port Phillip Bay in October 1803 and to which Buckley was sent, the *Hobart Town Almanack and Van Diemen's Land Annual* goes further. It includes Buckley among a group of mutineers from Gibraltar, who 'turned out to shoot the Duke of Kent – a statement which is confirmed by Mr R.L. Murray, who was there at the time'. In fact, Knopwood doesn't mention Buckley specifically in relation to the incident, and Buckley himself denied the slur.

In any case, the settlement in Port Phillip under Lieutenant Governor David Collins struggled to survive, in large part due to the failure to find reliable supplies of good water. Buckley, meanwhile, was using his bricklaying skills to build a government storehouse. However, while consideration was being given to moving the entire settlement to Sydney or Hobart, the youthful Buckley decided he'd had enough of prison life. 'Dissatisfied with my condition as a prisoner of the Crown,' he later confided to Langhorne, 'and finding that the ship was about to sail for Van Diemen's Land, I resolved to make my escape, and if possible find my way overland to Port Jackson.'

Buckley and a small group of fellow prisoners secretly gathered food, equipment and a gun they'd been allowed to use for hunting game. Then, as Robert Knopwood recorded, on the stormy night of 27 December 1803: 'At 9 p.m. six convicts endeavoured to make their escape. They were beset by a lookout party, and one man [Charles Shaw] shot – very badly wounded. At 10 much lightening and rain.'

Accounts vary as to how many of the men escaped into the darkness. It appears that one man may have been captured with Shaw, leaving four. In later accounts Buckley suggests that he was left in the company of two men, but he may have forgotten the fourth, Daniel McAllender, who, according to Knopwood, on 16 January 1804 'went to the Governor's garden and surrendered himself'.

As for the men who continued, according to the *Hobart Town Almanack and Van Diemen's Land Annual*, 'At first they experienced great privations living on cockles and mussels, which they found on the beach at Port Phillip, hoping vainly to make their way to Sydney. One of them, however, was so ignorant that thinking by keeping westward he would soon reach China, he separated from them at Mount Villamanata.' Many convicts escaping from the early settlements mistakenly believed China was just a few hundred kilometres away. In the hope of reaching it, they headed off into the bush, or sailed off in stolen boats, only to learn the truth, usually at a terrible price.

In an article for the Royal Geographical Society, titled 'On the Country around Port Phillip', Melbourne settler John Wedge has Buckley in the company of two men, Marmon (not listed as one of the original absconders) and Pye.

In *The Life and Adventures of William Buckley*, which Buckley wrote in 1852 with the assistance of former newspaper editor John Morgan, he relates how:

> we reached to about 20 miles [32 kilometres] distant from what is now the City of Melbourne, and halted there until the morning, when we crossed the Yarra River; and, after passing over extensive plains, reached the Yawang Hills [the You Yangs], where we finished the last particle of bread and meat that we had, not having divided our rations properly, and taken the precautions necessary to avoid starvation.

They continued to the west. However, in the account he gave to George Langhorne around 1836, Buckley states:

> I wished to direct our course to Sydney, which I believed was not far off. Here we differed, and my two companions taking one direction, I took the other.
>
> When, however, I had gone some little distance my heart failed me,

> and in a desponding frame of mind I again directed my steps towards the sea.

The account given in 1852 differs on this point, stating: 'I told my companions that we must make for the beach to look for food, or death was certain. They agreed with this suggestion, and after a long and weary march we again made the shore of the bay, and finding a few shell fish, with them appeased our hunger.' Why these inconsistencies? Were they due to the passage of time and the consequent fading of Buckley's recollection of events? Or were there other more sinister explanations?

Meanwhile, Buckley continued his journey with his two companions, as detailed in his *Life and Adventures*:

> At a place the natives call Kooraioo [present-day Corio], in an extensive bay, we were so fortunate as to find a well of fresh water, and here we remained the night – the following day continuing our course along the beach gathering shell fish, until we reached a place called Woodela [Clifton Springs], signifying rock. Here we again rested, if rest it might be called, suffering as we were from the want of the absolute necessaries of life: the fish although preserving it, affecting us all very severely. The next day our route was the same, and as we saw several native huts in our journey, we were hourly expecting to fall in with one of the tribes, hunting or fishing on that part of the coast. Another day's travel brought us to a little island, called Barwal [Swan Island], which we could reach at low water, and here we halted several days to recover our strength, which was by this time greatly exhausted. We found about this place a sort of gum, which, when placed over a fire became soft, and palatable; on this, and fish, we subsisted. From Barwal, we could see the *Calcutta* at anchor on the opposite side of the bay.

However, the *Calcutta* had left Port Phillip Bay in mid-December 1803, at least a week before Buckley absconded. This vessel would have stuck in Buckley's memory as it was the very ship the convicts had travelled in to Port Phillip. The ship the absconders now saw was likely to have been the *Ocean*, which was at this time preparing to ferry the settlement to Hobart (Risdon Cove), with the assistance of the smaller *Lady Nelson*, from Sydney. As it turned out, the name of the vessel hardly mattered:

> The perils we had already encountered damped the ardour of my companions, and it was anxiously wished by them that they could rejoin her, so we set about making signals, by lighting fires at night, and hoisting our shirts on trees and poles by day. At length a boat was seen to leave the ship and come in our direction, and although the dread of punishment was naturally great, yet the fear of starvation exceeded it, and they anxiously waited her arrival to deliver themselves up, indulging anticipations of being, after all the sufferings they had undergone, forgiven by the Governor. These expectations of relief were however delusive; when about halfway across the bay, the boat returned, and all hope vanished. We remained in the same place, and living in the same way, six more days, signalizing all the time, but without success.

Buckley's account in *Life and Adventures* has his fellow escapees deciding to try and walk back, returning the way they'd come around the head of the bay. Having failed to convince Buckley to return with them, they eventually set off, leaving him alone, determined to retain his freedom.

Beset by doubts, faced with an environment in which he knew little of what was edible and where to find it, Buckley continued on around the shores of Port Phillip Bay. Not long afterwards he saw a large group of Aborigines in an encampment, only managing to elude them by swimming a river – in so doing, extinguishing his firestick.

Fortunately, it was still high summer and warm, but he now had no means of cooking the shellfish that he found.

For the next four days he travelled on, out past the entrance to Port Phillip Bay, through what is now the holiday resort of Barwon Heads, on to the world-renowned surfing spot Bell's Beach and over the Anglesea River, searching for food and water, but finding little. At night he slept under the stars, chilled and haunted by the howling of wild dogs. Then came the day when his lack of fire for cooking was the least of his worries:

> This day I was more unfortunate than the one preceding, for I could not find a single fish, or particle of any other kind of food or water, and in great pain and misery that day ended. The following was one which I anticipated would be my last, for I could scarcely move my limbs along, and the stages I made, were in consequence, very short.

Though near death, Buckley continued doggedly pushing on. Parched with thirst and completely exhausted, he came to a stream near present-day Aireys Inlet. Unfortunately, it was tidal and salty. Adding to his difficulties, he had to cross it. It was on the other side of the stream that his luck finally turned. Aboriginal people had been burning the scrub there not long before and Buckley started searching for anything that was still smouldering and might give him a fire and the comfort of some warmth:

> At length to my great joy, discovered a tree still smoking, and by this means again provided myself with a fire-stick. For a time, however, this was useless, as I had no kind of eatables to cook, and was still without fresh water. At length I discovered a high shrub bearing a kind of berry; many of which I knocked down; but not knowing what effect they might have upon me, I ate of them very sparingly. These berries I found very refreshing, and soon after I was so fortunate as to discover a native

> well near the bank of the stream, and close to the beach, in which there was excellent water – of which I drank abundantly. The Almighty indeed appeared that day to favour me – especially, as I thought, in pity to my sufferings, for I found also a great supply of shell fish: so that I had now food, and fire, and water.

Having a good supply of the necessities of life, Buckley remained at the site for some time, recovering his strength, and eventually finding a cave where he could shelter. He started to lose track of time, unsure as to whether he'd been there a couple of weeks or much longer.

When he had sufficiently recovered his strength, he moved on, following the spectacular coastline that is now traversed by the Great Ocean Road. For the next two days he found plenty of fish, but little water, until he came to a large rock and a sheltered spot with a good stream, where he established a permanent camp. Travel was now out of the question. Poor nutrition had left his body covered in sores and eruptions, and every movement was extremely painful. He managed to build a rough shelter of trees and seaweed. Then, while foraging for food, he discovered a creeping plant that seemed edible, as well as a kind of currant. With these and his shellfish, he rapidly built his strength, and his condition improved. He was starting to qualify as the first European bush-tucker man.

With his prospects rapidly improving, Buckley imagined he might be able to live as he was for the rest of his days. However, he now began to realise that man doesn't live by bread alone. He missed human companionship, even if it was intent on putting him in chains and flogging him. As luck would have it, he was in one of the most densely populated parts of Aboriginal Australia and it would be only a matter of time before the locals found him.

'Gazing round from my Robinson Crusoe hut upon the surface of the waters,' Buckley wrote in *Life and Adventures*, 'I thought I heard the sound of human voices; and, on looking up, was somewhat startled at seeing three natives standing on the high land immediately above me.'

They carried spears and had obviously seen him, but Buckley still tried to hide, crawling into a crevice in the rocks. The natives gathered round, calling to him to come out. He was trapped:

> With but faint hopes of meeting with good treatment at their hands, I crawled out from my shelter, and surrendered at discretion. They gazed on me with wonder: my size probably attracting their attention. After seizing both my hands, they struck their breasts, and mine also, making at the same time a noise between singing and crying: a sort of whine, which to me sounded very like premeditated mischief.

The three men then turned to Buckley's little hut, and went inside. Soon they were making themselves at home, one of them nipping out to dive into the sea to gather some crayfish, another getting a large fire going. Buckley felt sure that the fire was for a local specialty, barbecued white man, but instead, the crayfish was cooked and distributed among them. According to the local custom, Buckley was given the first and best portion.

After the meal, the locals insisted that the still-reluctant Buckley accompany them to their huts, which they reached at nightfall. He spent a sleepless night, and the next morning refused to go on with the men. They eventually left him, one of them returning with a basket of the berries of the sort he had discovered earlier. When he was left alone, he finally made his escape to the seashore.

Standing on the lonely coastline, he may have realised that far from threatening him, the Aboriginal men had been good company, so he returned to their huts, but they were gone. Trying to follow them, he became completely lost in the thick forests that cover most of the area around Cape Otway. For the next three days he had no food or water as he wandered back and forth through the trees, trying to find his way back to the coast and the food supplies he knew. At last he found a lake, then a stream, and good sense told him it would lead him back to the sea. Following it he at last found the shore, and soon the huts and his former home.

The Aboriginal men didn't return, and Buckley was still living in his seaside hut several months later when concerns about his food supplies and his own wellbeing started to gnaw at him:

> My clothes were all in tatters, my shoes were worn out, my health was much impaired by want and exposure, and my spirits broken – so much so, that I determined on retracing my steps in order to regain the ship [by then regaining the ship was a forlorn hope, the ships having deserted the bay long before] in the event of her remaining in the bay, and with the hopes of rejoining my companions, should they be still in existence. The winter was fast approaching, the weather had set in dreadfully cold and tempestuous, so that it was not without great difficulty I could go down amongst the rocks for shell fish, which . . . were now, from some cause or other, getting very scarce in that locality. I therefore bade good-bye to my lonely habitation and started on my return.

The journey back was harder than the original. Hungry and feeling winter's icy bite, Buckley found he could manage only short distances each day, but he forced himself to go on. Creek crossings were hardest of all, the freezing water and swift-flowing currents threatening to overwhelm him. It was while he was gathering his strength to cross one stream that he noticed the burial mound of an Aboriginal, with a spear protruding from it. He decided to take the spear, not for hunting, but to help him as a walking-stick. It was soon to help him in ways he couldn't imagine.

> The next day I reached the Kaaraf [Bream Creek] at high water. In attempting to swim across I had nearly lost my life, the stream being too rapid for my enfeebled state, so that I was carried some way down by the force of the current. I however succeeded in reaching the opposite bank, and then crawled on my hands and feet into the bush, where I laid myself down nearly exhausted, and perishing with cold and hunger, not expecting to see the light of another morning.
>
> At daybreak I went again onward, looking for any kind of food by which to appease my hunger, and at length came to a place the natives call Maamart, where there is a lake, or large lagoon, surrounded by thickly growing scrub and timber . . . I was seen by two native women, who watched me unperceived. At length I threw myself down at the foot of a large tree to rest. On observing me thus prostrate, and helpless, these women went in search of their husbands with the intelligence that they had seen a very tall white man. Presently they all came upon me unawares, and seizing me by the arms and hands, began beating their breasts, and mine, in the manner the others had done. After a short time, they lifted me up, and they made the same sign, giving me to understand by it, that I was in want of food. The women assisted me to walk, the men shouting hideous noises, and tearing their hair. When we arrived at their huts, they brought a kind of bucket, made of dry bark, into which they put gum and water, converting it by that means into a sort of pulp. This they offered me to eat, and I did so very greedily. They called me Murrangurk, which I afterwards learnt, was the name of a man formerly belonging to their tribe, who had been buried at the spot where I had found the piece of spear I still carried with me.

One of the common characteristics of first contact between Aborigines and Europeans is the Aboriginal belief that white people were the spirits of the dead, returning to live among them. Rather than fearing these spirits, Aboriginal people welcomed them back into the tribe, observing the position and relationships of the individual believed to have returned. However, it was clear to the people who'd found Buckley that he was in bad shape, even for a ghost:

> In a short time they went away, making signs for me to remain; and on returning, they brought with them several large fat grubs, which are found buried in decayed trees, and more particularly about the roots. These grubs they gave me to eat, and by this time, so changed was my palate, that I did so, thinking them delicious.
>
> I remained with them all that night, but in great anxiety, not knowing their intentions. I thought several times of endeavouring to make my escape, but in my weak state it was impossible. The women were all the time making frightful lamentations and wailings – lacerating their faces in a dreadful manner. All this increased my anxiety and horror, which was added to in the morning, when I saw the frightful looking demons they had made themselves. They were covered with blood from the wounds they had inflicted, having cut their faces and legs into ridges, and burnt the edges with fire-sticks.

The mourning continued into the next day, and while Buckley was appalled at the pain the people inflicted upon themselves, he knew there was nothing he could do. Their self-injury was an expression of sorrow for his absence, and for the terrible sufferings he himself must have endured during his death and in the afterlife.

The mourning was then followed by celebration, with a large group of Aboriginal people gathering to sing, dance and chant, long into the night. Throughout these observances, the ailing Buckley was well cared for – provided with food and warmth, his prospects improving all the time.

It soon became clear to him that rather than being a danger to him, the Aboriginal people who had taken him in were his best chance for survival. He started helping out wherever he could, carrying water and collecting firewood. Always, though, he was watched over, and if he went missing a search ensued. He was eventually taken into the care of his 'brother' from his previous life, and his 'brother's' wife and son:

> That night was another great corrobberree [sic], with shakes of the hand, and congratulation at my return. When these ceremonies were over, I went with my new relations to their hut, where they hospitably regaled me with roots, and gum, and with opossum roasted after their fashion. This was the first animal food I had taken since parting with my companions from the *Calcutta*, and it was to me a most delicious feast. They presented me also with an opossum-skin rug, for which I gave my new sister-in-law my old jacket in exchange, although it was by this time very much the worse for wear.
>
> My not being able to talk with them they did not seem to think at all surprising – my having been made white after death, in their opinion, having made me foolish; however, they took considerable pains to teach me their language, and expressed great delight when I got hold of a sentence, or even a word, so as to pronounce it somewhat correctly; they then would chuckle, and laugh, and give me great praise.

They also started teaching him the wide variety of bush skills that make Australia's Aboriginal people among the greatest survivors in the world, skills many a bushie was to learn and utilise as they pressed further into the wilds of the country. Buckley was taught how to throw a spear, skin kangaroo and possum, and prepare animal sinew for use in sewing. He learned how to catch eels and fish:

> They generally catch them with lines – the bait being a large earthworm. Having these worms ready, they get a piece of elastic bark, and some long grass, on which they string them; this is tied to a rod, and as the eel, after biting, holds on tenaciously he is thrown or rather jerked

upon the bank, in the same way as boys catch the crayfish in England. They used to take me out on calm evenings to teach me how to spear salmon, bream, etc. Their manner is to get some very dry sticks, cut them into lengths of ten or twelve feet, tie several of these together into a kind of faggot, and then light the thickest end; with this torch blazing in one hand, and a spear in the other, they go into the water, and the fish seeing it, crowd round and are easily killed and taken. This – as the reader is perhaps aware – is the general practice throughout all the world.

They cook their fish by roasting, but they do so somewhat more carefully than their other food; for they put thick layers of green grass on the hot ashes, and lay their fish upon them, covering them with another layer, and then some hot ashes upon the top.

Apparently Buckley was not only given valuable information on how to survive in the Australian bush, he was also given a wife, but the details of what happened vary widely. In Langhorne's *Reminiscences*, 'They gave me a black woman for a wife but observing that this occasioned jealousy among others of them I relinquished her to the native and contented myself with being single – this seemed to please the men much – and I was no longer apprehensive of danger from them.'

J.H. Wedge's 1836 article 'On the Country around Port Phillip' gives us more background:

The natives gave him a wife, but discovering that she had a preference for another, he relinquished her; though the woman and her paramour forfeited their lives, having violated the custom which prevails amongst them: for, when a woman is promised as a wife, which generally happens as soon as she is born, it is considered a most binding engagement, the forfeiture of which is visited with most summary vengeance.

In his *Life and Adventures*, Buckley was more casual about her loss, saying she was taken away from him by a group of men from another tribe, by force, but that the woman went willingly. He maintains that she was later killed by another man, whom she had betrayed in a similar fashion. Her activities provoked numerous conflicts between the tribes, several of which were serious, and Buckley observed that it was not uncommon for fights between the various local groups where he was living to be over women. In his *Life and Adventures*, he describes one such battle:

> I had seen skirmishing and fighting in Holland; and knew something therefore, of what is done when men are knocking one another about with powder and shot, in real earnest, but the scene now before me was much more frightful – both parties looking like so many devils. Men and women were fighting furiously, and indiscriminately, covered with blood; two of the latter were killed in this affair, which lasted without intermission for two hours.
>
> The bodies of the dead they mutilated in a shocking manner, cutting the arms and legs off, with flints, shells and tomahawks. When the women saw them returning, they also raised great shouts, dancing about in savage ecstasy. The bodies were thrown upon the ground, and beaten about with sticks – in fact, they all seemed to be perfectly mad with excitement; the men cut the flesh off the bones, and stones were heated for baking it; after which, they greased their children with it, all over.

In Langhorne's *Reminiscences*, however, he described such battles in more shocking detail:

> It is true they are cannibals – I have seen them eat small portions of the flesh of their adversaries slain in Battle – they appeared to do this not from any particular partiality for human flesh but from the impression

> that by eating their enemies they would themselves become more able warriors. Many of them are disgusted with this ceremony and refusing to eat, merely rub their bodies with a small portion of fat as a charm equally efficient. They eat also of the flesh of their own children to whom they have been much attached should they die a natural death.

While such behaviour may be abhorrent, it is similar to evidence of ritualised consumption of enemies and loved ones in many other societies, even those regarded as civilised. The Christian mass, for example, includes rituals involving the body and blood of the son of God. As for conflicts over women, Aboriginal society certainly doesn't have a monopoly there.

For example, in his *Reminiscences*, Buckley describes how he discovered one of his fellow absconders some six months after falling in with his Aboriginal protectors. The absconder was, in turn, taken in by Buckley and the tribe, but the absconder's inability to behave himself, both with his Aboriginal benefactors and especially in his relations with the Aboriginal women, led Buckley to ask him to leave. The convict did so, and Buckley heard later that he'd been killed – due, Buckley suspected, to his inability to get along with the people he met.

This was a pattern that was to become established throughout decades of European–Aboriginal relations, especially when the former found themselves in life-and-death situations in the Australian bush. Those who showed Aboriginal people some respect had a much better chance of survival than those who didn't, as the Aborigines were consummate bushies, with the benefit of over 50 000 years of experience behind them.

Where Buckley was concerned, that Aboriginal lore helped him to thrive on the abundant food that surrounded him. It was just a matter of knowing where to look. On one occasion, his tribe went to visit some friends at a nearby lake:

> Here we had as many swan's eggs as we could consume; and there were many more: they were the first I had eaten, and I thought them, by way of change, a great treat. The first day we passed at our new locality, the other tribe said they would take us home with them and have a Corrobberree [sic] after visiting the island. On arriving there we found it literally covered with eggs, so that we very soon filled all our rush baskets.
>
> We next went about 40 miles [64 kilometres], I should think, to a place they call Kironamaat; there is near to it a lake. We here made nets with strips of bark, and caught with them great quantities of shrimps. We lived very sumptuously.

They also feasted on possums (or opossums as Buckley described them), which were a little trickier to lay their hands on than eggs or shrimp:

> My brother-in-law, as he considered himself to be, had shown me how to ascertain when these animals were up the trees, and how the natives took them; this was, in the first place, by breathing hard on the bark, so as to discover if there was any opossum hairs left attached to it when the animal ascended. This found, he next cut a notch in the bark with his tomahawk, in which to insert his toe, and then another notch, holding the tomahawk in his mouth after making the incision, and so on upwards; by this means climbing the highest trees, and dragging the animals out of their holes, and off the branches by their legs and tails, and then throwing them down to me at the foot; my business being to kill, and carry them. At the former I was tolerably expert, so that he often cried out from aloft, Merrijig; which means well done. We lived in clover at this place, getting plenty of opossums, and a very excellent root, which, when roasted, I found as sweet as a chestnut, and as white as flour.

Koalas, or karbor as they were known in his locality, were also fair game: 'They are very harmless, making no resistance when taken, might be easily domesticated, are excellent eating, and very much resembling pork in flavour.'

Slightly less appetising was a species of ant called the kalkeeth:

> In order to ascertain where they are, the trees are struck with the tomahawk, and, at the noise, they show themselves at the holes. An entrance for the hand is then made, and so they are taken out and put into baskets, being, at the proper season, as fat as marrow. These creatures are prepared for eating, by placing them on slips of bark about 3 feet [90 centimetres] long and 1 foot [30 centimetres] wide, and so, burnt, or roasted. It is only for about one month in each year they can be had.

Buckley's stories relate how over several years he travelled around a wide area, but he had lost track of how long exactly he had been living in the Port Phillip Bay area, being able to gain some impression of the passing of time only from the slowly changing seasons. Winter in particular was recognisable, mainly due to the cold and the scarcity of food. It was a hard time – even for the Aboriginal people, who often went hungry after fruitless foraging.

As time passed he became fluent in the local dialect, while realising that he was losing his ability to speak English. However, when it came to the cultural matters of his hosts, he chose his words carefully. 'The subject of Religion I was careful not to introduce, as I was afraid that they would kill me if I meddled with their customs or superstitions,' he relates in his *Reminiscences.* 'I have frequently entertained them when sitting around the camp fires with accounts of the English People's Houses, Ships – great Guns etc. to which accounts they would listen with great attention and express much astonishment.'

Despite his caution, he still had sufficient courage to step into the numerous fights that occurred and try to act as a mediator. His status as a ghost accorded him some respect among the Aboriginal people, and he claims to have had some success. However, violent confrontations still took place with monotonous regularity, with the result that death or serious injury was common.

One savage battle, provoked by the death of an elder due to a snakebite, resulted in the slaughter of his brother-in-law, the man's wife and son. Few of Buckley's group were spared, though Buckley wasn't touched. Nevertheless, it was the last straw, and now well able to look after himself, he escaped from the tribe at the first opportunity. Now free, he returned alone to some of his haunts on the sea fronting Bass Strait.

He found a place where there was fresh water and plenty of fish, built a hut, and settled down for several months. Then he moved to the Karaaf River (Bream Creek) and got himself well established. Unable to hunt kangaroo on his own, he lived mainly on fish. It was in ensuring his food supply that he applied the knowledge he'd gained from the local Aboriginal people in ways even they hadn't imagined:

> One day, whilst watching the fish, I saw a great shoal of bream come into the mouth of the river, making their way up a long distance to a bend where it branches off, and where it is of considerable depth. When the tide turned, they came down with it again, and it occurred to me that if I could by any means stop them in their retreat by a sort of wear [weir], I should have a great supply of food, thus placed at my command.
>
> I caught in this way, considerable numbers, and consequently was in great delight; for with them and the roots growing thereabout, I had food in abundance. I gathered – or rather caught, I should say – heaps of them, and employed myself in drying and preserving them – many of these fish weighing three pounds each and more – being also of very delicious flavour.
>
> It was necessary, I found, to consult the moon, so as to judge of the

> ebbing and flowing of the tides; for the fish, I ascertained came and went accordingly; and therefore, in order to prevent a scarcity it was proper I should dry them in the sun, by spreading them about on the trees, and on the roof of my hut, taking them inside on every appearance of rain. There was another sort of food very useful to me; this was a particular kind of root the natives call Murning – in shape, and size, and flavour, very much resembling the radish.

Some time later, the other members of his original tribe happened to come across Buckley, and when they saw what he had achieved, were both delighted and subsequently well fed. They were so happy that they set up camp with Buckley and stayed for some time. So much for wanting to be alone.

However, tiring of the fish, and quite likely aware that utilising only one food source could eventually exhaust it, they urged Buckley to move on with them. As a group they went after kangaroos and wombats, which his tribe called norngor:

> The natives take these creatures by sending a boy or girl into their burrows, which they enter feet first, creeping in backwards until they touch the animal. Having discovered the lair, they call out as loud as they can, beating the ground over head, whilst those above are carefully listening – their ears being pressed close to the earth. By this plan of operations, they are enabled to tell with great precision the spot where they are. A perpendicular hole is then made, so as to strike the extremity of the burrow: and having done this, they dig away with sharp sticks, lifting the mould out in baskets. The poor things are easily killed, for they offer no resistance to these intrusions on their haunts. The animal is generally roasted whole.
>
> So we kept wandering along for several days, until we made a lengthy halt at Mangowak where we lived on shell fish, and a sort of wild grape which grows in great abundance thereabout. It being the

height of summer, we did not suffer much privation; for, as far as I was concerned, I had now been many years accustomed to all the habits of my extraordinary life.

At one point in this 'extraordinary life', Buckley believed he saw a creature that so frightened the Aboriginal people that they avoided the places where it lived: 'In this lake, as well as in most of the others inland, and in the deep water rivers, is a very extraordinary amphibious animal, which the natives called Bunyip, of which I could never see any part, except the back, which appeared to be covered with feathers of a dusky grey colour.'

The years became decades while Buckley lived among the Aboriginal people, or on his own, yet he encountered no Europeans other than the one man with whom he'd absconded. During this period, however, the Australian penal colonies were rapidly growing and changing in nature. Explorers discovered vast areas where European animals and farming practices might flourish, and increasing numbers of settlers were arriving to take up land grants in areas from which Aboriginal people had been removed, either by force, inducements or through the decimating effects of European diseases.

From Sydney in particular, every year, settlement spread further and further, over the Blue Mountains, up and down the New South Wales coast, and inland to vast grazing areas that extended towards what would one day be Victoria. Earlier opinions on the quality of land around Port Phillip Bay were starting to be reconsidered as Tasmania failed to meet growing needs for land. The larger world was edging ever closer to Buckley and his Aboriginal friends, threatening to encroach on their isolation, as this episode from his *Life and Adventures* indicates:

One day when I was at Bangibarra, some distance in the interior, I saw some natives coming along, one of them carrying a flag over his shoulders. On anxious enquiry, I was told by them that they had seen a vessel laying at anchor in Port Phillip Bay, and near Indented Heads; watching her for several days, they observed her remove to another anchorage, soon after which, a boat was hoisted out and all hands left her, proceeding up the river. After watching several hours to see the coast clear, three of them swam alongside, and hoisted themselves on board, one, one way, and another, another. The first object that attracted their attention was the colours; these they soon hauled down: then they purloined rope, sails, and other things they thought would prove serviceable such as glass bottles to bark and sharpen their spears with. There were many other articles they took but fortunately they were afraid to go down into the cabin, and so considerable property was saved from plunder. Having completed their marauding excursion, they carried what they had to land, and far back into the bush.

This was the story they related, and great anxiety was expressed that I should lend a hand to decoy the people on shore, so as to get them into our power, with the vessel, boats, and cargo also. I did all possible to divert their attention, telling them that if they went to where the ship was, they would be fired upon, and all killed. A few days after I saw the vessel still laying at anchor, and became almost nervously wild with desire to make myself known to those on board, so as at length to be released from captivity, and with that hope I went alone, taking with me merely my spears and other instruments for hunting and fishing. When I got to the beach abreast of the vessel, I made a large fire, thinking I should attract their attention, as several persons could be seen walking up and down the deck, occasionally looking attentively toward me, as I thought. All my efforts however were useless – the crew no doubt supposing, after the robbery on board by the natives, that the object was to entice them on shore for some murderous or mischievous purpose. I could not hail them, having lost all my English language.

Some months later, Buckley found a rowing vessel abandoned on the seashore. He thought it was from a whaler, but there were signs that it had been used as a lifeboat, with blankets rigged together to make a sail. It was probably all that was left of one of the victims of treacherous Bass Strait or the shipwreck coast (on the north-western approach to the Strait).

Buckley salvaged the blankets, and not far away found a group of Aboriginal people, with whom he shared them. They told him more about the boat. It had contained two white men, still alive. They were suffering from exposure, starving and thirsty, and it was clear from their gestures that they had suffered some terrible calamity. The natives took care of them, feeding them well on fish and kangaroo, and tried to indicate that there was a ghost like them living not far away. The Aboriginals attempted to explain that they'd go and find Buckley, but the men didn't understand and instead set off in the general direction of Sydney. Buckley later heard they'd been killed by a particularly hostile group that lived around the Yarra River.

It appears that just a year or two later the next contact came. Buckley was out gathering roots with an old man of the tribe, as he relates in *Life and Adventures*:

> We discovered two young natives coming through the marshes, and in our direction: each having a coloured cotton handkerchief fastened to the end of his spear. It was evident they had met with civilized people; and, on coming up, it was explained that they had met with three white, and six black men, they had never seen before. I enquired if the strangers had any boat? and was told they had a Koorong, meaning a ship, but that she was gone, leaving the men behind; – that they had erected two white houses, which I supposed to be tents; – that they had plenty of provisions, blankets, tomahawks, and such articles; – that they had asked for some of the Kallallingurks (tomahawks) but

> were refused; although presents were made to the tribe near Indented Heads, of knives, and scissors, and other things.
>
> The next piece of intelligence was very alarming – the men saying they were in search of another tribe, to enable those they had left behind to murder the white people the more easily, and by doing so to get possession of their property.
>
> That night was one of great anxiety to me, for I knew not how, without danger, to apprise the strangers of their perilous situation – as the least appearance of such an intention would, to the natives, have seemed like treachery. I was at a loss what to do for the best, but at length determined on hazarding my life by going to them at the earliest opportunity for their protection. So when the two men who brought the intelligence had left us to go in search of the other tribe, I hastened off on my journey to where the strangers were – which, as the natives had described, was about fifteen miles [24 kilometres] distant; but it must have been much more, for I did not reach it until the next day; the weather being cold and very tempestuous.

What he found wasn't the camp of some shipwrecked sailors. There were tents, stores, and a flagpole flying the British flag. These people looked like they were there to stay. However, Buckley knew that, if the tribe that was headed their way attacked without warning, the settlement was doomed. For a while he agonised about what to do. He was, after all, an absconder and, if caught, would quite likely still be clapped in irons and flogged.

While he considered his position, he saw a European go for water at a nearby well. While he was watching, the Aborigines who were with the Europeans noticed Buckley, and pointed him out. The decision about what to do was made for him:

> I walked away from the well, up to their place, and seated myself there, having my spears and other war and hunting implements between my

> legs. The white men could not make me out – my half-cast [sic] colour, and extraordinary height and figure – dressed, or rather undressed, as I was – completely confounding them as to my real character.

John Wedge picks up the story in 'On the Country around Port Phillip':

> On being observed, Buckley caused great surprise, and, indeed, some alarm; his gigantic stature, his height being 6 feet 6 inches [1.98 metres], enveloped in a kangaroo skin rug, his long beard, together with his spears, shield and clubs, it may readily be supposed presented a most extraordinary appearance. The Europeans believed him to be some great chief, and were in no little trepidation as to his intentions being friendly or not. William proceeded at once to the encampments, and seated himself amongst the natives, taking no notice of the white men, who, however, quickly detected, to their great astonishment, the features of a European: and after a considerable difficulty, succeeded in learning who he was.

Buckley explains in *Life and Adventures*:

> At length one of them came up and asked me some questions which I could not understand; but when he offered me bread – calling it by its name – a cloud appeared to pass from over my brain, and I soon repeated that, and other English words after him. Somehow or other I soon made myself understood to them as not being a native-born, and so the white men took me to their tents, and clothed me, giving me biscuit, tea, and meat; and they were, indeed, all very kind in every way.
>
> My sensations I cannot describe; and, as I could not explain to them in my mother tongue, I showed the initials W B on one of my arms, by which they began readily to sympathize and look upon me as a long cast-away seaman – treating me accordingly, by giving me well-cooked food, shelter, and raiment.

It took some time for the people to realise that Buckley was from the ship *Calcutta* and the first attempt to settle the Bay in 1803. The people were the advance party of free settlers of the Port Phillip Association, lead by John Batman from Launceston, Tasmania, who had found a site for a settlement on the Yarra River. He had then negotiated a 'treaty' with the Wurundjeri tribe for rights to a 243 000-hectare area in return for an annual payment of some blankets, knives, mirrors, axes and other items. It didn't take long for the people who'd cut that deal to do the maths and work out how long Buckley had been living around Port Phillip. The year was now 1835. William Buckley, aged fifty-five, had survived in the wilds of Australia for thirty-two years.

Buckley's return to civilisation caused a sensation, and he quickly became known as 'the Wild White Man'. Yet he had more immediate concerns, in particular the imminent danger that threatened these settlers. It seemed to him natural to do whatever he could to prevent bloodshed, as he reports in *Life and Adventures*:

> At length these [Aboriginal] people came in great numbers, and seeing the very few English, and small party of Sydney natives, their determination to destroy them was communicated to me, with a positive desire that I should aid them, and with a threat that I should be sacrificed with the weaker party on my refusing to do so.
>
> The policy I adopted therefore, was, to seem to fall in with the views of the savages, but to induce them to delay carrying them out until the ship [returning with many more settlers and supplies] arrived, when I said, in support of my argument, the amount of plunder would be much increased.
>
> This manoeuvre succeeded for a few days, but at the end of that

> time they became very impatient, so that I told the white men to be on their guard; and arming myself with a gun, I threatened, in strong language, the life of the first native who raised a hostile hand against the strangers, telling them afterwards, that on the arrival of the vessel they should have presents in abundance.

Faced with a determined William Buckley, and the increasing likelihood that their journey might have been in vain, the Aboriginal people thought they might go and check out the fishing in that part of the bay. When the ship did make its appearance, everyone was happy – the natives because it had turned out Buckley was right and they were going to get presents, the Europeans because they were still alive.

When John Batman and John Helder Wedge disembarked, they were stunned to meet Buckley, but grateful for the service he'd rendered. Wedge, in particular, made representations to the authorities for Buckley to receive a pardon. In the meantime Buckley acted as the settlers' go-between with the restless local population and showed them some of the local sights, as he recalls in *Life and Adventures*:

> At length Mr Wedge expressed a wish that I should accompany him on an exploring excursion inland. [At Lake Connewarre] Mr Wedge here took some sketches, and I pointed out to him the falls, near a place called Woorongo, where I had caught a vast quantity of eels. Of these falls he also took a view, calling them Buckley's Falls, out of compliment to me.

Wedge also wrote of the excursion, as quoted in James Bonwick's book, *William Buckley, The Wild White Man, and His Port Phillip Black Friends*, published in 1856:

> On one occasion Buckley accompanied me on an excursion for a week, during which we fell in with the family he had lived with. If I had any

> doubts as to the fact of his never having seen a white man during his residence with the natives, (and I confess, knowing that the sealers were in the habit of sometimes visiting this part of the coast, I was not without them at first) they were now entirely removed. Nullaboin and his family had never seen a white man with the exception of Buckley, till he saw me. He received and examined me with great curiosity, opening my waistcoat and shirt to see whether the whole of my body was white.

Not long after a supply ship arrived and John Batman went aboard, assuring Buckley that if there was any good news about a free pardon he would fire a gun as a signal. There were a tense few minutes as the boat rowed out and Batman climbed aboard the vessel. There was more delay while the gentleman opened and read the mail. And then, with a mighty roar and a burst of smoke and flame, a ship's gun told Buckley that he was a free man.

Not only was Buckley given his freedom, he was also given a job, as the Association's interpreter, on a pay of £50 a year, plus rations. He organised the distribution of gifts to the local population and to groups from around the region drawn in by stories they'd heard about the new settlement. He also put his former training as a bricklayer to use, superintending some of the work on Batman's residence.

At first, things progressed smoothly, but increasingly there were skirmishes between the new settlers and the firmly entrenched indigenous population and Buckley found himself between a rock and a hard place. Usually the Aboriginal people came off worst, but not always, as events in 1837, as related in *Life and Adventures*, were to show:

> About this time we received intelligence that Mr Gellibrand [a settler] had again arrived from Hobart Town, in company with a Mr Hesse,

a Solicitor of that city. It appeared that shortly after landing at Geelong, they had left that place on horseback for Melbourne; but, at the end of a fortnight, great alarm was excited by the news, that they had not arrived at the latter – nor found their way back to the former. Although greatly fatigued after a very long journey, I was immediately sent on horseback in search of them.

[With Gellibrand's son and others] we now struck across the country, still hoping to gather some intelligence; and falling in with a native encampment, and having reason to think it was not a tribe likely to receive the white men in a friendly manner, I requested them to remain where they were, whilst I endeavoured to obtain some information.

At first [the Aborigines] did not know me, but ran away in great alarm, having never seen a horse before. After a time, however, I made them understand who I was, and dismounting, they all came round me in a friendly manner. Just when I was explaining the object of my visit, our white party rode up, and one of them began asking questions in a jargon of language no one could understand.

The abrupt appearance of our people on horseback, so much alarmed the natives, that I could do nothing, except accompany them alone to their camp as they wished, but this my companions would not allow me, as their guide, to do, not feeling safe in my absence. Our efforts to trace the lost travellers were all in vain, and at length I returned to Melbourne to report our ineffectual efforts for their rescue.

While that search was going on, another was also being organised by a group of Gellibrand's friends, recently arrived from Hobart. On Buckley's return, they urged him to give them information and accompany them. He told them all he knew but refused to go on the trip, sure that he'd do better without an entourage that thought bullying was the best way to deal with the local population.

Gellibrand's friends were less than impressed and, ironically, the man who had survived thirty-two years in the bush, failed to detect the sound of knives being sharpened behind his back. In *Life and Adventures* he continues the story:

> I was summoned before the Commandant to give my reasons; to whom I said, those who were with me before had most improperly interfered, endangering my life and their own, by not having placed confidence in me and allowed me to do with, and say to the natives, what I thought best on the matter. The Commandant agreed with me, but the persons who had taken the affair in hand decided on having their own way; and they accordingly engaged several blacks to go with them, who strange to say, they furnished with fire arms.
>
> Three days after they had left the place, I had permission from Captain Lonsdale to proceed alone on my search; but my horse having a sore back, I was obliged to remain a short time until it could bear the saddle. In the meantime he was tethered in the rear of my quarters, where the animal was very happy during his temporary rest; until one day a native came running to me in great sorrow, saying he was bleeding very much and nearly dead. Mr. Batman happening to be near, we went away together to where the horse was, and found he had been, what is called, ham-strung; all the hind sinews of his legs having been cut through by some white, or other savage.

The horse died, but worse was to come. Buckley went to Geelong by boat to continue a search he was increasingly sure was futile. What he found, however, was that the Aboriginal men who'd accompanied the other search party had shot a man and his daughter, whom Buckley knew had absolutely nothing to do with the disappearance of Gellibrand and Hesse. Describing their murder in *Life and Adventures* as inexcusable, he wrote: 'This affair gave me great pain, because, from my long association with the natives, I thought such destruction of life anything but creditable to my countrymen; but on the contrary, that they were atrocious acts of oppression.'

It was soon obvious that, while he enjoyed some support from the settlement's authorities, those intent on the dispossession of the Aboriginal people by any means were openly and covertly questioning Buckley's loyalties. The organiser of another band of settlers, John Pascoe Fawkner, accused him of having too much influence over the natives. Yet Buckley feared the Aboriginal people no longer trusted him. In the end: 'I could not calculate on one hour's personal safety from either one party or the other, under such circumstances, for if lives had been lost, or cattle stolen, in any locality where I happened to be stationed, prejudice or vindictive feelings might have been brought into play, and I should have been sacrificed.'

In 1837 he resigned his job and left the colony for Hobart, where he got a job as an assistant to a storekeeper. In 1840, he married Julia Eagers, a settler whose husband had died and left her with a young daughter. Buckley later worked as a gatekeeper at the Female Factory. In later years, he was reduced to a pension of £12 a year, which was barely enough to live on. However, the people of Melbourne didn't forget William Buckley. Not by a long shot.

In 1852, *The Life and Adventures of William Buckley, Thirty-Two Years a Wanderer amongst the Aborigines of the Then Unexplored Country round Port Phillip*, was published, partly in the hope that Buckley and his co-author, John Morgan, would profit from a book they hoped might be as successful as the then popular *Robinson Crusoe*, based on the real-life story of shipwreck survivor Alexander Selkirk.

Unfortunately, the book's reception was lukewarm, except in Melbourne, where they weren't going to take kindly to the suggestion they'd been a bunch of murdering bastards. Prominent Melbourne historian James Bonwick led the charge in his book, *William Buckley, The Wild White Man, and His Port Phillip Black Friends*, published in 1856. He starts by questioning the veracity of *Life and Adventures*, insinuating that from his knowledge of Buckley the man was practically a vegetable:

> When Governor Bourke saw him in 1837, he could make nothing of him. A few monosyllabic replies only could be obtained. Captain Lonsdale, to whose regiment he was attached, vainly sought some knowledge of his career. Mr George Arden, the earliest writer on the colony says, 'His extreme reserve renders it almost impossible to learn anything from him of his past life, or of his acquaintance with the Aborigines.' Captain Stokes, the Australian voyager, observes of Buckley: 'His intellect, if he ever possessed such, had almost entirely deserted him, and nothing of any value could be procured of him respecting the history and manners of the tribe with whom he had so long dwelt.' We [Bonwick] lived for seven years in the same town [Hobart] with Buckley, almost daily seeing his gigantic figure slowly pacing along the middle of the road, with his eyes vacantly fixed upon some object before him, never turning his head to either side or saluting a passerby. He seemed as one not belonging to our world.
>
> When we had first the honour of his acquaintance, in 1841, he was a sort of constable at the Female Factory in Liverpool Street, Hobart Town. He had just before married the widow of an emigrant. It was amusing to see the two walking together; the lady could just reach up her fingers to lay hold of his arm, and seldom was a word exchanged between them.

There was more. On Buckley's work in Melbourne, Bonwick confides: 'The truth of it was, he was seen to be thoroughly useless.'

Yet at least three people (Langhorne in 1836, Wedge around the same time, and Morgan in 1852) had conversed with Buckley and, while acknowledging that the information he gave was disjointed, managed to construct narratives of his life that broadly agree with one another, although there are some inconsistencies.

It's worth noting that though Bonwick's book did a hatchet job on Buckley, its title gave him pride of place, setting him up as the major figure. The truth is the book has only a small section on Buckley, the main portion being about his 'Port Phillip friends'. So even though Bonwick didn't like him, he knew a good hook for book sales when he saw one. Meanwhile, Bonwick introduced a few inconsistencies of his own, writing in his derisive style, 'The Wild White Man always said that he never had a child of his own. Several parties attest to the knowledge of his children.'

Bonwick then cites the narrative of John Wedge, in which Buckley admits to having a daughter. The *Hobart Town Almanack and Van Diemen's Land Annual*, whose account is also based on Wedge, wrote in 1837, 'Buckley states that he has no family legitimate or illegitimate. He has since, however, pointed out a young woman not quite so dark as the others as his daughter.' Bonwick also relates that an Aborigine who didn't know Buckley had met his son.

When Bonwick's book came out, Buckley was no longer in a position to defend himself. In January 1856, the year of its publication, he had been riding in a gig when he was thrown out and seriously injured. He died on 2 February.

The slurs on his character didn't end there. In one of the best-known novels on the convict era, *For the Term of His Natural Life*, first published in 1870 in serialised form, Marcus Clarke models one of his characters, Gabbett, on William Buckley:

> 'How many mates had he?' asked Maurice . . .
>
> 'Three, sir.'
>
> 'Three, eh? Well, give him thirty lashes, Vickers.'
>
> 'And if I ha' had three more,' growled Gabbett, mumbling at his tobacco, 'you wouldn't ha' had the chance.' . . .
>
> As he sat there gloomily chewing, he was a spectacle to shudder at. Not so much on account of his natural hideousness, increased

> a thousand-fold by the tattered and filthy rags which barely covered him. Not so much on account of his unshaven jaws, his hare-lip, his torn and bleeding feet, his haggard cheeks, and his huge, wasted frame. Not only because, looking at the animal, as he crouched, with one foot curled round the other, and one hairy arm pendant between his knees, he was so horribly unhuman, that one shuddered to think that tender women and fair children must, of necessity, confess to fellowship of kind with such a monster. But also because, in his slavering mouth, his slowly grinding jaws, his restless fingers, and his bloodshot, wandering eyes, there lurked a hint of some terror more awful than the terror of starvation – a memory of a tragedy played out in the gloomy depths of that forest which had vomited him forth again; and the shadow of this unknown horror, clinging to him, repelled and disgusted, as though he bore about with him the reek of the shambles.

William may not have been entirely forthcoming about the fate of his accomplices, and the accounts he gave, as has been shown, reveal some curious inconsistencies. There were other cases where absconders were suspected of devouring their colleagues as they staved off starvation, yet the slur falls short of explaining Buckley's extraordinary survival. He didn't perish when his supply of mates ran out. Resourceful, possessed of common sense, and willing to accept the help of the indigenous people around him, Buckley became one of Australia's first real bushies. The way he was immortalised in literature is unfortunate. Yet as will be seen throughout this volume, another characteristic of bushies is their ability to inspire. For good and ill, Australia's literature returns to their exploits time and time again.

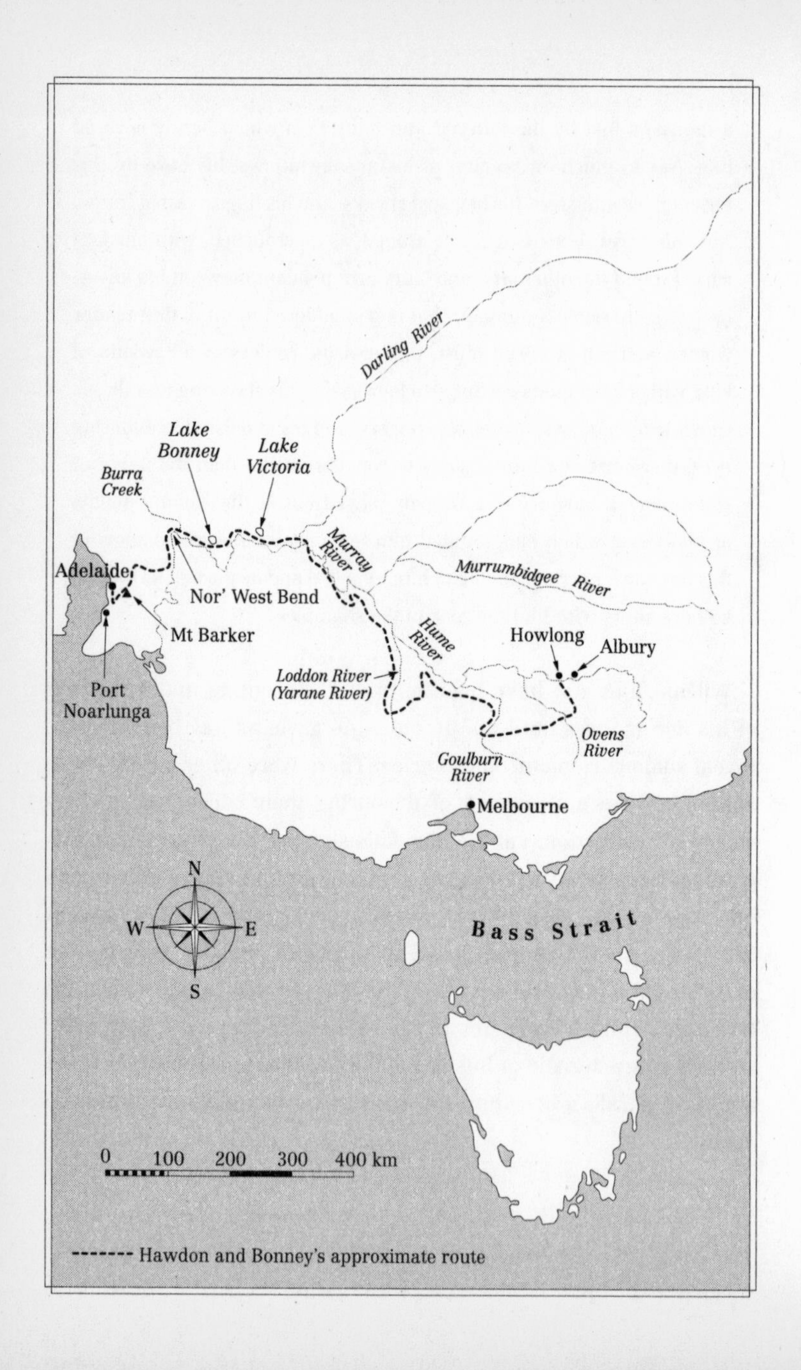
Darling River
Lake Bonney
Lake Victoria
Burra Creek
Murray River
Murrumbidgee River
Adelaide
Nor' West Bend
Mt Barker
Hume River
Howlong
Albury
Port Noarlunga
Loddon River (Yarane River)
Ovens River
Goulburn River
Melbourne
N
W
E
S
Bass Strait
0 100 200 300 400 km
Hawdon and Bonney's approximate route

Portrait of Charles Bonney, 1859 by S. Solomon. Original held by the City of Norwood, Payneham and St Peters, Norwood, South Australia *(State Library of South Australia, SLSA: B 7390)*

Joseph Hawdon, circa 1836 *(State Library of South Australia, SLSA: B 7389)*

2

THE OVERLANDERS, 1838:

Joseph Hawdon (1813–1871) and Charles Bonney (1813–1897)

Even as William Buckley was making himself known to the first settlers of Melbourne, the pace of settlement was increasing. A year after the establishment of Melbourne, in 1835, a settlement at Adelaide was begun. The tiny outposts rapidly grew as new arrivals either seized tracts of land or negotiated ownership with the local Aborigines, who still considered the European presence a novelty, and had not yet appreciated how great would be their hunger for land. Only in the unsettled areas between the nascent state capitals, and away from the large expanses of farming country around Sydney, did the Aboriginal way of life continue undisturbed, except for the passing of an occasional explorer. Yet even in these remote locations, time was running out.

A new breed of European was beginning to venture beyond the fringes of civilisation, heading across the great unknown, droving mobs of cattle and sheep to the fledgling communities. What little they knew of the country ahead of them came from the sketchy reports of the explorers. For the rest they relied on their own resourcefulness and bush skills, and a healthy dose of courage. They soon became known as 'overlanders'.

The first of them was an English gentleman, Joseph Hawdon, who hadn't been long in the colony. Born in Durham in 1813, he wrote in his 'Journal of a Journey from New South Wales to Adelaide':

> I have arrived in Sydney, New South Wales, in the Brig *Children*, Captain Durochier, in November 1834, having been induced to emigrate in consequence of the favourable report that had been forwarded to me of the advantages for the investment of capital in grazing pursuits by my brother, Mr John Hawdon, J.P., of Burgalia, near Batemans Bay.

Lured by the chance of making a quick quid, although he put it in a more quaintly ornate style, 1836 saw him on the road from New South Wales bound for Melbourne with 300 cattle:

> the first expedition of the kind ever performed between that Settlement and the parent Colony. The distance I travelled over that portion of the country which was uninhabited was rather more than 300 miles [500 kilometres], which I accomplished in three weeks and five days, arriving with the stock in perfect safety.

Young Joseph arrived just as Melbourne was getting on its feet, and he was therefore very welcome, especially as the substantial profits from his initiative, and his appreciation of the quality of the grazing around Melbourne, saw 5000 head of cattle and 150000 sheep overlanded in the next eighteen months. The value of land around the tiny township rose rapidly, and one of the new landholders was Hawdon, with a property near Western Port.

Yet Hawdon's greatest journey still lay before him. In 1837, the twenty-four-year-old came up with a new scheme. 'I determined on making the arduous experiment of driving Cattle, for the first time since the colonisation of New Holland, from Eastern to Southern Australia, an undertaking which, for a private Individual relying upon his own resources, was generally considered rash and Quixotic.'

People may have thought him as quixotic as a cut snake as he rounded up some 300 cattle for the expedition from his and his brother John's property at present-day Howlong, near Albury. The men Hawdon hired for the expedition, at 20 shillings per week, double the usual pay for such work, had a more sober outlook of a journey into the potentially hostile unknown. Hawdon wrote:

> It was amusing to witness the solemnity with which the men signed the Articles. It seemed as if they were signing away their very lives! The distribution of their labours was thus: four of them were to drive the cattle (consisting of 340 head); two to drive the drays, one to have charge of the horses; one to cook, and one to act as my body servant, having the care of my tent and its appurtenances. Each man was armed with a carbine, a pair of pistols, and a bayonet.

While he was organising his expedition, Hawdon also got the job as Melbourne's first postie. His postal service was as audacious as his overlanding – a fortnightly service between Melbourne and the nearest New South Wales settlement at Yass, 650 kilometres north. The men he hired for the job faced 300 kilometres 'through a country inhabited only by native savages'.

On 4 January, the cattle men left Melbourne for Howlong to pick up the cattle:

> After seeing the drays start, I rode on with the Post Boy through the beautiful open down of Port Phillip, by way of Mercer's Vale; a great portion of the country through which we passed being good, covered with a thick coating of grass, but poorly watered. We halted at the rich and well-watered stock station of Messrs Bonney and Burton, 36 miles [58 kilometres] northward of Melbourne. Mr Bonney having just given up sheep farming, I proposed to him to accompany me on my journey to Adelaide to which he readily acceded.

While Charles Bonney, who was the same age as Hawdon, oversaw the journey of the drays filled with supplies, Hawdon rode on to Howlong to get the cattle, and meet his mail carrier from Yass – a stockman named John Bourke. The mails were exchanged, then Hawdon and his men started driving the cattle back to a meeting place with Bonney on the Goulburn River.

Hawdon hadn't got far, though, when he discovered just how tough Australian conditions could be. He was certainly never going to forget 14 January 1838. First, he discovered the country's ability to strike down even the fittest:

> One of my men getting blinded with what is termed land blight, I was obliged to send him back to the station. This disease, which appears to be infectious, is very prevalent on the banks of the Hume [as that upper section of the Murray was then known], and frequently continues exceedingly painful for fourteen days. From this accident I was under the necessity of sending only one man forward with the Cattle.

Next, he discovered what can happen if you drove cattle at the height of summer, even in relatively temperate Victoria. Mad dogs and Englishmen might go out in the midday sun, but if they do, they're on their own:

> About noon, the heat being most intense, we halted for an hour; but on attempting to proceed the Cattle would not move. The wind began to blow with great violence, and was perfectly hot. Mounting our horses and driving the spare ones before us, we started in search of water. Our kangaroo dogs began howling and could not be induced to follow. Fortunately for me, I was riding my favourite horse, which in twenty minutes carried me 6 miles [10 kilometres] when I came to a water-hole. Short as the ride was, the heat and violence of the gale made it truly dreadful; it was like riding through a furnace; and so intolerable was my thirst that if I had to go half a mile further, I certainly must have fallen from my horse. In a quarter of an hour from my arrival at the water-hole Mr Weatherall (who started with me from my brother's station on the Hume) came up with the man [suffering land blight], when we made some tea, and rested for a couple of hours. The man went perfectly blind owing, I presume, to the intensity of the heat; we therefore placed him in a hollow tree, the best place of shelter we could find, whilst Mr Weatherall and I rode back to bring up the Cattle. We found them in the position in which they had been left with the exception of one, which, being too fat to bear the heat, had dropped dead.

Finally, the weather showed Hawdon that it was saving the worst for last:

> It was now quite cool, with every appearance of a coming thunderstorm; we had arrived within a quarter of a mile from the water-hole where we had left the blinded man, when a tremendous peal of thunder burst over our heads. The electric fluid [lightning] passed along my

> head, causing me to feel as though struck with a heavy bludgeon. Two of the bullocks, within four yards of us, were killed on the spot, one of them standing stiff and dead some seconds before he fell. I exclaimed, 'That beast is standing up after he is dead' but on looking round for Mr Weatherall I saw him supporting his head with his hands. He also had felt the shock, but more severely than myself. A second peal roared and crashed around us, killing another beast about 15 yards [14 metres] from where I stood. To prevent the whole herd from being killed we galloped among them to scatter them in various directions. One fell struck with the electric fluid whilst I was on the point of striking it. We dismounted for the purpose of bleeding those that had fallen, and while so employed, the tree under which I stood was shivered to pieces. The thunder continued rattling around us, resembling a constant fire of cannon, branches and limbs of trees falling in all directions. We remounted our horses which stood trembling with terror, that we might better view the surrounding scene. Two hundred of the Cattle had huddled closely together, each trying under an instinctive sense of danger, to screen himself behind his neighbour; the rest, in separate groups of thirty and forty, were flying over the ground in the wildest state of alarm, now running towards us, then bounding away again, as each successive peal of thunder burst.

It was an inauspicious start to their adventure, though not an isolated incident. Some years later, Lightning Ridge in New South Wales was so-named following a similar incident involving a flock of sheep. Miraculously, neither Hawdon nor Weatherall were badly injured – Hawdon received a small cut. Six cattle had been struck by lightning, three of them were dead. When they got to the tree where the blinded man huddled, they found him utterly terrified. Yet rather than retreat with their tails between their legs, Hawdon and his men pressed on.

Three days later, on 17 January they reached the place on the Goulburn River where they were to meet Charles Bonney and the men with the drays (and coincidentally 1200 sheep bound for Port Phillip). They encamped while all their supplies caught up with them, and the blind man, who had partially recovered, joined them. While they waited, Hawdon and Bonney talked over the planned journey.

In his 'Account of the Hawdon and Bonney Trek with Cattle from New South Wales to Adelaide 1838', the more restrained Bonney wrote:

> The course we had intended to take was to follow the Goulburn to the point where [explorer] Mitchell supposed he had left it when he turned to the southward after exploring the River Darling, and then to take his track to the southward, to follow the course of some of the rivers which he had crossed, and which he described as flowing to the westward, hoping that we might thereby avoid what was anticipated to be a difficult country to get through with cattle, in the neighbourhood of the Murray Cliffs, described by [explorer] Captain Stuart.

The overlanders finally set out on 22 January 1838, as Hawdon wrote:

> Entering upon the entirely new country, hitherto untrodden by the foot of civilised man . . . The distance from Melbourne 80 miles [130 kilometres], from Sydney 500 miles [800 kilometres]. At 8 o'clock the van of my party, headed by Mr Bonney, moved off in rude procession. First went the light dray drawn by six bullocks, then the heavy dray drawn by six bullocks, laden with nearly two tons [1800 kilograms] of stores; each team had a driver with the first of whom walked the cook, and with the second the servant of my tent; behind the drays went a man driving a few sheep for our supplies of fresh mutton; then came the whole herd of cattle, driven by four horsemen, each rider having a spare horse, and last of all followed the dogs.

It may have been Hawdon's expedition, but it was soon obvious who was leading it. Charles Bonney himself wrote that he 'had undertaken the duty of leading the drays and choosing the line of route, the cattle being generally some little distance in the rear'. Some distance behind them, Hawdon kept himself amused by riding about on his thoroughbreds, harassing the wildlife with his guns, and writing extensively about the journey in his diary, as on 26 January:

> The hot wind again prevailed all day. So fiery was the air that the oxen in the dray frequently fell down, and after travelling 13 miles [21 kilometres] I was obliged to halt for the day. Kangaroos and emus are here plentiful amongst the lagoons. On pursuing them with my dogs they immediately took refuge in the thick box forest, and thus spoilt my sport. One of my kangaroo dogs today disappeared, and never afterwards joined our party, but after my return to the Colony I heard of his having found his way back to our station on the Hume nearly dead with hunger and fatigue. In the evening we caught, with hooks and lines, as many cod as would have supplied a hearty meal for five times our number.

The expedition followed the Goulburn River first north and then along its course to the west until it joined the Murray (which was known at that time and along that stretch as the Hume). Bonney chose a route that balanced the cattle's need for water with the drays' preferred open and flat terrain. The extreme heat, however, dictated that they stay closer to the river than he would have liked. In fact, the country was in the grip of a severe drought, and the rivers were far lower than usual, which was causing the mob considerable stress. As Hawdon explained on 29 January, on his return from exploring the countryside: 'I returned to the party who, during my absence, had suffered one of the Oxen to get drowned. It appears that being devoured by thirst, the brutes rushed into the river before the men had time to unyoke them, and two of the men had a narrow escape of their lives while trying to disentangle them.'

While Bonney had his hands full with the cattle, the group was also in frequent contact with Aboriginal people, who weren't particularly pleased to see them. On one occasion Hawdon shot a 'white macaw' (actually a cockatoo) and gave it to an old Aboriginal man, who accepted it but continued to tell him 'Yanika', meaning 'Go away'.

The Murray/Hume flowed away to the north-west, the reeds on its banks providing succulent feed for the cattle, while the plains remained parched. Finally, the party left the river, as Bonney records:

> We then followed the course he [Mitchell] took to the southward, passing the hill he named Mount Hope, because from the summit he saw a line of trees which seemed to mark the course of a large river flowing to the westward. We also had a view from the summit of Mount Hope, but it was Mount Disappointment to us. The line of trees described by Mitchell evidently marked the direction of a watercourse flowing to the northward to join the Murray. However, we followed Mitchell's track till we came to a log bridge, which he had thrown across the river, seen from Mount Hope, which he named the Yarane [now known as the Loddon]. His grand river had dwindled down to a dry creek, with only a little water left in some of the holes at distant intervals. The question then was: what course should we follow? Go on to some of the other rivers which Mitchell had described, or return to the River Murray, which we had left, and trust no more to Mitchell's accounts? My advice to go back to the Murray was followed.

It wasn't an easy decision. Mitchell had also reported that the Aboriginal people along the Murray were particularly hostile. Yet in the ferocious heat, the cattle had to have water. Meanwhile, unknown to Bonney and Hawdon, another group of overlanders led by Edward Eyre was following in their tracks, having left two weeks after them, and was also using Mitchell's accounts. However, Eyre's group decided to stick with Mitchell's descriptions and continued westward. It wasn't a race as such, though whoever got to Adelaide first would be greeted with the best market. More significantly, the wrong decision risked men's lives and those of their stock.

On 11 February, Hawdon and Bonney reached Swan Hill, so named by Mitchell. The place was thick with bird life – pelicans, swans, ducks, wild turkeys, parrots and emus. They also met a large number of Aboriginal people who contested their progress. As the men and cattle advanced, however, the Aborigines fell back. All but one, wrote Hawdon: 'a fine fellow, about 6 feet [1.83 metres] in height, was actually foaming with eagerness to get his tribe to stand their ground, but on my putting my horse into a gallop to go up the hill to him, he also thought proper to retreat among the reeds, shaking his spear at me as he disappeared.'

The overlanders camped in the vicinity that night, during which they induced the hostile Aborigines to join them. The Europeans made clear their peaceful intentions, and gave a small gift to the warrior who had defied them during the day. Wrote Bonney: 'We had no trouble whatever with the natives. At Swan Hill we established friendly relations with them, and from that point until we left the river they always sent forward messengers to the next tribe, to give notice of our approach.'

But it wasn't entirely as friendly as Bonney's account makes out. Passing through country that was home to sufficient numbers of Aboriginal people to slaughter all of them, Hawdon and Bonney knew they had to do all they could to maintain peace. Indeed, as they pressed on the next day, they met a group of forty whose intentions were particularly threatening. As Hawdon wrote:

> We were at the moment going through a thick brush; they at first stood at a distance of about a hundred yards [90 metres] to our right, but as we passed on, the men fell back to the rear of our party, raising a loud

> shout, which was answered by other Blacks hidden from our view by the scrub. Supposing it to be a sudden attempt to attack by surprise, my men closed together with their firearms. As I came up out of the scrub the Blacks were standing opposite to my men with their spears all stripped, and threatening to throw them, and one old hoary headed savage was on the very point of darting his spear at one of my party, who in return had his musket levelled at his assailant and in four seconds more would have fired. I had just time to ride between them, and prevent what might have proved the commencement of hostilities throughout the remainder of our journey. On my first interference the old Black lowered his spear, but instantly raising it again, I discharged my gun close over his head, which had the desired effect of causing him and the whole tribe to fall back while we passed forward to our encamping ground.

In Bonney's account of a similar incident with these Aboriginal warriors, he emerges as the hero:

> I had left the drays and proceeded in advance to look out for a road, and the party had come up with a tribe of blacks, drawn up, as usual, at the edge of a lagoon, which the drays had to go round: and the blacks wishing to have another look at the strange white creatures, took a short cut across the lagoon to meet them, when our men became frightened, and took it into their heads that the blacks were going to attack them, and halted the drays and got out their firearms. The blacks, seeing what was going on, handled their weapons in self defence. Fortunately at this moment I returned, just as the fight was about to commence. Having been a great deal among the blacks, and being well acquainted with their habits, I at once saw the mistake the men had made, and ordered them to put down their guns. I then rode up to the natives, and by signs induced them to lower their spears, and so peace was restored.

Not long after this encounter, the overlanders were joined by the group of Aborigines from the night before, who stepped in to act as ambassadors on their behalf, explaining the white men's peaceful intentions to the warriors. Soon the hostility of a few moments earlier appeared to have passed, although Hawdon and Bonney remained on their guard. The importance of maintaining good relations was crucial. As William Buckley had found (see Chapter 1), once the cycle of violence was begun, it knew no end, as reprisal followed reprisal without respite.

More incidents demonstrated the differing styles of Hawdon and Bonney in handling relations with the Aborigines. According to the more gung-ho Hawdon, an Aborigine 'told Mr Bonney, as a great secret, that after dark the Blacks intended to spear us. We laughed at him, and told him that if they came near us for such a purpose, we would kill them all with our guns. I think the scamp only wanted to try whether we should be frightened'. On another occasion, Bonney amused a group of Aborigines by playing to them on a small flute he carried.

The most serious incident came on 17 February and showed Hawdon's lack of diplomacy:

> One old chief asked me where I intended to sleep; I told him when he gave me a rude push with his staff, pointing for me to return to my party; an impertinence which I resented with the butt end of my pistol, when Mr Bonney came forward, and by passing a few cheerful jokes put some of them into good humour, whilst others remained doggedly sulky. Whether their intentions were really for war or peace, we did not much care.

When the overlanders set their cattle into some grass to graze, the Aborigines set fire to it. They'd worked out what cows ate and knew they could deny food to them. For the next three days, everything edible in the direction the cattle were travelling was found to have been burned.

One thing that the Aborigines couldn't understand about the overlanders was why they had no women with them. A group of men travelling without women was, naturally enough, considered by them to be a war party; but as the Europeans were peaceful, it didn't make sense. Finally, clarification was sought, as Hawdon reports:

> One of them asked me in perfect seriousness whether the heifers, pointing to the cattle, were our wives! This sage question so amused my fancy that I called to Mr Bonney, telling him what the black had said, and we both of us indulged in a hearty laugh, on which the old fellow turned away, seeming quite ashamed of his ridiculous blunder.

Not that it was a good idea to laugh at a tribal elder. 'Some of the others began to get rather troublesome,' Hawdon continues, 'and one was nearly shot by Brian, one of my men, who saw him raise his spear at me while my back was turned.'

The Murray was by now so low that on 28 February, Hawdon and Bonney were able to cross it easily – a thing they had expected would be one of their major obstacles. After allowing the stock to graze on good herbage for a day, they pressed on westward. They thought they had already passed another obstacle, the Darling, but just 5 kilometres downstream it cut across their path. Drought, however, had rendered the river a thin vestige of itself, and the cattle again crossed easily.

At the junction, Joseph Hawdon saw the words 'Dig Under' carved into a tree. He wrote on 1 March:

> The direction was instantly obeyed, when we dug up a small phial in which was deposited a slip of paper written by Major Mitchell, dated 3rd January 1836, and stating that from this point he commenced his

> return from the Darling; that he was surrounded by hostile tribes, and was very anxious about the safety of his party at the depot near the junction of the Murrumbidgee [further east], and giving the name of eleven persons with him. I again buried the phial in the same spot, after taking a copy of the Major's memorandum, and adding to it another of my own, to the effect that I had arrived at this point in safety, and with a fair prospect of my having a prosperous journey to St Vincent's Gulf, should I only find sufficient food to keep alive my stock.

It wouldn't be the last time a bushie followed hotly on the footsteps of an explorer.

As Hawdon and Bonney continued west, they encountered numerous sandhills that made things particularly difficult for the drays, and would make travel a supreme challenge for the generations of bushies who came after them, pressing further into the interior.

Joseph Hawdon surmised that the dunes must relent a little to the north of his line of travel, and that good country might be found there. Little did he know that the country grew ever more marginal, if not desert, the further one went. However, he soon had other problems of his own. On 3 March the trigger-happy English gentleman recorded that:

> In the evening a fatal [sic] accident had nearly put an end to my travels, and to my career in this world. Having singled out a fat bullock with a view to having it slaughtered for the use of the party, I fired a ball at him, which entered near the eye, but the shot not having the expected effect of bringing him down, he made a rush towards the river. Two of my men seized hold of his tail to keep him back, but in vain. Another man was standing close by the river bank in the direct line the bullock was taking, and a tree growing upon the water's edge prevented the possibility of his moving in time out of the enraged animal's way. Seeing the danger the man was in, I also seized hold of the beast's tail,

> for the purpose of checking his career; but the man suddenly perceiving his danger, without a chance of escape, snatched a horse pistol out of his belt and fired at the bullock's head. The ball missed the beast, and grazed along my own breast! I at first thought from the sensation I felt, that I was shot through, but though the pain continued rather severe for some time, the injury was not serious. I had, however, a hair-breadth escape of my life. We at length managed to shoot the bullock effectually.

Had Hawdon or the other man been badly injured, they would have been among the first to suffer the fate of so many Australians who have found themselves far beyond any hope of medical assistance, and an inevitable and often painful death would have followed. Not until the establishment of the Royal Flying Doctor Service in 1928 did a 'mantle of safety' begin to extend over much of the outback.

In some areas, Hawdon and Bonney's journey was made easier by the Aborigines they befriended along the way. As Bonney recalled:

> The natives on many occasions proved very useful to us, and the paths which they had made in travelling up and down the river afforded an unfailing guide as to the direction we ought to take in order to cross the great bends it frequently makes. On one occasion we came to a point on its course where the river swept away to the south as far as the eye could reach, without any appearance of a return to its general western course. A well-beaten native track led off north of west, and it became a weighty question whether we should trust to the usual guidance of a native path or keep to the river. It was evident that if the path led to the river it would not reach it for many miles, and I was inclined to adopt the safer course of keeping to the river; but Hawdon thought we might venture to follow the path, and we did so. We travelled on until late in the afternoon, and still there was no appearance of the river gums in the western horizon. Hawdon, who had ridden on ahead, anxious to

> look out for the river, came hurriedly back, and wanted me to turn to the southward and strike in for the river; but I showed him that it was too late then to alter our course, and that we should probably find the river further away to the south than in the direction we were going. We accordingly pursued our course along the native track, and just before dark we were fortunate enough to come upon a fine sheet of water, which Hawdon named Lake Bonney.

Continuing westward, they again hit the river, their shortcut saving them nearly a week. Indeed the native track is still in use today, connecting the towns of Berri (on the Murray) and Barmera (on Lake Bonney), though it's now known as the Sturt Highway.

The overlanders also relied on the local Aboriginal population when they came to a section of the Murray where a series of high cliffs often barred their route. It was a constant question whether to stay on the river flats or head for higher ground, with a 5-kilometre backtrack being the consequence of a mistake. Bonney describes one of their more fortunate encounters:

> At last we fell in with three natives, who gave us to understand by signs that they belonged to a tribe lower down the river, and that they would accompany us. One of them I adopted as a guide, and made him understand what I wanted, and such was his intelligent and quick understanding that, though he had never seen a white man before, he seemed to know almost by instinct where a dray could pass and where it could not.

The Aborigine's name was Tenberry, and he would later assist other overlanders through his country.

On 19 March Hawdon and Bonney reached the section of the Murray where it turns south, towards the sea. They found they were leaving the sandy country behind and were entering areas of better grass. Two days later it rained, for the first time since the thunderstorm that had nearly killed Hawdon some nine weeks and 1600 meandering kilometres earlier. At last, on 23 March, the overlanders turned away from the Murray, striking west for Adelaide. Not long after they came to hilly country, with better vegetation, although it made their journey more difficult. Eight days of slow progress later, they sighted St Vincents Gulf.

On 2 April the men descended the ranges and approached the sea. Since their route was blocked by a steep range, the men split up – Hawdon went one way, Bonney the other – to look for a way around or through it. The former, who was successful, and was subsequently followed by Bonney and the cattle, recorded:

> On coming to the seashore we observed the fresh print of a horse's hoof, and following the track thus obtained, we came upon a tent and hut, in which were residing three young men, who were just commencing a settler's life, their chief occupation at this time was hunting of Kangaroos for the Adelaide market, which they disposed of at a shilling per pound. On my first appearing before them they were at a loss what to make of me; but on my telling them that I had come across the vast wilderness of the interior, they shewed me every possible attention and hospitality.

In a colony whose inhabitants were destined to be called 'crow-eaters', someone turning up with 300 head of cattle was bound to get a very warm reception. On 4 April, just a day after reaching Adelaide, Joseph Hawdon dined with Governor Hindmarsh, 'who expressed himself highly delighted with my arrival, and with the advantages which my arrival with stock would, both immediately, and in its future consequences, entail upon the new Colony'.

Charles Bonney enjoyed his reception so much that he eventually settled in South Australia. Bonney records how three months after he and Hawdon had arrived, Edward Eyre's party straggled into town after a much harder journey:

> He saw our tracks going back towards the Murray, and not having had so much experience of Mitchell's inaccuracies as we had found, he placed accordingly more reliance on his description of the rivers he had met with further south, and in consequence he continued on Mitchell's track, and tried to get to the westward by following the courses of several rivers one after the other, but they all ran out in the scrub until he came upon the Wimmera, which he found to end in a lake, to which he gave the name of Lake Hindmarsh, after the then Governor of South Australia. He next tried to push through the scrub to reach the River Murray by a northerly course, but he was foiled in the attempt, after destroying many of his horses and losing some of his men by desertion. He was at length compelled to retrace his steps, and after much suffering he reached Mitchell's Bridge on the Yarane, about three months after he first saw that watercourse. Weakened as he was by the loss of his horses and the desertion of some of his men, he persevered on his journey, and following on our tracks, arrived at the settlement in Adelaide free from further troubles.

Adding to Bonney's account, in his book *Early Experiences of Life in South Australia*, stock agent J.W. Bull noted the condition of the cattle:

> I must state that Hawdon and Bonney brought in their cattle and horses in fine condition, but Mr Eyre and his party, men and stock, arrived in a weakened state . . . Although I was able to put these cattle on splendid feed, it took many months before they recovered from the hardships they had undergone.

Bonney overlanded more of Hawdon's stock through Portland, Victoria, further south, the following year, finding the route much tougher due to the lack of water. One of his party on that journey was a young Scotsman, John Ross, who was to go on to perform even greater overland feats, but in the interests of technology, not cattle (see next chapter).

Bonney eventually went into partnership with Edward Eyre, and also took up several public offices in South Australia (he was for a time mayor of the inner-Adelaide suburb of Norwood), as well as pursuing a political career. He died in Sydney in 1897.

Joseph Hawdon raised sheep and cattle in Victoria until 1858, when he moved to a property in New Zealand. He, too, became a member of the landed gentry. He followed a political career while pursuing his pastoral interests, until his death on 12 April 1871.

Near the junction of the Murray and the Darling, a plaque now indicates the position of Hawdon's ford, and records the first overlanding expedition. It was by no means the last. As subsequent chapters will show, the great stock routes became the proving ground for generations of bushies – men and women of great skill and endurance. The first of them, though, were two young English gentlemen who pressed into the unknown with courage, determination and a common sense that ensured they thrived where others were to struggle or perish. They may not have been bushies in the sense we understand them today, but they certainly led the way.

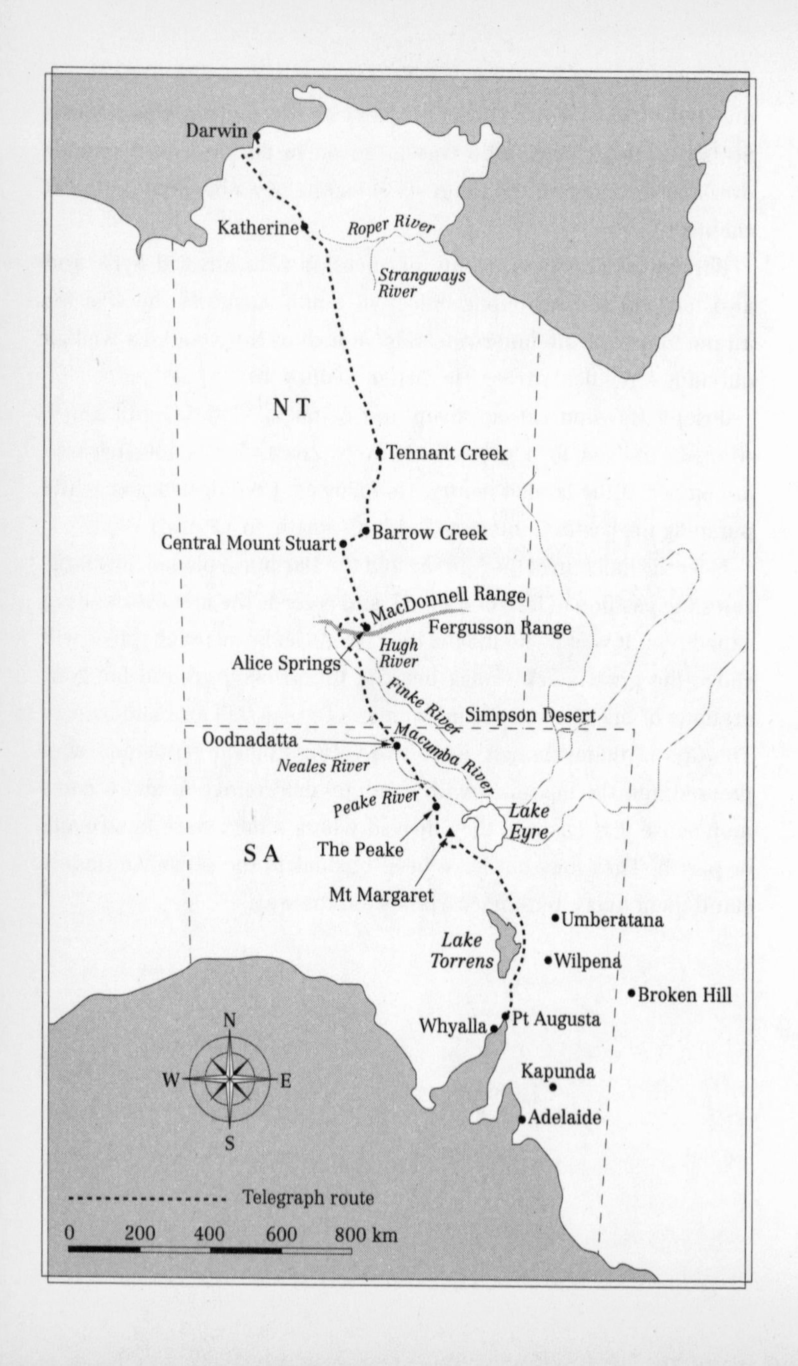
Darwin
Katherine
Roper River
Strangways River
N T
Tennant Creek
Barrow Creek
Central Mount Stuart
MacDonnell Range
Fergusson Range
Alice Springs
Hugh River
Finke River
Simpson Desert
Oodnadatta
Macumba River
Neales River
Peake River
Lake Eyre
The Peake
S A
Mt Margaret
Umberatana
Lake Torrens
Wilpena
Broken Hill
N
W
E
S
Whyalla
Pt Augusta
Kapunda
Adelaide
Telegraph route
0
200
400
600
800 km

John Ross, circa 1836
(State Library of South Australia, SLSA: B 14129)

3
THE BUSHIE'S TELEGRAPH, 1870–1871: John Ross (1817–1903)

'Are you sound in mind and limb? Can you live on bandicoot and goanna?'

The questions may have been confronting, but the questioner, John Ross, was a man in a hurry.

'I have already done so,' an eager, young Alfred Giles replied.

'Then you'll do,' said Ross.

Young Giles was overjoyed. It was 4 July 1870, and he'd just been hired at £1 a week by the leader of the exploration party that would precede construction of the telegraph line from Adelaide to Darwin, across the continent of Australia.

For Giles, it was the adventure of a lifetime. A successful trans-continental crossing of any kind had been achieved only once before, by explorer John McDouall Stuart, nine years before. Now a major infrastructure project was proposed, spanning 3200 kilometres of trackless desert, mulga scrub and tropical swamps. There'd been a flurry of activity ever since the South Australian Parliament's decision, just two weeks earlier, to ratify its agreement with the British–Australian Telegraph Company. The agreement required the line to be completed by the South Australian Government by 1 January 1872, in time to connect to the undersea line being laid from Timor. That gave the project's prime mover, Charles Todd, South Australian Postmaster-General and Superintendent of Telegraphs, just eighteen months to realise his long-held dream. The clock was ticking.

The 53-year-old station manager, John Ross, had been a candidate to lead the exploration party for some time, but had not been appointed until earlier on the day that he hired Alfred Giles. As mentioned in the previous chapter, his experiences in the bush started as one of the first overlanders back in the 1830s. A highland Scot and an agriculturist by trade, he'd arrived in Australia, aged twenty, on 1 September 1837, aboard the *Earl Durham*. Then, as he later wrote: 'I lived on the Murrumbidgee, manager for Mr George McLeay's sheep in 1837 and part of 1838, when I left to go to South Australia with Joseph Hawdon's cattle in charge of Mr Charles Bonney, and he being the pilot overland by the sea coast to South Australia.'

He'd been managing South Australian properties ever since, but had also explored the possibilities for sheep when he'd gone north to Lake Benagerie and Lake Yantaweena, where he'd found water. He'd visited the Barrier Ranges, explored the country north-west and north-east of Lake Eyre, and taken sheep to the Macumba River, in an effort to escape drought. As soon as Alfred Giles heard that John Ross had been appointed, and was already hiring men at Adelaide's York Hotel:

> I lost no time, but wheeled round . . . made a bee-line for the York, and there, for the first time, met Mr Ross, and took a liking to him immediately. He appealed to me as one bushman to another. A typical Highlander he was, standing over 6 feet [183 centimetres] in height, with a full black beard and bald head . . . I remembered that he explained the duties as well as the difficulties that might occur on the journey he was about to undertake into an entirely new country, and that I might expect many setbacks and obstacles. We might be often short of water as well as provisions. How I thrilled!

Giles was South Australian born and bred, raised on local properties. He was a bushie, as were two other young men, Thomas Crispe and William Hearne. The only member of the party who lacked bush skills was its second-in-command, surveyor William Harvey. He was green as they came, but his work would be vital in plotting the route the Overland Telegraph would take.

Three days after they'd been hired, John Ross received Charles Todd's formal letter of appointment and instructions for the first exploration trip. Basically, he was to go as far as the eastern MacDonnell Ranges in the hope of finding a pass through them and then return south in time to meet the construction parties heading north. His mission was to find a route for the construction parties to follow, timber for them to use for poles along the route, and water to keep them, their horses and dray-hauling bullocks alive.

The next day, 8 July, the party was on its way north from Adelaide. The expedition, with Harvey following some days behind, travelled to Kapunda by train, to Wilpena by coach, then from Blinman in a horse and buggy to Umberatana Station, south-east of Lake Eyre.

There, as Giles wrote in the diary he kept throughout the expedition (and published much later, in 1926):

> The outfit supplied to us by the Government was simply abominable and totally unfit to withstand the rough treatment it was bound to receive in such a prolonged trip as ours . . . the present day cattle drover prides himself on his splendid outfit, consisting of solid leather packbags and his strong and durable packsaddle trees . . . but in our case the packbags were made of a poor canvas with short flaps that would not cover the contents in the bags when full . . . Our water-bags were just plain canvas . . .
>
> If our saddles, packs, and other equipment were of the poorest quality, it was quite the reverse with our horses. They were indeed a splendid lot, and no better sample for the work they had to do could have been selected in Australia. Mr Ross knew what he was about when he selected the mob. Having been the manager of Umberatana, he knew the qualities and stamina of each horse.
>
> Mr Harvey was given two of the quietest we could find in the mob, as he was a poor horseman.

With their mounts, the exploration party moved on to Mount Margaret Station, just west of Lake Eyre – quite a journey in itself – but it was just the beginning. As with many major projects, the Overland Telegraph was initiated with an optimistic view of the obstacles ahead. Thus, when Ross and his fellow bushies, and their surveyor, left Mount Margaret on 14 August 1870, they attempted to take the shortest route north, east of the route Stuart had taken, in an effort to shave 400 expensive kilometres off the length of the line. What they found was the Simpson Desert.

'Everlasting and horrible porcupine grass and sand!' Giles wrote in his diary, his excited notions about overland adventure returning to earth with a thud:

> When would it cease? For the whole day we had been travelling up and down sandhills, and it had a most desert look about it, and no sign of water whatever. We reached [a] range at sundown, and a very high and rugged one it was, with sandhills right up to the very foot of it. There was no water for the horses, but, fortunately, we carried enough for ourselves in the waterbags.

Waking thirsty, and increasingly concerned for their animals, they pressed on. Looking for timber for poles and a good telegraph route soon took second and third place to the search for enough water to support their immediate requirements, let alone those of the telegraph crew. There was none. They did, however, startle an Aborigine who'd been catching goannas. The presence of a man meant there had to be water nearby, but they were unable to find it. That night when they camped, the horses had been two days without a drink. The men drank the small amount they had left for themselves, knowing that from then on they were in the same plight as their mounts. The next day's diary entry was all about water:

> Mr Ross sent me to follow up a gum creek to search for water. I followed it up among the ranges, and passed blacks' camps about a fortnight old, with their pads leading to places where they had been getting water, but which were now all dry. Mr Ross followed the creek out on to the plain, but neither of us found water. We then struck out in a direction we had noticed smoke on the previous day, and after going round the range we could see smokes at no great distance ahead. This gave us hopes that we were not far from water, for, as we often used to say, 'where there is smoke there is fire, and where there is fire there are blacks, and where there are blacks there is water' . . . We kept straight on for a peaked hill, where on reaching we also found a large creek with magpies and black cockatoos flying about, but not a drop of water. Hobbling out the poor horses, Mr Ross, Hearne, and myself went out in

> search of it. I took the shovel to dig in the sand, but all returned at dark with the same tale of no water. This was the third night our poor horses went without a drink of water, and we had not had a drop that day ourselves or a mouthful of food. It was a most extraordinary country, showing all signs of water, but none was to be found . . . Daylight had scarcely appeared when Mr Ross and Hearne mounted their horses and started away down the creek, in the direction where we had seen the blackfellow on the previous day, in search of water. To our extreme delight they returned in about three hours with a bag of water each, and tidings of plenty more where they had got it. They also reported having surprised two camps of natives, who bolted in every direction at their approach.

The expedition returned to the waterhole, the horses getting their first drink for three days, the men for a day and a half. Soon, though, they discovered that out in a desert every drop of water belongs to someone. When the Aboriginal people who'd been surprised realised that the white men had increased in number and brought their horses to drink their water as well, they regrouped on top of a nearby hill. As Giles recorded:

> Their chief signs conveyed to us appeared to be an urgent demand for us to depart, and more particularly our horses, of which they seem to have had the greater dread. Mr Ross, on the other hand, endeavoured to get them by signs to come down, but they did not, or would not, understand, and repeatedly pointed to us, and then to the horses, which they did not like going near the water.

The exploration party remained at the waterhole, which was also used by huge numbers of birds, especially pigeons. The men shot thirty-six 'flock pigeons', which they boiled to take with them as they headed north. It wasn't bandicoot or goanna, but it wasn't far off.

The exploration eventually reached the MacDonnell Ranges, some 800 kilometres north of Mount Margaret. The MacDonnells are a rampart of barren crags that form a barricade to north–south travel in Central Australia. For several days the men searched in the Fergusson Range, now known as the Eastern MacDonnells, for a much-needed pass through which the supply trains could travel. All they found were awesome cliffs of sun-baked red stone, deep and shadowy gorges, spinifex and dry creek beds.

They again found themselves short of water, the horses going without for two days. The hot days, the search for water and digging in dry creek beds added to their suffering. Finally, they turned back to a water source they'd found previously:

> We kept a south-east course, making for the gorge we had entered on striking the Giles Creek [a tributary of the Todd River that Ross had named after Alfred Giles], three days before, and where we knew we would get water. Upon reaching the gorge we found Mr Ross waiting for us, and there at a point of a cliff was a little hole a foot or more deep, sunk in the sand, and full of delicious cold water. With a quart of it in my hand, I said to my companions, 'See that cliff up there? If it was solid gold I would not exchange it for this quart of water.'

Giles should have dug around a bit. At the time he wasn't far from what was to become the Arltunga gold diggings.

It was on their way south, again travelling through the western reaches of the forbidding Simpson Desert, with its rank upon rank of red sandhills and spinifex, that the men were to be reminded just how precious water could be. On this occasion Giles wrote:

> While having breakfast one morning we noticed four blacks poking their heads over a hill in front of our camp. We made signs to them, which they answered. Their appearance assured us that water was

> not far distant, and Mr Ross, Hearne, and I mounted our horses and struck off in different directions in search of water. Mr Ross met with most success, a mile and a half [2.4 kilometres] from our camp. We surprised a mob of blacks – five men, two or three women, and about a dozen piccaninnies – but their only water was a muddy claypan, and they had most ingeniously made the water to filter through sand by digging holes on the upper side of the claypan. Mr Ross got off his horse to fill a waterbag, but while in the act of doing so he became sensible of something from behind, and was surprised on looking around to see three savages flourishing their spears and waddies, and making signs to him to go away, which he very prudently did without firing at them. The fact of about a dozen blacks subsisting upon so precarious a water supply proved beyond doubt its scarcity in their neighbourhood, and the hostile attitude in which they placed themselves can be attributed solely to that cause, and not to any hatred, but to guard their precious supply, which was threatened by an enormous animal and its rider which they had never previously looked upon.

After considerable hardship, and a sightseeing trip to Chambers Pillar, the men reached the Hugh and Finke rivers. It was mid-October, and they were out of everything except flour for making damper. Giles was so desperate for a cup of tea that he scraped together all the dust and grains in the bottom of the tea box to make a weak brew. As he'd written earlier, when they'd been soaked by a sudden storm, 'Bushmen are possessed of a large stock of patience, especially when their favourite pot of tea hangs at the end of a lucifer match.'

The men returned to civilisation, in the form of the Peake Station, west of Lake Eyre, on 19 October. While the other men recuperated, John Ross and William Harvey went on to Mount Margaret Station. At a meeting with Todd on 24 October, they explained where they'd been, and strongly advised, 'Don't go there.' The desired shortest route would see the line pass through waterless, burning desert. Better to follow the Neales River up from Lake Eyre to the Macumba, then head for the Finke and the Hugh. The bushies were starting to appreciate that water, more than anything else, was going to decide the route of this section of the telegraph.

Back at the Peake, Giles also wrote of his lost illusions: 'So far as we had been and seen of the interior, it meant facing tremendous and unforeseen difficulties.' He didn't know the half of it. He'd been travelling in the cooler months of winter and spring. Yet as bullock drays and men arrived, ready to push north along the just-established route, he and the men in the spearhead of the project prepared for their second expedition north, in the fierce heat of summer.

All the time, supplies poured into the Peake. One consignment was of tinned beef from Booyoolee Station. It was as tough as the tins it came in. The men first referred to it as Booyoolee Beef, then, when they realised just how tough it was, Bully Beef. The camp also received camels and Afghan camel drivers, who would become famous in their own right throughout the Centre.

The search for a pass through the MacDonnell Ranges now loomed large in the Overland Telegraph's priorities. The line was getting closer to the mountains every day, and no way through had yet been found. Todd was still determined that it should pass through the Eastern MacDonnells, and he issued instructions to John Ross on 15 November 1870 to that effect:

> No effort should be spared to find a good route on this course, but should the result of your outward exploration north of the Fergusson Range [the Eastern MacDonnells] be not sufficiently encouraging, you are to return from Mt Gwynne or thereabouts, along Stuart's route

> [through the even more daunting Western MacDonnells] carefully examining the country on either side . . .

Despite having given the Eastern MacDonnells a pretty thorough exploration, John Ross and his men set off again, on 16 November, heading up the Alice Creek, an offshoot of the Hugh, then skirting the fearful Simpson, and heading into the region of their previous expedition. At their previous camp on Giles Creek they met Aboriginal people, who they were able to entice into camp, including one of the elders. Giles wrote:

> Mr Ross made the old man a present of a brand-new and bright tomahawk, which he examined very carefully, feeling the bright steel edge, and, no doubt, wondering what sort of stone it could be. After he had examined it, he returned it to Mr Ross, seemingly unaware of its use. Mr Ross told me to go and lop off a small limb of a tree near by, which I did with one blow, to the astonishment of the old savage, who examined the limb and then eagerly took back the tomahawk.

The country was not so amenable, as Giles explained:

> Near the Finke we were at war with the ants. The whole country was black with the little pests, and regiments invaded every nook and crevice. We had to spread hot ashes across our paths.
>
> Another event occurred that day that might have proved more serious. Crispe and I were sitting down by a packbag when I noticed, as I thought, a large snake curled under the bag, but on turning it over we found it to be a death adder of a light orange colour with hook [sic] on its tail and black rings around its body. It must have been within 6 inches [15 centimetres] of Crispe's foot, and was some 18 inches [45 centimetres] long. I broke its back, chopped off its tail, and put it in the fire.

Soon John Ross and his men were to discover just how tough the Centre could be, on man and beast. By 9 December summer was upon them and the day was terribly hot. They were again without water. In the afternoon, they made camp, then fanned out in search of it. Giles got caught by darkness and only just found his way back, parched with thirst and hoping someone had been luckier than he had:

> The first glance at the camp fire told me it was a dry camp. Mr Ross had been up to the old Warlock Swamp, but had found it and others all dry, and, what was worse, the waterbags were all nearly empty, leaking through the rubbishy canvas. We unrolled our swags and flung ourselves on the blankets, drank half a pint of water each, and slept until morning without eating anything. We were all very thirsty. It had been a fearfully hot day, and we had come 30 miles [48 kilometres].

According to modern medical knowledge the first symptom of dehydration comes with a loss of just 1 per cent of body fluid, or about half a litre for the average person. You start getting thirsty. With a loss of 2 per cent, the thirst grows stronger, appetite is lost and the body feels discomfort. The men were clearly at that stage when they went to bed. The next day was to get much worse. In the morning:

> Our horses looked miserable and tucked up, and apparently had not fed very much during the night, as the feed was very dry, and they were very thirsty after the previous day's long and terribly hot journey. We kept following up this dry creek. The weather was frightfully hot. Mr Ross left us, going towards a low range, and shortly afterwards Hearne left, and a little later Crispe – all in search of water. Mr Harvey kept the course and the lead, while I drove the mob of packhorses behind him until about 3 p.m., when so scorching and burning was the

> sun that the horses kept clustering under every shady tree, and my thirst was increased by my shouting at the poor brutes to get them along.

At 3 per cent fluid loss, the mouth becomes dry. At 4 per cent, you'll feel sleepy, apathetic, nauseous and suffer headaches. Giles's journal notes:

'Mr Harvey was so exhausted that we both got off our horses; we felt so weak. We stopped for half an hour. The horses clustered together nose to nose, and sucked each other's breath – a thing I had never seen or heard of before.'

At 5 per cent concentration wanders. At this stage Giles comments that Harvey was weak and dizzy, and said he was unsure he could follow the right course. Anyone who's had a taste of Central Australia's heat would be aware of the danger the men were in. Where the low scrub provides no shade at all, the sun not only beats down from the sky, it reflects up off the rocks and sand, doubling its intensity.

With a fluid deficit of 8 per cent the symptoms – some of which Giles observed in Harvey – are dizziness, mental confusion, weakness, mumbled speech and laboured breathing. Over 10 per cent fluid loss, there are muscle cramps, delirium and the tongue swells. Then they would be in danger of kidney failure and death. In the heat that Giles described, it wasn't far off.

With the other men searching all around them, Giles and Harvey raised themselves and pushed on. They had just got going when Giles exclaimed: 'There's a smoke! A smoke!'

It was some way off, but Giles tried to encourage Harvey to an extra effort to reach it.

'It might only be blacks,' the surveyor replied disconsolately.

'Well,' Giles said, 'you know where there's smoke there is fire, and where there is fire there are blacks, and where there are blacks there is water.'

Giles felt certain it was a smoke signal from John Ross, that the bushie with the uncanny knack of finding water had done it again. After a while they reached another creek that had a rocky bottom and tea-tree along its banks. Even better, there were doves, crows and parrots flying about. Then Giles spotted a tiny diamond sparrow. As he wrote: 'A sure sign of nearness of water, although often only a very small supply. There also was the fire blazing up not half a mile [800 metres] down the creek. Crispe overtook us. Both he and his mare knocked up. He, too, had seen the signal, and steered for it.'

As they staggered forward, they saw John Ross coming towards them. To their great relief he called out to them, 'Plenty of good water just ahead.'

Giles felt compelled to explain the circumstances that had got them into such a dire condition so quickly. It is as valid today as it was in 1870:

> Readers of this, whoever they may be, and whether they ever have or have not felt the pangs or, I might say, the agonies of thirst, will understand with what joy and thankfulness we listened to those few magic words . . . To city dwellers, and even to some bushmen, it might appear that the sufferings of ourselves and horses for want of water during only some 36 hours might appear extraordinary, and even exaggerated, but bushmen generally will quite understand and confirm that while on our former expedition we were 72 hours without water, we did not suffer one-quarter as much as we did on this 36 hours' trip, and this was only and entirely accountable to the difference in temperature.

The parched Eastern MacDonnells still refused to give up a suitable route for the telegraph. As John Ross wrote in a diary written some years after the journey, 'the mountains at the head of the Todd and the Fergussons are impassable for teams of any kind. It gives us enough to do to get our pack horses over the Ranges, and Stuart speaks of the ranges at the head of the Hugh as being equally impassable.'

Unable to find a suitable route, John Ross pushed on to the north of the ranges, seeking water sources. By the end of December, they were nearing the northern limit of their trip, knowing that their southern journey would be well west of the desired route of the telegraph line, through the Western MacDonnells that Stuart had described.

On New Year's Day 1871, they were close to the route Stuart had taken north and south nine years previously. Then, incredibly, they found his party's tracks, which they followed for nearly 2 kilometres. If they wanted an indication of how little it rained in the area, it lay in these tracks that hadn't been washed out in nearly a decade. For a while they were quite literally following in the footsteps of the explorer.

Not long after, Harvey made an announcement, as Giles records:

> 'Well, comrades,' he said brightly, 'You see yonder mountain. That is Central Mount Sturt, discovered and named by John Ross McDouall Stuart, who led the first exploring party across Australia from south to north and back again. Our party is the second to sight it since he named it ten years ago. To-night or to-morrow we shall reach it, and I think that this being a very special occasion we ought to celebrate it by drinking someone's health and one another's too.'

Then the man who had almost died of thirst a few weeks before reached into his swag, pulled out a package wrapped in a shirt, and unwrapped a bottle of overproof rum. The bushies eagerly clustered around what was certainly the only bottle of grog in the entire Red Centre. They drank John Ross's health, and each others'. Giles wrote:

> None of us had the slightest suspicion that such a beverage was within 1000 miles [1600 kilometres] of us, and it certainly was a marvel to us how Mr. Harvey had carried it safely all those hundreds of miles,

> through dense scrub, rocky gorges, and bumping against trees and anthills without smashing it.

The bushies, and their surveyor, later ascended the mountain and located the stone cairn Stuart had erected. They found a bottle Stuart had left, containing a message for those who came after him. John Ross didn't open it, but eventually returned it to Charles Todd. It read:

> John Ross McDouall Stuart and party consisting of two men and himself arrived from Adelaide in the Centre of Australia on Saturday evening the twenty-first day of April 1860, and have built this cone of stones and raised this flag to commemorate the event, on the top of Mount Sturt. The Centre is about 2 miles [3 kilometres] south, south-west at a small gum creek where there is a tree marked facing south.
> John Ross McDouall Stuart, Leader
> William Darton Kekwick
> Benjamin Head
> 21 April 1860 Centre of Australia

On 5 January John Ross and his men left Mount Sturt – which was named by John McDouall Stuart after explorer Charles Sturt, but which is known these days as Central Mount Stuart. Water continued to be a major problem, but the bushies were by now adept at finding it by watching birds in flight, especially those that couldn't go far without a drink. Thousands flying in one direction could mean only one thing.

Following Stuart's route south, they found themselves among tea-tree gorges and gullies, where water was plentiful, if you knew where to look. They reached the first steep ramparts of the Western MacDonnells on 13 January, and took the day off. The hills might be rugged, but there was plenty to eat. John Ross got them fresh meat in the form of a euro (wallaroo) and a rock wallaby. As Giles put it, 'We emptied a bucketful of delicious wallaby soup, pronounced by all to be unbeatable among soups.'

However, one thing was lacking in their diet: green vegetables. The lack of vitamin C was especially telling on John Ross, who often ranged far beyond the men and the packhorses, seeking water, poles and a good route for the telegraph. His health was suffering, which may explain why he didn't ride out on the search that followed the loss of their surveyor on 14 January. Harvey had ridden a short distance away from the party to get a second bearing on their course, and hadn't returned. The bushies made camp and waited, assuming Harvey would realise he'd gone the wrong way, turn around and follow his and their tracks back to them. Night fell. No Harvey.

At dawn, there was still no sign. Ross set off up a creek, on foot, while Hearne rode back along their tracks. Nothing. The bushies were getting concerned. They all knew what they should do in such a situation, but as Giles wrote:

> It was hard to conceive what an inexperienced bushman might do, but [Harvey] must surely recognize that he must reverse his course. We feared if he were not found that day he would be completely exhausted, as he was rather of an excitable nature, not an experienced bushman, and not one who could withstand unusual hardship. The worst of it, too, was the fact that we had scarcely a horse fit to look for him, as they were so tender-footed and the country so terribly stony that it was difficult to get them along at all.

At dusk, Hearne and Crispe (who had also ridden out) returned. They'd tracked Harvey for nearly 20 kilometres along the range. He didn't appear to have camped or turned back. His horse had thrown all its shoes, but still he'd kept going. That night he still didn't return, and at dawn everyone set out again. John Ross remained in camp, possibly as his health wasn't good, in case Harvey returned.

Finally, the bushies found where Harvey had turned around on his tracks. Then it became clear he'd been confused by the crisscrossing tracks of the searchers. As the bushies rode back and forth like bloodhounds on his scent, he finally found the camp on his own, just on lunchtime, utterly exhausted. Ross gave him a shot of rum, some coffee and stewed wallaby. By the time the others returned, he was tucked in a swag, sound asleep.

The episode had sorely tested both horses and men. The packhorses having become scattered, the bushies took the next day off while they found them, and everyone recovered. Yet their rations were now running very low. They'd been travelling for nine weeks, and had supplies left for only one.

When they got going, they had an encounter with an Aborigine who set fire to the grass in front of them, in an attempt to hinder their progress. Then, wrote Giles: 'We passed through terribly rough country, and our poor horses were sore-footed and limped along like cats on hot bricks. It will take some fossicking to find a route for the telegraph line through these wonderful ranges.'

John Ross was more pessimistic, writing: 'It is not possible to bring the line through this mass of precipitous mountains.'

It wasn't good news to be bringing back to the lead camps of the telegraph, but first they had to get there. Out of flour, dried beef and coffee, they had a handful of tea and two kilograms of oatmeal between the five of them. They were also out of gunpowder, and could only watch potential meals wing past unmolested. As Giles put it:

> Should there be no-one at Alice Creek we would be approaching the starving stage. We were about 18 miles [29 kilometres] from Alice Creek, but were doubtful whether we would find anybody there. Upon our arrival we were disappointed to find no-one there, nor any message for us as to where to find them with the provisions. We rested there a short time, and then started down the Hugh, and at 9 miles [15 kilometres] reached our

> old camp, and managed to catch a dozen or two of fish . . . One more pot of oatmeal, and we would have to subsist on roots and lizards . . .

John Ross's question back in Adelaide months before, about eating bandicoot and goanna, was looking less and less like a joke. While starvation loomed, the men faced more immediate concerns. That night they heard a cooee and five Aboriginal men strolled into camp. Three of them they'd met before and the greetings were friendly, but the bushies feared the Aborigines' intentions. As darkness had fallen they motioned them to leave, and gave them firesticks to light their way, but the men only camped some 30 metres away. The nervous Europeans assigned watches before going to bed. As Giles's journal makes clear, this was a prudent move, particularly as they had so little left to lose to a raid:

> During Crispe's watch, from 10 to midnight, he noticed one fellow creeping about the row of packsaddles. On seeing Crispe he sneaked back to his mates . . . The best way to handle wild blacks is never to allow them within spear distance of the camp. We could have got rid of them quicker by sharp and rougher methods, but our instructions were to treat them as peaceably as possible everywhere, especially, as the first party through, we should set the best example possible for the sake of those to follow.

Finally, on 26 January 1871, the bushies and their surveyor found the tracks of the supply party and followed them back to their camp near the junction of the Finke and Hugh rivers.

The lack of a route through the MacDonnell Ranges was now looming as a crisis. A way had to be found, and despite having followed Todd's instructions scrupulously, John Ross and his men were criticised. One letter writer from The Depot, the forward base at the Hugh and Finke, said:

> His previous explorations have not been of the least service to us, nearly every inch of the road being over new country, and it will be so right on . . . The delay – the whole of which may be fairly attributed to Mr Ross – will tell heavily on us, and especially the further sections.

It was partly true, but written by someone who wasn't dying of thirst in the Simpson Desert, as they might have been but for the explorations of John Ross and his team. The bushies, and their surveyor, meanwhile, had their own problems. Harvey, the well-educated lowland Scot, and John Ross, the practical highlander, had reached the point where they couldn't face another expedition together. John Ross probably found Harvey an impediment, if not a dangerous liability. Harvey may have found life in the wilderness more than he could handle. Whatever the reasons, Harvey decided to leave and efforts began to find a replacement.

North of The Depot, activity was intensifying. Several parties were probing the MacDonnells, seeking a route through, while John Ross and the others prepared for the major trip all the way through to the Roper River, in the Northern Territory's Top End. Their third trip would link the northward advance of the telegraph with the line being driven south from the tiny outpost at Port Darwin.

Life at The Depot, though, was no picnic, as Giles recorded:

> The flies were an awful pest, driving the horses nearly mad . . . Nearly everyone had bunged-up eyes; the flies were a constant torment and nearly all the party were attacked by severe vomiting . . . Life in the interior is all right, but one wanted to keep moving; it was less exhausting than idle camp life, and it dodged the flies . . . I was about to step

> on a large snake in the dark and close to the camp fire, but I just saw it in time. The scorpions there were an enormous size, and I was stung twice within 15 minutes at Mr Knuckey's camp – on my arm and back of the neck. The sting is very painful, like a coal of fire, and lasts for about 20 minutes, but fortunately they were not large ones.

On 9 February 1871, G.R. McMinn and W. Whitfield Mills set out specifically to look for a route through the MacDonnells. Without instructions to search to the east or west, they went straight up the middle. They split up and soon found themselves pinned down by, of all things, severe storms and floods. McMinn, however, managed to get a brief view from Simpsons Gap of the MacDonnells to the east of Stuart's track, and the country looked promising.

The parties returned to The Depot with the news; then Mills set out again to confirm the possibility of a route. Finally, in a letter to Todd, he was able to report with relief:

> On the 11th [March] I again arrived in the MacDonnell Ranges and was successful in finding a pass about 30 miles [48 kilometres] east of Stuart's track with numerous waterholes and springs, the principal of which is the Alice Spring which I had the honour of naming after Mrs Todd. Before returning to the drays I pushed across the mulga plains in the north side of the Macdonnell Ranges to the Strangways Ranges . . .

Hot on their heels were John Ross and company, who had left The Depot on 7 March for their fifth crossing of the MacDonnells, each time by a different route. They were without a surveyor, as every effort to find one had come to nothing. Crispe had also departed; and two new men – Robert Abrahams (who was a former Ross employee) and William Gregory – had joined John Ross, Giles (now second-in-command) and Hearne. Without a surveyor, navigation depended more on the sense of direction of John Ross and the other men, aided by equipment no more sophisticated than a compass, a protractor, a pencil and a tracing of Stuart's map.

As always, most of the expedition's efforts revolved around water. At one point, John Ross went off to look for it on foot. As Giles noted, he returned 'quite exhausted. He had been unwell for some time. The extra exertion and thirst told on him.' He was actually suffering from scurvy, due to months on an unbalanced diet. Yet he drove himself on.

By 31 March they were in new country 10 kilometres north of their previous expedition's furthest point, in the vicinity of Barrow Creek. Giles was still capable of a starry-eyed sense of adventure when he wrote: 'It was a long way to the Roper. We wondered what was ahead of us, and what would be our experience, and what we would discover.' Not long after he found out:

> When about 2 miles [3 kilometres] from a waterhole we heard a yell. Looking back, we saw a mob of savages, about a quarter of a mile [400 metres] in our rear, armed with spears and boomerangs. When we halted they made signs that they wanted to speak to us. One youngish man took the lead, and held out a dead bandicoot in his hand. Mr. Ross and Bill Gregory dismounted, and went to meet him. They had a short conclave which neither party could understand, so we proceeded on the same course. The savages, of whom we counted fifteen able-bodied young fellows, with one old man, followed us, yelling and shouting, and making signs, that there was water a little way on ahead, and where we could 'sit down'. We cut a creek with plenty of water. Here the savages assembled on one side of the creek, and made all signs in their power to induce us to 'sit down', or camp. We only halted for a few minutes, proceeded on our course, and entered very high and dry porcupine grass, with low and thick gum scrub. We fancied we had shaken off our dusky acquaintances, but after proceeding a couple of miles

> we saw them again, and they soon overtook us, and followed within 50 yards [45 metres] of our horses' heels, and shouted at the top of their voices. We believed they meant mischief, which soon became apparent, for about a dozen fires sprang up behind us, and two of the wretches with immense bunches of flaming porcupine ran at their utmost speed, keeping parallel with us, and endeavoured to make a ring of fire around us. The wind was blowing a gale from the south-east, and the roaring of the flames in the tall dry grass and scrub, and the dense columns of black smoke, coupled with the yelling and shouting of the savages, with their naked and greasy painted bodies, gave the whole scene a most demoniacal tinge. We took no notice of them for a short distance, but they began to get bolder and bolder, and set fire to the grass within a few yards of the leading packhorses. The larger number followed behind, under cover of the dense smoke. At last they got abreast of Mr. Ross in the lead. He shouted out to them, holding up his gun. They took no notice, but kept on firing the grass. He then galloped to within 50 yards [46 metres] of the leading savages and fired off both barrels of his gun over their heads, and the whole mob turned and bolted for their lives, having had the biggest fright in their experience and their first sound of a gun. There is no doubt the savages fully intended to burn us . . .

It was the most serious incident in their expeditions, during which they'd been scrupulous in trying to maintain good relations with the indigenous populations whose lands they crossed. As with the overlanders of the previous chapter, at any time a strong force of Aboriginal warriors could have wiped out John Ross and his men, guns or no guns. Under the circumstances, respect and diplomacy were clearly a better policy than hatred and brute force.

As John Ross and the others probed north of Barrow Creek, they missed their rendezvous with a supply party sent south from Port Darwin to the junction of the Roper and Strangways rivers, in the

Top End. The supply party arrived at the junction on 4 April, not knowing that John Ross's departure had been delayed until early the month before. The party waited a week, then buried the stores for Ross and left.

Through April, May and into June, there was no word of John Ross, Giles and the others. While the northern party desperately needed information on the route south, more worrying questions loomed: Had the expedition perished? Were the Aborigines of the interior so hostile that the entire project was in danger?

Finally, on 19 May, a ragged party of men emerged on the southern bank of the Roper River, 100 kilometres west of its junction with the Strangways. John Ross had got through. He was off course, in part due to his lack of navigational equipment, but he had some very good news. With just over seven months before the deadline for the line's completion, he'd found a more direct route which would greatly accelerate construction. What they'd lost because of the Simpson and MacDonnells, they'd gained in the northern hinterland.

Not finding the supply party or his supplies, John Ross and the men had no choice but to press on to find the northern section of the line. On 2 June they found the line of poles, but there was no sign of any activity, and no line they could use to transmit news of their arrival. A few days later, they found two police, the first Europeans they'd met in almost three months. What the police had to tell the men, whose epic journey had achieved so much, left them gutted. At the beginning of the dry season, when work should have been proceeding at a furious pace, work had been abandoned. The work parties and supervisors had taken ship to Adelaide. The reason was a lack of supplies with which to continue the work.

When John Ross finally found a part of the line that worked, he sent a telegram to Port Darwin announcing that he'd made it through alive. In response, Captain Douglas, the Government Resident in Port Douglas, replied, 'Congratulations to Mr Ross on his safe arrival in the Northern Territory after one of the most successful expeditions ever undertaken.'

Giles was particularly chuffed by this: 'This was most gratifying, and endorsed my opinion of Mr Ross's leadership, and consequently the unbroken comradeship that had existed among us all through the trip.'

Then, after reporting all they had learned, the bushies prepared to turn around and do it all again. They proposed to return to Adelaide overland, further improving on the route. Giles waxed lyrical:

> Exactly twelve months had passed since we started from Adelaide, and there we were, at the opposite side of the continent, still wondering at its vastness, with its marvellous changes of scenery and climate. We had experienced the scorching heat of the sandhills, as well as the icy chills of the vast gorges of the great MacDonnell Ranges, and the steamy nights of the tropic regions. Pangs of thirst and pains of hunger had assailed us, but not impaired us. Our bodies were still strong and lithe and our ambition undimmed. Our clothes were scant, but our minds enriched. Our track had been parallel with that of Stuart, a faint line from south to north. We had seen the centre and the trunk, but what of the branches – the east and west? What possibilities are there? We could not guess, but we felt it was the magnet that drew us on, and we were ready.

But the truth was that John Ross, in particular, had been ground down by illness, months in the saddle, and the pressures of keeping his men alive. The young and enthusiastic Giles eventually had to admit as much on 22 July 1871, at Strangways River: 'Mr Ross, who had been very unwell, and also considering the low condition and shortage of our horses, decided, and I think wisely, to give up the trip of recrossing the continent.' Ross left his men (who continued south) and made his way to Port Darwin. From there he took ship to Adelaide.

As it turned out, the 1 January 1872 deadline for getting the Overland Telegraph through to Port Darwin was missed. It wasn't until 20 June 1872 that messages started being passed, with a pony express bridging the gap. The service ran for only four days, because on 24 June 1872 the undersea cable went dead. While it was being repaired, the Overland Telegraph continued to be laid. It was finally joined on 22 August. Then, on 20 October, the underwater cable was repaired and for the first time Australia was connected to the world. It was the work of many men, but crucial among them were a small band of bushies who utilised all their skills and resourcefulness to determine the route. As the *Adelaide Observer* noted of John Ross in February 1903: 'On his return from the Northern Territory a banquet was given him at the Town Hall. The Governor (Sir James Fergusson), who was a great admirer of him, occupied the chair.' The article, prompted by John Ross's death in Adelaide Hospital on 5 February following a fall, described him as 'one of the oldest and best bushmen in South Australia.'

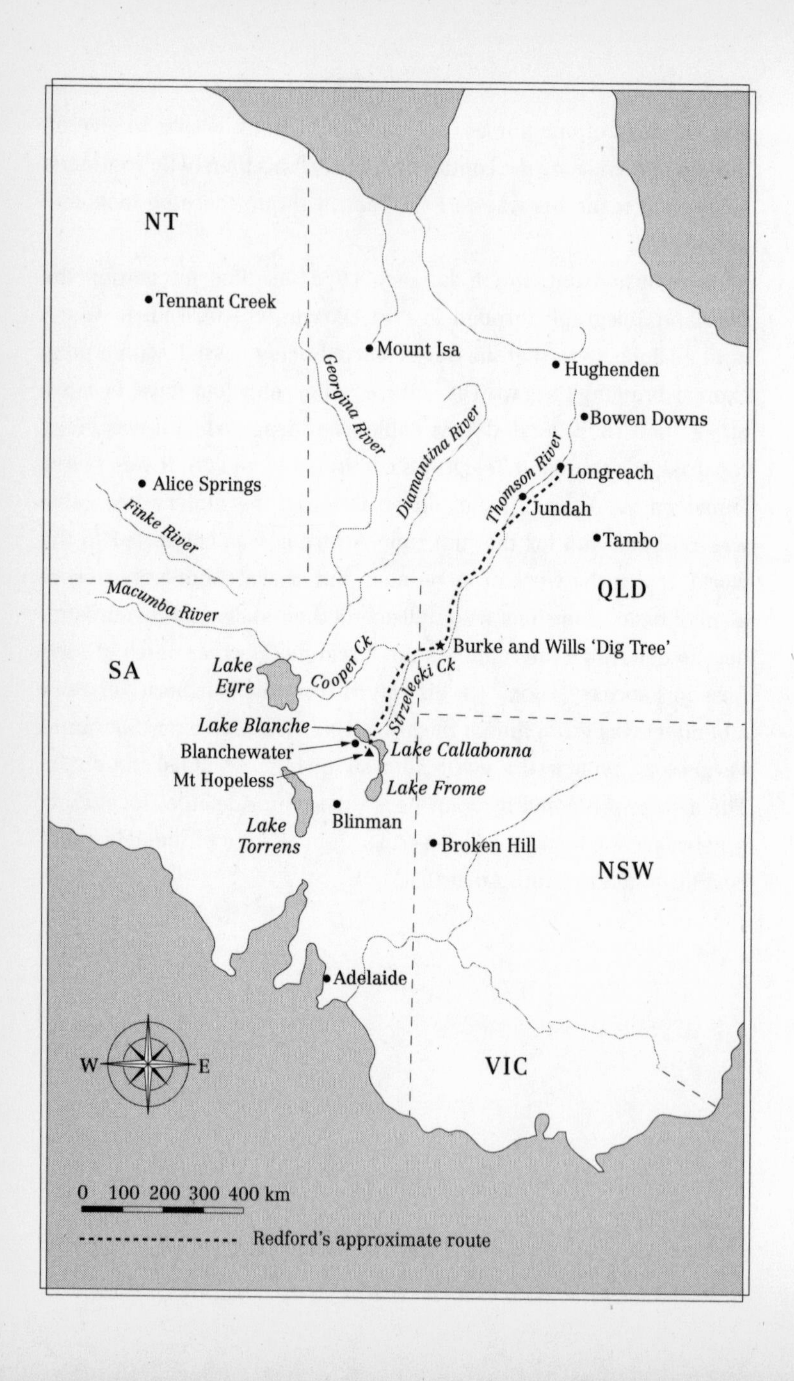
NT
Tennant Creek
Mount Isa
Georgina River
Hughenden
Bowen Downs
Diamantina River
Thomson River
Longreach
Alice Springs
Jundah
Finke River
Tambo
QLD
Macumba River
Burke and Wills 'Dig Tree'
Cooper Ck
SA
Lake
Eyre
Strzelecki Ck
Lake Blanche
Blanchewater
Lake Callabonna
Mt Hopeless
Lake Frome
Lake
Torrens
Blinman
Broken Hill
NSW
Adelaide
W
E
VIC
0 100 200 300 400 km
Redford's approximate route

Harry Redford (also Readford) studio portrait, date unknown

4

THE BIG STEAL, 1870: Harry Redford (1842–1901)

From the time we halted Mr Burke seemed to be getting worse, although he ate his supper; he said he felt convinced he could not last many hours, and gave me his watch, which he said belonged to the committee, and a pocketbook to give to Sir William Sawtell [chairman of the Burke and Wills expedition's Exploration Fund Committee], and in which he wrote some notes. He then said to me, 'I hope you will remain with me here till I am quite dead – it is a comfort to know that someone is by; but, when I am dying, it is my wish that you should

> place the pistol in my right hand, and that you leave me unburied as I lie.'
>
> That night he spoke very little, and the following morning I found him speechless, or nearly so, and about eight o'clock he expired.

So wrote the sole survivor of the Burke and Wills expedition, John King, as he described the death of Robert O'Hara Burke at Cooper Creek in 1861, after their ill-fated crossing of the Australian continent from south to north, and back. When King returned to where he and Burke had left William Wills, he, too, was dead. Both men might have survived their terrible ordeal had they reached Cooper Creek just a few hours earlier. Their relief party had abandoned the site on the morning of the day the beleaguered men had staggered in. All the starving explorers found was a note and some buried supplies at the now famous Dig Tree.

It is well recognised that the expedition members, especially Burke, were in large part the architects of their own demise: burdened as they were with excessive equipment and supplies, and too suspicious of the Aborigines they met to enlist their help in finding precious food and water. However, the fate of Burke and Wills underlined just how harsh the Australian interior could be, and would make the exploits of the bushie Harry Redford that much more remarkable.

Henry Redford (or Readford), known as Harry, was quite a character. Born around 1842, the twelfth child of an ex-convict, he was raised on the fertile farmlands around the Hawkesbury River in New South Wales. By 1870 he'd grown up to become a huge man, by some accounts 6 foot 3 in the old money, 190 centimetres in the new, with a small property of his own in western Queensland. He was also doing some work for William S. Forrester on his run, Balaclave, which lay between Redford's own property, Wombunderry, near Jundah and the larger Bowen Downs to the north. Redford and four men – John McKenzie, James McPherson, William Rooke (who is variously referred to in the documents of the time as Rooke, Brooke, Rourke, and O'Rourke) and George Doudney (also referred to as Dewdney, Dowdney and Dewdbury) – were hauling goods across from the railhead at Tambo to the station at Bowen Downs.

However, this was just a sideline to Redford's principal activity. He was, to put it bluntly, a thief. More specifically, he was a horse thief and cattleduffer, but a cattleduffer like no other. Cattleduffing had been on the rise throughout the 1860s. This was in part due to the increase in cattle prices, caused by several Queensland gold rushes, but was also a consequence of many runs falling into the hands of absentee landlords who squeezed everything they could out of their properties while putting very little back. A lot of the locals, struggling to survive on their much smaller holdings, came to regard the absentee landlords' understaffed and overstocked properties as fair game.

Harry Redford was one of those locals, and the 250-square-kilometre Bowen Downs was one of the fattest targets. It was 'owned' by two gentlemen whose address was given as Sydney. Messrs Young and Morehead (who managed Bowen Downs) were the Queensland representatives of the Scottish Australian Investment Company, which controlled fifteen other Queensland properties, all ranging in size from 100 to 260 square kilometres.

With so much land, and literally thousands of cattle wandering over its vastness, it was little wonder that duffing was rife. Redford had come close to being caught and convicted on several occasions, but he hadn't been deterred. Now he was about to embark on an exploit that was destined to make him famous, or infamous, depending on your point of view. In fact, it is one of the boldest heists of its time.

According to Hector Holthouse in *Up Rode the Squatter*:

> The full story of their activities was never sorted out, but according to evidence later given in court, Redford put it to his four mates that it would be fairly simple to round up about a thousand head of Bowen Downs cattle and overland them to Adelaide, where the Bowen Downs brand would not be known.

Certainly Redford and his mates started rounding up cattle and shifting them to yards they'd built in secret on properties to the south of Bowen Downs. However, a slightly different version has been put forward by Patrick McCarthy in his thoroughly researched *The Man Who Was Starlight.* It's the more believable, as Redford understandably kept his cards close to his chest:

> It was only six days after he and his men began moving cattle further south that he revealed the grand plan of taking them to South Australia in a daring episode that nobody would anticipate. With this, several of 'the McKenzie lot', including John McKenzie himself and James McPherson, a 34-year-old itinerant labourer from New South Wales, refused to venture further.

Two men at least decided to go with Redford: William Rooke and George Doudney. They had come up to Queensland from South Australia, following the tough Strzelecki Track. McCarthy contends that these two knew enough about the route to assure Redford that the feat was at least possible.

Still it was an ambitious plan. Adelaide was 1500 kilometres away as an indefatigable crow flies, and much of that distance was through virtual desert inhabited by potentially hostile Aborigines. It was the same country that had killed Burke and Wills just nine years before. But Redford was undaunted. At the time there had been extraordinarily good rains, and he was confident there'd be plenty of feed for the cattle. Water, or rather the lack of it, wouldn't be a problem either.

Also believed to be in on Redford's scheme were stockmen James Johnson and Harry Merrick, and a much more noticeable character called Whitey. Whitey (known as The Duke of Marlborough) was a striking pure-white Shorthorn bull that was taken along to keep the other cattle quiet or, given the large number of cows he'd have for company, because he couldn't be kept away.

The great drive south probably began in early March 1870, although police eventually decided it was 1 April. It isn't clear whether one of the investigators was having a private joke, but in any case the choice of April Fool's Day turned out to be appropriate.

Accounts of the journey south vary widely, not helped by the fact that there are few records of Redford talking about it. The usual story has him initially splitting the mob into three, and driving them south separately, to reduce the likelihood of detection. According to Holthouse:

> Slowly now, the three [sic] men with their thousand head of cattle began the long trek southward, down the almost dry, many-channelled course of Cooper Creek. They passed the stockade at Fort Wills – Burke and Wills' old base, crossed the border into South Australia, and continued down to Strzelecki Creek. Here also, the season had been good. Water was running and pasture was knee-deep. Geese, duck, and plain turkeys were to be had for the shooting.

Patrick McCarthy, however, doesn't think the men had it that easy:

> Readford continued southwards along the general route that he, Rooke and Dewdney had formulated, but in many places they had to make wide detours to keep the mob at a safe distance from the flooded Cooper Creek . . . At what was normally the Callamurra Waterhole, Readford and his mates turned the cattle south-southwest along Strzelecki Creek.

Redford was understandably reluctant to discuss his activities. However, many years after, he appears to have talked to a writer, Alec Marsh. In an article published in the 1 May 1936 edition of *Walkabout* magazine, long after Redford had passed away, Marsh quoted him as saying:

> Once we were a month gone, I knew danger of being followed had passed; but I took no risks just the same. At daylight every morning I'd start the others off with the cattle, and then I'd climb to the top of the highest hill about and look over the back track. Only once did I get a real scare. We were away down in the sandhill country in South Australia at the time, and, just after I'd climbed to the crest of a big sandhill, I felt my heart jump. What appeared to me to be a party of mounted men were riding along one behind another a few miles back along the track. I imagined I could see a policeman on each horse, and the longer I looked the more certain I became the game was up.
>
> I did not know what to do, and thought of mounting my horse and galloping after the cattle and then getting the other two and making off bush. Still keeping my eyes on the mounted party, I weighed up all possibilities, and I had just decided to make off and give the alarm, when to my delight I saw what the presumed police party really was. A mob of emus were coming along one behind another, apparently on their way to water! The yell I let out must have carried far; it stopped the emus for a few minutes and they were at least two miles off.

The men pressed on through often flooded country, having to make extensive detours that delayed their progress, until they reached South Australia's Hill Station, in the state's north-east. Water had proved to be a problem after all – there was far too much of it. On the plus side, the rain and floodwaters obscured some of the cattle's tracks, and made things difficult for anyone who might be on their trail. However, all the detours meant the men had taken some three-and-a-half months to cover a little over 1000 kilometres. Their clothes were in tatters and their supplies were running low. Not that they were starving, but they must have been fed up with nothing but steak for breakfast, lunch and dinner.

Redford and company were now at the northernmost settlement in South Australia, where they found a bush store. What happened next is contained in evidence given in court proceedings in Roma on 11 February 1873, and then reported in the *Brisbane Courier* of 18 February:

> Allan Walke proved that he lived in South Australia, at a place called Walleldeerdine [no such place can be found in the records of any era, but it is thought to be near Artacoona Well]; he knew the prisoner, and first saw him at Streletzski [sic] Creek in that colony about June, 1870; two men were with prisoner at the time he first saw him, whom he (witness) knew previously; they were named Doudney and Brooke; they had a large number of cattle with them; he and his brother kept a general store at Streletzski Creek, and the prisoner, at the time mentioned, with his mates, came there to purchase clothes and stores; after selecting what articles they required, they proposed to sell witness two cows, branded LC; he agreed to purchase the animals provided they would also dispose of a bull they had in their mob; to this the prisoner and his mates consented; before completing the purchase witness asked who the cattle belonged to, and prisoner replied that they belonged to himself, in conjunction with his brother who owned a station in an adjoining colony; he gave his name as Henry Collins; witness' brother then drew up a receipt, which the prisoner signed.

The LC brand was one used by Bowen Downs, and stood for Landsborough and Cornish. Redford, alias Henry Collins, really did have a brother named Lawrence, which supplied him with the explanation for the bulk of his cattle being branded LC. He also told Walke that the station's name was Wilbe Wilbe. The bull, meanwhile, had a special running A branded on each rump, plus an S, that would have meant nothing to Walke.

After disposing of the white bull at Artacoona, Redford and his men spent a week recuperating before continuing 250 kilometres south with the rest of the cattle. Their route probably took them past Carraweena, between Lake Blanche and Lake Callabonna, and on past the discouragingly titled Mount Hopeless. It had been named in 1839 by overlander-turned-explorer Edward Eyre (referred to in Chapter 2), who wrote of the outlook from the summit: 'Cheerless and hopeless indeed was the prospect before us . . . I had now a view before me that would have damped the ardour of the most enthusiastic, or dissipated the doubts of the most sceptical.'

Feeding the cattle on the succulent saltbush that Eyre hadn't realised was excellent for fattening stock, Redford continued on to Blanchewater Station, owned by the Honourable John Baker, a member of Parliament who'd briefly been South Australia's premier.

Presenting himself to Blanchewater's manager, again as Henry Collins, he offered to sell his cattle. The manager there, J. Mules, may have had his doubts about their origins, but he was also in the middle of unprecedented rains, with feed abundant, and here he was being offered over 1000 head of cattle at a bargain price. Considering most of Blanchewater's cattle had been killed by severe droughts in the preceding years, Mules bought the lot for between £3500 and £5000. However, Redford didn't get the cash up-front. He was given a promissory note for the full amount to be paid six months later. Down in Adelaide, though, he'd be able to cash the promissory note with a money dealer, at a discount rate. So Redford and the boys headed for the moderately big smoke.

Along the way, according to Patrick McCarthy, Redford (under the alias Henry Collins) couldn't resist giving an interview about his remarkable exploit to a newspaper in the South Australian town of Blinman:

> He claimed he was owner of the Wilbe Wilbe cattle and had just sold them at Blanchewater after a trek of four months. This involved repeated detours of more than 50 miles [80 kilometres] to escape floodwaters; on the way, according to Henry, they encountered tribes of friendly Aboriginals, 19-foot-long [5.8 metre] snakes and 'alligators'. Apparently he mistook the 6-foot-long [1.8 metre] desert goannas for their larger saurian cousins.

The reference to friendly Aboriginals is significant. Burke and Wills had perished while spurning their help. Expedition member King had survived by accepting it. Of course, with a large amount of protein on the hoof, Redford would have been able to make friends easily. As several generations of bushies before him had also found, had he not established good relations, his passage may well have proved much more difficult.

So far, so good. Redford and company made it to Adelaide, where they could relax, but sooner or later someone at Bowen Downs was going to notice they were missing 1000 head of cattle. Someone might even discover the substantial tracks left by 4000 hooves heading south into the uncharted wilderness. When they did, though, they would still have to assemble a puzzle whose pieces were scattered across half a continent.

Evidence of the lax management of Bowen Downs was all too apparent in the fact that it took months before the theft was noticed. In fact, it was a bushie looking for good grazing land along Cooper Creek who first became suspicious. Sometime in the middle of

1870, John Costello was taking a close interest in the Wombunderry Channel country in south-west Queensland (he was later to lease a 140-square-kilometre chunk of it). While carrying out a close inspection, he happened upon the tracks of a large mob of cattle heading towards the South Australian border.

Costello had himself been one of the first to overland horses on the Strzelecki Track, so his interest was piqued by someone's attempt to go even further with cattle. He also knew enough to suspect that the only mob of such size must come from Bowen Downs. He dutifully reported as much to the police, who passed the news on to Bowen Downs. Incredibly, it wasn't believed.

In truth, the stockmen at Bowen Downs had their hands full with the McKenzies who hadn't accompanied Redford. They were duffing cattle, too, though in much smaller numbers, and Bowen Downs was doing everything it could to catch them. They weren't about to go on a wild goose chase over thousands of kilometres just because of a rumour started by some crazy bushman. That is, until they started mustering towards the end of 1870, and noticed a remarkable lack on their normally overstocked property.

By January 1871 South Australian police were making inquiries and the following month they arrested a drover from Blanchewater Station who was taking a number of cattle along the stock route to Adelaide. They were branded LC. The agents for Bowen Downs, Elder-Smith, also noticed LC-branded cattle being sold at the Adelaide saleyards. All were traced to Blanchewater Station.

On 17 February, Boyd Morehead of Bowen Downs arrived in Adelaide by ship, and along with stock agent Robert Barr Smith went to visit John Baker. The honourable gentleman told them they could inspect his LC cattle, but he wasn't giving them back. When the men tried to work out a time that would be convenient, Baker became increasingly difficult. Possession is, after all, nine-tenths of the law.

While the Bowen Downs people tried everything to recover their cattle, Baker tried everything to flog them to the butchers of Adelaide as fast as he could. In this he proved remarkably efficient. Morehead of Bowen Downs ended up getting a legal opinion about going onto Blanchewater and retrieving his cattle. He was advised he risked being charged with duffing himself. In the end, and at considerable expense, he managed to recover only a dozen or so LC cattle. He did, however, get the information that the cattle were sold by one Henry Collins.

In February 1871 police in South Australia and Queensland issued notices that read:

WANTED

For the stealing of cattle from Bowen Downs. Warrants have now been issued for the arrest of the following:

COLLINS alias JAMES COURTLEY: 32 years old, 6'1" [185 centimetres] tall with broad shoulders, large hands, high cheek bones, brown hair, dark whiskers, moustache, nose slightly hooked at the point; shows upper teeth when laughing . . .

The management of Bowen Downs offer £200 for information leading to the arrest of the culprits.

Redford was also mentioned in connection with the matter, but was not recognised as Henry Collins, the ringleader. However, amid all the other manoeuvrings, a party of stockmen was despatched from Bowen Downs to follow the fading trail south and maybe get more of the cattle back. They were led by Edmund Butler and included stockmen John Vernon and John Craigie. James Henderson and an Aboriginal tracker, John Allen, may also have been included. Without the burden of having to drove a large mob of cattle, they made much faster time than Redford had on his journey south, although they did so in great discomfort. The rains had brought a time of plenty to the inland and the wildlife was rampant. Specifically, the pursuers found themselves in the middle of a rat plague.

The journey was not without its rewards, however. At Artacoona Native Well, they found Whitey. An initially hesitant Allan Walke gave up the bull, plus the receipt of sale signed by Henry Collins, and a description of the man himself. More significantly, stockman John Craigie had happened to be in Adelaide the previous July on family business. Incredibly, he'd bumped into Redford, the notorious duffer, whom he knew from Bowen Downs. Redford had told him that in Adelaide he went by the name Henry Collins. At the time, as no-one knew about the theft, it mean little to Craigie. Now it meant a great deal.

For Redford, the chance meeting with Craigie had been a shock. Knowing Craigie was from Bowen Downs, Redford assumed the bloodhounds were hot on his trail. As quickly as he could, he'd cashed the promissory note and boarded the SS *Aldinga* on 20 July, bound for Melbourne.

Redford was by now a rich man, but it was obviously too hot for him back in Queensland, so he headed for central New South Wales, where he had family and friends. Good sense should have told him to keep a low profile. However, as a larger-than-life character, he may not have been able to help himself. On 13 April 1871 he got married to a girl he'd gone to school with, Bessie Skuthorpe. They opened a pub near the mining town of Gulgong. They even advertised. As the licensee, Redford's name had to be published in the police gazette. Incredibly, even then no-one noticed that the publican was wanted in New South Wales, Queensland and South Australia. Under the circumstances he could be forgiven for thinking the law was an ass.

Finally, though, he was undone. On the night of 20 October 1871 there was a robbery in Gulgong.

Two men, Fred Howard and Bill Osborne, had stolen a safe from a store, taken it across the road and removed the valuables it contained to the value of £60. Howard was arrested soon after. Osborne was never located. However, under questioning Howard fingered Redford. Howard said they'd got the tip about the safe from him. When they'd had trouble making off with it, they'd borrowed Redford's horse. Then, unable to get the safe onto the horse, they'd got Redford to help them.

Redford was arrested on 7 November, but with no-one to confirm Howard's story, the case against him wasn't particularly strong. Not that it mattered. An investigation of the publican's background revealed the warrants for much bigger crimes and he was rearrested on 13 November for cattle duffing. It had taken the law 18 months to catch up with him.

Redford's luck, it appeared, was up. To make his arrest more worrying, his wife was by then seven months pregnant. At the beginning of January he was taken aboard the ASN ship *Queensland*, bound for Rockhampton jail. On 20 January 1872, Jemima Redford was born.

To make matters worse for Redford, the incompetence the law had shown in not being able to apprehend him, even though he'd made little attempt to hide, continued when it came to preparing the case against him. It took months while witnesses were found, lost, offered deals, escaped, recaptured, brought from South Australia, or rounded up from stations near and far. At one point the trial was ready to go but floods prevented the judge and legal officers from reaching the court.

The prosecution's difficulties didn't end there. All the cases brought against those of Redford's co-accused who'd been captured had failed. Cases against the McKenzies had also struggled to secure verdicts. There were suggestions the jury in the Roma Court, where the cases were being tried, was being bribed. This incensed the jurors, who vigorously defended their decisions.

Another problem for the prosecution was working out exactly what the charge against Redford should be. Very few cattle had been recovered, so no-one knew exactly how many had been stolen. Baker had sold most of the cattle by April 1871, which meant most of the evidence wasn't so much destroyed as char-grilled. What the prosecution did have, though, was Whitey, the bull. The men from Bowen Downs who'd been sent to South Australia in pursuit of Redford had eventually returned by the even more rat-plagued route by which they'd come, with the much-travelled bull in tow.

So, finally, before a packed courtroom the final act of Redford's extraordinary drama got under way. The king of the cattleduffers went to trial over a year after his arrest, on 11 February 1873. At that time of year in Roma, everyone, accused and accusers alike, would have been feeling the heat, especially in the close quarters of the old wooden courtroom.

The most substantial surviving account comes from the *Brisbane Courier*'s correspondent, who recorded the trial as taking place on 11 February. Other accounts suggest it was 10 February. In any case the unnamed correspondent captured the formality of the occasion with a report that began:

> Regina v. Redford
>
> Henry Redford was indicted that he, in the month of March, 1870, at Bowen Downs station in the colony, 100 bullocks, 100 cows, 100 heifers, 100 steers, and 1 bull, the property of Messrs Morehead and Young, feloniously did steal, take, and carry away, and in a second count for receiving the same knowing them to be stolen.
>
> Messrs Pring, Q.C., and Hely prosecuted on behalf of the Crown; and Mr Paul, instructed by Mr C.J. Blakeney, defended the prisoner.

As the saying goes, the wheels of the law grind slowly, but they grind exceedingly fine. Unfortunately, in Queensland in 1873 the grinding machinery was pretty thin on the ground. Legal practitioners were scarce, thus Charles John Blakeney was the son of the judge, Charles William Blakeney. Ratcliffe Pring, the prosecutor, had run the successful defences for all Redford's accomplices, with the exceptions of Doudney and Rooke, who were never apprehended. It has been suggested the prosecution secured Pring's services in hopes of weakening Redford's defence.

Before the trial even got under way, though, it hit trouble. The case required the services of twelve jurors, but out of a panel of forty-eight potential jurors, only seven made it through the objections of the prosecution and the defence. George Paul, who was allowed a total of twelve objections for the defence and had used all of them, then suggested all the panel objected to by either side return so they could go through them again. However, he reserved the right to make more objections. The judge instead ruled that only those names objected to by the Crown should go in, and Paul would not be allowed to object to any as he hadn't objected to them before. When Paul 'strenuously objected', Blakeney replied that, if he hadn't applied the law correctly, Paul was free to take the matter to the Supreme Court and his client 'could have the benefit of a mistrial'.

Eventually the trial continued with a jury composed of James Nimmo, John Carmichael, John Maguire, George Young, Thomas Mogridge, James O'Brien, William Spence, Patrick McKenna, Dugald Carr, Michael Mullavey, William Downes Jnr, and Alexander Robinson. One of the jurors had himself been found guilty of stealing cattle in 1869. Others were suspected of having previously been bribed. However, at least one, James Nimmo had been involved in cases where convictions were recorded.

From the start, the prosecution built its case around Whitey. Edmund Butler, overseer of Bowen Downs, positively identified it as the bull that was even now outside the courtroom. As the *Courier* reported:

> During the months of March, April, and part of May, 1868 [actually late 1870], a muster of the cattle was made on the part of Bowen Downs where the bull was kept, and about one thousand head of cattle, together with the bull in question, were at that time missed from the station; the next time he [Butler] saw the bull was in South Australia, about 1000 miles [1600 kilometres] distant from the place where he had been missed; it was at a place called Strezeltzki [sic] Creek; he was in the possession of a man named Allan Walke; he, Walke, told witness that he had purchased the bull with two cows from a man who gave his name as Henry Collins; there were with Collins at the time two other men whom he (Walke) knew to be named Doudney and Brooke [sic]; Walke then produced to witness a document which he said was the receipt given to him by Collins for the purchase of the cattle, and which document he, witness, then produced before the Court.

John Vernon, the stockman from Bowen Downs who'd accompanied Butler to Artacoona, identified the bull. The owner, Boyd Morehead, identified the bull. He also maintained that the bull had never been sold, cutting off any possibility of escape for Redford if he said that he bought the bull legally. John Craigie also identified the bull, and Redford, who he'd always known as Henry Redford.

The prosecution even called in 'expert' witnesses, as the *Courier* reported:

> Mr Lukin, the Police Magistrate at Roma, produced the recognisance of bail signed by the prisoner as 'Henry Redford', in his presence. Mr J.K. Cannan [the local bank manager] was examined as an expert, and gave it as his opinion that the signatures 'Henry Redford' to the recognisance and 'Henry Collins' to the receipt given to Walke were written by the same person.

The prosecution was constructing a rock-solid case. Then they called Allan Walke, who they'd brought all the way from South Australia, and kept in Roma for months at the expense of Bowen Downs. Apart from the evidence described earlier, it was reported that:

> He [witness] had no doubt whatever as to the prisoner being the man who sold him the cattle and signed the receipt, as he remained at his [witness'] place for some days afterwards; the bull he then purchased remained in his possession for over three months [it was more like six] until delivered to the authorities, having been identified by Messrs Butler and Vernon and claimed as the property of Messrs Morehead and Young, the owners of Bowen Downs in this colony; the next time he saw the animal was at Mount Beagle station, near Roma, about 2000 miles [3200 kilometres, but actually more like 1700 kilometres] from Adelaide, where he identified him amongst 70 other bulls, a great many of whom were of the same colour – white.

Another witness, identified in the *Courier* report as Buch, but actually Charles Birch, testified that the prisoner 'was known about Tambo, the Thomson, and Bowen Downs, as Henry Redford'.

The prosecution also called one of Redford's accomplices, James McPherson, who was remarkably forthcoming with his evidence:

> Witness, in company with Redford, and three other men, named McKenzie, Doudney, and Brooke [sic], were on Bowen Downs station in the year 1870, in charge of drays and horses belonging to a man named Forrester; they all went 25 miles [40 kilometres] up the Thomson River, and there built cattle yards; when the yards were completed, he, with the others, mustered a large number of the Bowen Downs cattle, and filled the yards with them; the cattle were afterwards drafted off in mobs of two or three hundred at a time to Forrester's camp; the white bull outside the Court was amongst the cattle taken at that time, the object being

> that he would keep the cows and heifers quiet, of which there were a large number in the mob; ultimately the whole of the cattle were driven off by Redford, McKenzie, and Brooke, towards the southern colonies.

It was all pretty damning, despite the error that described McKenzie as having gone with Redford. However, it was McPherson that Paul for the defence had in his sights. The *Courier* reported: 'Mr Paul's examination of this witness occasioned some amusement. The witness stated that he was not a cattle stealer, although he might have stolen some, though not to his knowledge.'

Under Paul's questioning, however, McPherson was forced to admit that he had been charged with stealing the cattle from Bowen Downs, about which he'd just given testimony. Had he been committed for trial? Yes, he had. What had happened in his case? He'd pleaded not guilty. Then what? He'd been discharged on the grounds of insanity and sent to Brisbane as a lunatic. And then? He'd escaped.

As an escaped lunatic, McPherson's credibility was starting to fray, but Paul wondered how he'd wound up giving evidence in the current case. As the *Courier* reported:

> He also stated that he was re-arrested at Armidale, in New South Wales, and was brought up to this Court to give evidence against the prisoner, under a promise of a free pardon if he gave fair evidence at the trial; that he was there trusting to the honour of the authorities respecting the free pardon to be granted to him.

George Paul smelled a rat, and it wasn't one left over from the plague down on the Strzelecki Track.

After the prosecution had finished calling witnesses, the defence had its turn. And here was yet another surprise. Paul didn't call anyone – no character reference for Redford, no-one who might supply an alibi, no signature experts of their own, and not Redford himself.

Instead Paul went onto the attack. For more than an hour he talked, challenging every detail of the prosecution's case, bolstered by the fact that much of it rested on an escaped lunatic bribed to give evidence. Unfortunately, the trial proceedings have since been destroyed (probably in the 1950s), but it is likely that he attacked the credibility of other witnesses, some of whom were no less disreputable than McPherson, while others had a vested interest in making Redford an example to others. He certainly made much of the fact that Redford had already been held without bail for more than a year while the prosecution struggled to build a case, even though all the cases against his co-accused had failed.

A re-enactment of the trial, written by Rachel Matthews and performed in the new Roma courthouse (built in 1901), in August 2002, attempted to capture the substance and style of Paul's closing remarks:

> Gentlemen of the jury, you appreciate the potential of this unexplored, untapped and untamed colony you live in. You understand its riches and its terrors. Henry Redford is one of those rare men who is sufficiently fearless and skilled in the arts of the bushman to face death and beat the harsh challenges of the uncharted inland. Henry Redford should be hailed as a daring hero, which he is, not treated as a common criminal. Did the prosecution mention the astonishing feats of survival that Henry Redford accomplished in opening up the stock routes to the southern colony of South Australia? No! But we all benefit from his journey of discovery. Harry Redford should be honoured and decorated by the Crown, not punished!
>
> – Extract reprinted by permission of Rachel Matthews

Matthews may have been close to the mark with her reconstruction, for the *Courier* reported that the judge, in directing the jury: 'Observed that he trusted that the jury would not be led away by the specious although clever address of the counsel for the prisoner.'

Indeed, Blakeney went considerably further. He also trusted:

> That they would dismiss from their minds the hardships said to have been endured by the prisoner, no doubt placed before them with a view to making him a martyr . . . He next would submit that, supposing that the jury accepted Mr Paul's recommendation, and gave no credence to McPherson, yet the case was plain against the prisoner. The bull had been identified beyond all question as the property of Messrs Morehead and Young; it is also identified as being the one sold by the prisoner to Mr Walke, and the evidence of that gentleman could leave no doubt on any reasonable mind that the prisoner at the bar and the person who sold that animal in South Australia were one and the same person. He would, with these remarks, request them to consider their verdict.

The jury filed out of the crowded courtroom at 9 p.m. on the evening of the trial. If they'd listened to Judge Blakeney, there was nothing to discuss and they'd only need a minute or so to 'decide'. However, the minutes ticked by. What were they considering? Certainly they'd have weighed McPherson's evidence, and the fact that the prosecution had dangled a carrot to get it. However, they may also have talked about the reputations of other witnesses.

Walke, for example, had made a name for himself around Roma during his long stay there. He'd been described as a gentleman loafer, even as a despicable character, who'd apparently suggested that the simplest way to deal with the case was to give him some money or do the bull in.

They may also have known about Birch. Implicated in duffing with the McKenzies he'd also given evidence in return for a pardon. He was also a disreputable alcoholic and the jury probably was aware that the police had actually kept him in a stable, under guard, to prevent him becoming drunk before he gave his evidence.

Even Judge Blakeney had a reputation. Born and raised in Ireland, the seventy-one-year-old was a Trinity College man who ended up bankrupt due to his inveterate gambling. He'd been forced to join his son in the colonies in 1859, at the age of fifty-seven.

An hour after they'd retired, the jury returned to the overflowing courthouse, now hushed in anticipation. Clearly a betting man, Judge Blakeney might have wagered London to a brick on the answer when the foreman, James Nimmo, rose and was asked for the verdict. The entire assembly was hushed in anticipation. And then . . . 'Not guilty,' he said.

Uproar. As the *Courier*'s correspondent described the scene: 'Much surprise was evinced at the verdict, in which the Judge joined; and after having requested the foreman to repeat it, observed, "Thank God, gentlemen, that verdict is yours, not mine".'

Harry Redford was a free man. He immediately headed south, back to New South Wales to be with his wife and baby daughter. In Queensland, though, the decision was already hitting the fan. Within a week, a Roma juror who had not sat on Redford's jury, John Grahame, had sent a petition to the Colonial Secretary regarding the case:

> We, the undersigned Jurors of the Western District Court of Queensland, having been present at the trial of Regina v. Redford, desire hereby, to express in the strongest manner our surprise and indignation at the verdict given in that trial and we consider that a more disgraceful miscarriage of justice never took place in any Court of Law. And we further consider that it is perfectly useless to bring cases of cattle stealing before this Court at Roma unless the present jury list is very much altered.

It was signed by Grahame and four others.

In the *Brisbane Courier* of 28 February 1873, the gossip-writer known as 'A Bohemian' mocked the Roma jurors:

> They have a curious practice out in the far west of 'pulling' fellows for cattle-stealing and taking them to Roma to be tried by a jury of their 'peers' at the District Court. The 'peers' seem to enjoy the fun amazingly and after going through the form of hearing the evidence and making a few bovine jokes at the expense of the prosecutors and their witnesses, they bring in a verdict of 'Not guilty'. Amusements are scarce about Roma, so an occasional diversion in the shape of a judge-and-jury trial for cattle-stealing is a delicious treat. The last sittings of the Roma Court were more than usually amusing as there were several cattle-stealing cases tried and the jurors enjoyed it much. They chaffed the prosecutors unmercifully and got rare old sport out of them. In one case a man was tried for stealing a cow out of a paddock by taking a panel out of the fence, driving out the cow, and putting up the fence again. There could be no reasonable doubt in the minds of either judge or jury or anyone else that the man was guilty, if that sort of thing was considered a crime at Roma, but the jury, as usual, brought in a verdict of 'Not guilty'. The jury got some fun out of the witnesses though. One of them asked the manager of the station which had been robbed if he would swear the fences had not been broken down by the sand-flies, to which the witness replied that he had never heard of sand-flies being guilty of such destruction of property, but that although they might have broken down the fence, it would puzzle them to put up the rails again so neatly as he found them the morning he discovered the loss of his cattle.

There is another story, unable to be verified, of a jury that acquitted a duffer with the verdict 'Not guilty, but he has to return the stock'. The judge was so outraged he demanded the jury go back and come up with a verdict that didn't make a mockery of justice. They grudgingly did as they were told and returned with the verdict 'Not guilty, and he can keep the bloody stock.'

Poor Judge Blakeney also expressed his displeasure in a report to the Queensland Attorney-General:

> Although, to my mind, no case could possibly be clearer for a conviction than this one, and my charge to the jury was decidedly against the prisoner, nevertheless, they returned a verdict of 'not guilty' . . . I fail to see the possibility of obtaining a conviction for cattle-stealing in any case before a Roma jury, if evidence placed before them in the cases referred to was not sufficient to convince them of the prisoners' guilt . . . The jury list for the Roma district is so constituted that when counsel for the prisoner exhausts the challenges allowed the prisoner under the Act, the more respectable persons mentioned in the panel are set aside and the remainder are of a class whose sympathies are almost always with the prisoner.

Prompted by Blakeney, on 4 April 1873 the Executive Council withdrew Roma's criminal jurisdiction for two years. Many of Roma's citizens were outraged. One wrote to the *Courier*:

> The jury consider the testimony of the witnesses so unreliable that they could not but find for the prisoner who, however morally guilty, failed to be proven so. The valuable services rendered to this district by Judge Blakeney in suppressing crime entitle him to a claim upon the Government, but it would tend to beneficial results if he were removed to some other district; and would better enable Roma juries to act with honour and without fear, who are now actually fearful of their verdicts giving satisfaction. Such a state of affairs can be remedied by only one course – the appointment of a new judge for this circuit; and one capable of standing that hardship of travelling which an old gentleman like Judge Blakeney is past bearing.

On a later visit to Roma, Blakeney was attacked by angry citizens and roundly abused. However, Roma got its court back within twelve months, because 1874 was an election year, and no candidate stood a chance whose party didn't support reinstatement.

The solution to the duffing problem was, of course, relatively simple. As had been done earlier in New South Wales, in 1872 the use of brands in Queensland was regulated. Brands had to be registered and their details were widely distributed. Cattle with unclear or unknown brands were considered unbranded and could be impounded until their ownership was clearly established. The spread of telegraphic communication, pioneered by the likes of John Ross (see Chapter 3), also made checks on stock movements and sales increasingly effective. Of course, this relied on cattle being branded. The absentee landlords who had cattle wandering over vast areas were easy targets for their less scrupulous neighbours until they fenced their properties and effectively controlled their stock.

And Redford? He didn't learn. He continued duffing cattle and horses, though the law finally caught up with him in 1877. He went before the court in Toowoomba only to find that his learned friend from 1873, George Paul, had been promoted. He was the judge trying his case, and when Redford was found guilty, Paul didn't hesitate. He gave his former client eighteen months' hard labour.

After his release, Redford pioneered another stock route, from Queensland to the Northern Territory, where he became manager of the newly established Brunette Downs station. He still couldn't mend his ways, and turned his hand to fixing horse races. He made a small fortune on a scam at the Tennant Creek races, and bought his own property, but it was eventually absorbed into Brunette. Employed as manager of MacArthur River, near Borroloola, he drowned in 1901 while trying to swim the flooded Corella Creek.

By then, Redford's exploits had become part of Australian folklore, in part due to the book *Robbery under Arms,* written by Rolf

Boldrewood and published in the 1880s. The first third of this tale of the bushranger Starlight is based on Redford's famous odyssey from Queensland to South Australia.

Redford's legend also continues to the present day, and excites the imaginations of Australians in every corner of the continent. In 2002, when a cattle drive was organised to celebrate Redford's famous exploit, riders from every state came to participate. As already mentioned, a re-enactment of the trial was also staged. Originally, it was planned to have two performances, but due to overwhelming demand, the production eventually staged nine sell-out shows. The performances were also filmed by the ABC television program *Landline.* To date it has been broadcast twice.

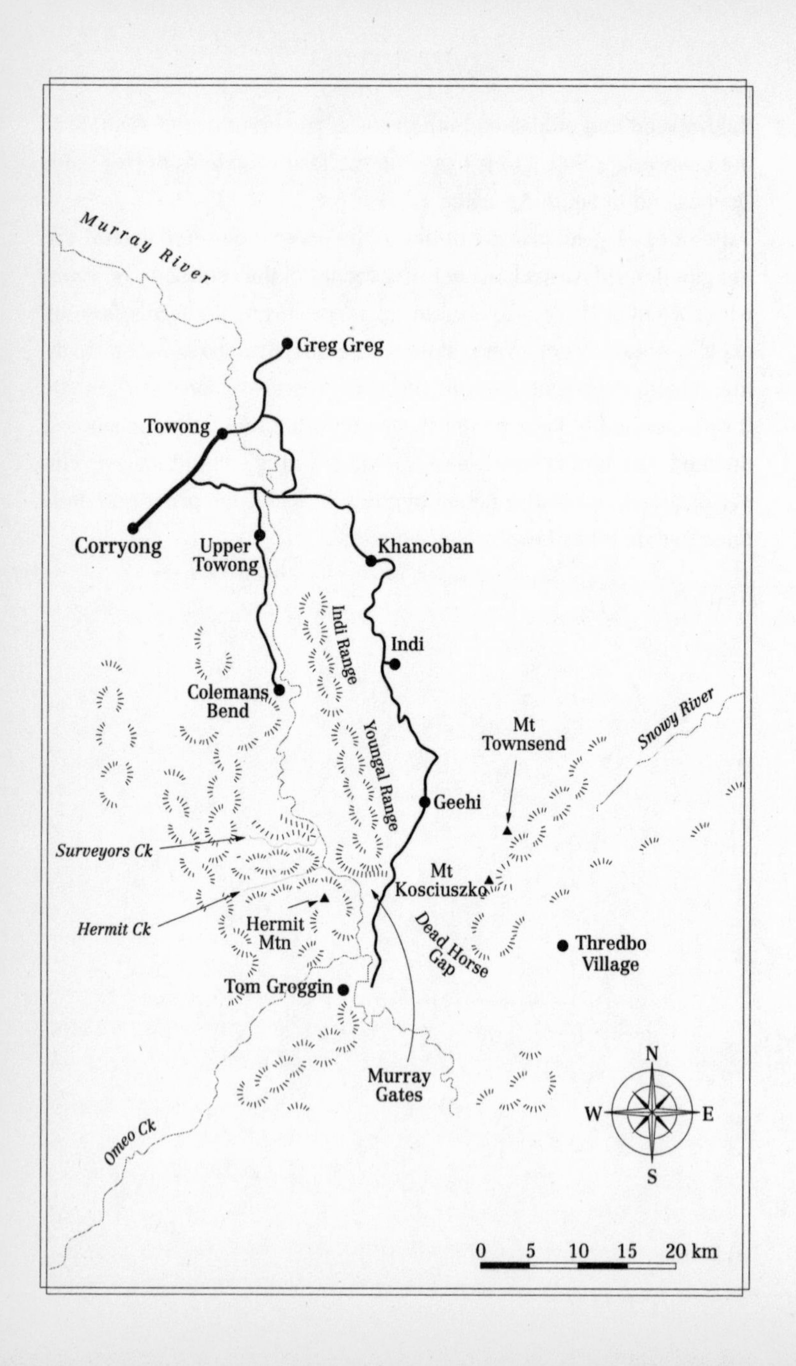
Murray River
Greg Greg
Towong
Corryong
Upper Towong
Khancoban
Indi Range
Indi
Colemans Bend
Youngal Range
Mt Townsend
Snowy River
Geehi
Surveyors Ck
Mt Kosciuszko
Hermit Ck
Hermit Mtn
Dead Horse Gap
Thredbo Village
Tom Groggin
Murray Gates
N
W
E
S
Omeo Ck
0 5 10 15 20 km

Jack Riley at his hut at Tom Groggin, date unknown
(Reproduced by James Nicholas, Corryong. Photo: Corryong Historical Society)

5
THE MAN FROM SNOWY RIVER, 1890: Jack Riley (1841–1914)

'Down by Kosciuszko where the pine-clad ridges raise their torn and rugged battlements on high,' where 'the Snowy River riders on the mountains make their home' and 'the river runs those giant hills between', on a chilly summer night in 1890, a bushie, a farmer and a young poet sat down in a bush hut for a bit of a yarn.

The bushie was John 'Jack' Riley, and the story of his life held his small audience spellbound. Born around 1841, he and millions of other Irish people had soon faced the appalling hardships of the potato famine that began in 1845. One of the lucky ones, Riley survived both the famine and the often horrific voyage on what became known as 'the death ships', transporting the destitute Irish to the four corners of the globe. Aboard the emigrant ship *Rodney*, Riley arrived in Sydney on 15 March 1854, aged only thirteen.

In those years the country was gripped by the fever of the first gold rushes, but not everyone who descended on the goldfields made their fortune. Riley ended up in the Southern Alps, around Victoria's remote township of Omeo, which had emerged out of the mountainous wilderness after gold had been discovered there in the early 1850s. He may have been there at the same time as police magistrate Thomas Browne, who under the pen-name Rolf Boldrewood became well-known for *Robbery Under Arms*, a novel in part based on the life and times of cattleduffer Harry Redford (see Chapter 4). At the time, the mountains around Omeo were also home to local bushrangers: Bogong Jack and Mad Dog Morgan.

For Jack Riley, it seems the attractions of the yellow metal were offset by the frustrations and the hard and dirty work of finding it, since he eventually set up a tailoring business with his sister, Mary Anne Jones. Then, after she married, he took a job that was better suited to his growing love of horses.

In a booklet published in 1995 to mark centenary celebrations of Corryong, the Victorian town west of the Snowy Mountains and Riley's burial place, Noel Gough relates that:

> The next stage in Jack's life finds him in the Monaro district, working for the Prendergast and Freebody families, and at a station called Eulamuna near the border of NSW and Victoria. A story is told in that district that Jack rode out into the wilderness of Tin Mine Creek, near Mt Pilot, to search for a missing cattleman, Christy O'Rourke. He found the injured rider and brought him back to Moonbah – a feat that did not go unnoticed by his peer group of Monaro horsemen.

Riley then drifted from job to job until, in 1884, he was offered work on the western side of the Snowy Mountains, on pastoralist John Pierce's 8000-hectare Greg Greg Station. Greg Greg was in the upper Murray (known locally as the Indi) valley near Corryong, but it also included the evocatively named Tom Groggin, the only piece of flat country in the almost impenetrably steep country 60 kilometres upriver at the foot of Mount Kosciuszko. It was soon to become Riley's home.

Some idea of how wild the country was comes from Jean Carmody's *Early Days of the Upper Murray.* A police report from 1881, written the year after Ned Kelly's capture and execution, detailed the police operation to surround the Kelly Gang with spies. Carmody writes:

> They had to be careful, however, not to arouse the outlaws' suspicions, as it was expected that they would then 'seek refuge in the inaccessible region near Tomgroggin [sic] in New South Wales.' This would indicate that the Kelly gang was known to have hidden out there on at least one earlier occasion.
>
> – Carmody quotes reproduced by kind permission, the estate of Jean Carmody

Tom Groggin's importance to cattlemen like John Pierce was that for many years it was the only way up to the high country's summer grazing, via the Leatherbarrel Mountain and Dead Horse Gap, then on to Mount Kosciuszko and Mount Townsend. In fact it wasn't until the 1920s that another track was opened, up Hannells Spur. That track had to be hacked through scrub so thick that in places the trail is only 2 to 3 metres wide.

Aside from stock routes, there was no proper road to Tom Groggin until the 1950s, when an access road was built for the Snowy Mountains Hydro-Electric Scheme. From Thredbo to Corryong via this road it is only 100 kilometres, but the drive by car can take more than three hours as one negotiates the steep and winding sections and is frequently compelled to stop and enjoy the spectacular scenery.

Initially Riley worked at Greg Greg, branding and drafting cattle. However, after a herd was taken to Groggin, Riley stayed on to watch over them and eventually ended up being put in charge of the run, the only accommodation being a rough bark hut. It was an incredibly isolated place to live, but Riley may have had his reasons for staying there. In his book, *Corryong and the Man from Snowy River District*, the late Tom Mitchell, husband of *The Silver Brumby* author Elyne Mitchell, relates a story told about Riley by an old stockman, Charlie Bingham:

> He was a queer old cuss . . . He used to live away up there on Groggin on a bit of a selection he had there. He'd had some trouble with the cops, or he'd been worsted in a law-suit or something and that's what made him clear out and live like that – no, by the Holy living Jesus I'm wrong – it wasn't that way at all – I remember it now . . .
>
> Jack Riley was working for a bloke who was a duffer, and one day this bloke sends Jack Riley off with a mob of horses to take to a sale or something somewhere. Jack Riley doesn't know that these horses have been duffed – he's quite innocent, he told me so himself – and here he is going along behind this mob of prads thinking of nothing at all, when a couple of troopers rides up and says, 'You're under arrest. You're our prisoner. Those horses that you have there you've stolen. We know all about you.'
>
> Jack Riley tells them that the horses aren't stolen, that they've made a mistake and that he can prove it, but they laugh at him and tell him to think of a better one before he comes up before the magistrate, and with that they whips the handcuffs onto him, and they takes him and locks him up 'behind the logs'. The bloody beak doesn't believe that he is innocent and gives him a year in the clink. He gets out after

> six months or so, but that finished him and he cleared right out and got away to hell up there in Groggin, and just lived there and got about the mountains.
>
> Now he was a man you should have met. He really could have shown you the mountains – after cattle and brumbies . . . He only used to come out perhaps once a year to go to Corryong for a spree and he would make it a good one, and then off back to the mountains he'd go and no-one would see him for months and months.
>
> – Mitchell quotes reproduced by kind permission, the estate of Tom Mitchell

Jean Carmody, who suggests Riley only used to go to Corryong for supplies, and that he was always honest and trusted, also described Riley's life at Groggin:

> At times he was joined by men employed to clear and fence on the run and, when the racing season was over for the year at Greg Greg, often the stable boys would be sent out to help him also. This nearly led to Riley's giving notice on one occasion, after the stable hands had had a wild night and left the hut almost in ruins. John Pierce, who did not wish to lose the services of such a reliable employee, promised to have another hut built for Riley over the river, and this is how Jack Riley came to live in Victoria.

Yet Charlie Bingham suggests Riley wasn't averse to an occasional nip himself, to ward off the mountain cold:

> He was a grey-whiskered old fellow, and if you fetched up to his shack in Groggin, you were all right as long as you had some whisky with you. If you had some whisky he'd give you the hut and everything in it, but if you had no whisky or the whisky you'd brought with you was finished, then he'd growl and he'd say – I can hear him just as plain as if he was

here today – 'See here now, it's time youse was going,' and he'd hunt you. He was a bit like them old blokes that lived on their own. He'd be that way that he'd prefer a couple of black snakes for company rather than a white man.

One time we were going up and we brought a bottle with us, so of course old Jack Riley gives us a great welcome. 'See 'ere now,' he says, 'I'm not one of them boozers. I likes it a little and often.' Well, we all goes to bed good and early as we had to be on the top of Kosciuszko the next day, but if Jack Riley was up once, he was up 50 times just drinking a little out of the bottle. He certainly liked a little but he certainly liked it often, and in the morning that bottle was empty. 'See 'ere now,' he says. 'It's time youse was going.' And with that he turns us out and hunts us away.

Though he preferred his own company, Riley was sometimes compelled to assist those less skilled in bushcraft. The Melbourne *Argus* wrote of Riley in 1914:

Gifted with the bushman's unerring sense of locality, he had a supreme contempt for the compass, and delighted to relate his experience with a party of city tourists which visited Groggin some years ago. The weather was treacherous, and Riley offered to guide the party to the top. They told him that there was no necessity to come, as they had a good compass. Foggy weather set in, and two days afterwards a party of bedraggled pedestrians returned to Groggin with only one desire – to get back to civilisation. Riley said never a word. He gave them food and a drink of tea, and catching his horse, led them over the Divide and put them on the Geehi track for home.

The *Corryong Courier* of 23 July 1914 added:

One of the tourists said he would like to recompense him, and offered Jack five shillings. Jack refused to take it, his reward was greater than

> that. Thirty years intimate acquaintance with Kosciusko had made him familiar with all the mountain's many moods, and if he warned a tourist that it was a bad day to try the ascent, the warning was worth paying attention to.

Giving further details, in 1914 the *Corryong Courier* reported: 'Your bushman is a philosopher, and life had many compensations for Riley. "See here, my boy," he would say, as he coaxed his horse off the track around a fallen tree. "There's never a tree falls in this country but it falls on the ——— track."'

Clearly there was room for differing opinions on whether Riley was a saint or sinner, but on one point there was no dissent. Riley could ride. Tom Evans recalled mustering stray bullocks with Riley and other Greg Greg stockmen up around Leatherbarrel Mountain:

> Old Jack says to me, he says, 'See 'ere now, young feller, youse goes that away and wees goes this way.' And off they went leaving me to look for the bullocks on my own. I was only a bit of a kid and I did not know the country and I was scared I'd get bushed, and I had a hell of a job getting through the big snow-drifts in the gullies, and I was having a hell of a time when I walked right onto the missing bullocks camped right against a big snow-drift. They were wild as hawks and my horse was a bit knocked up and had a shoe loose by this time, and it was a good time after dark before I got the brutes down to the mustering paddock at Groggin. Old Jack and the others won't believe that I have got the bullocks all on my own, but the next morning when they wake up here they are, and old Jack says, 'Looka here now, they needs a boostin'.' And with that he after them and into them with his whip, and there were no two ways about it, he could ride like the very devil, and he stayed with those bullocks no matter what they turned and did, and the whole time he was cussing them and taking pieces off them with his whip. They got boosted all right.

Another story, related by Gordon Williams in the *Argus* and reprinted in the *Corryong Courier* of January 1949, comes from John McInnes:

> Riley was chasing horses that had 'gone wild' from the Groggin homestead. All attempts to trap them had failed, the outlaws racing for shelter in a patch of venomous scrub country. Riley had grown tired of failure, so he resolved that he would head them off by careering through a patch of equally bad country littered with fallen timber.
>
> When the rest of the party came up with John, who was riding a bald-faced bay, [John] Pierce saw that the wild rider's legs were covered with blood. Examination showed that the horse, not John, was hurt – torn by a stake, a snag of timber beneath an arm, so severely that the shoulder seemed half severed. 'See here, now,' mused John, examining the injury, 'I was wondering what made her falter as we came through the timber patch up there.'

In the same article, H. Barlee of Khancoban, who as a boy had known Riley, had yet another tale of the bushman's exploits, as told to him by John Pierce:

> A station-bred horse, gone wild, was running on the Leatherbarrel Mountain, on the road to Kosciusko from Groggin. The horse had defeated every attempt to catch him, although all of his 'running mates' had fallen victim to the stockmen's strategy. However, his continuous challenge was too much for the stockmen. His capture became a matter of necessity, a needed balm for a wounded proper pride. So a council of war was held and a plan of campaign devised to trap the outlaw. A yard was built in a strategic position across tracks near a creek which the horse habitually crossed, and duties were assigned to each member of the chase.
>
> The hunting party found the magnificent outlaw high on a ridge.

They deployed, to sweep in on him from many angles with the intention of compelling him into the yard. But they had underestimated their quarry. He broke into a furious gallop, but for once abandoned his normal 'run' to the creek, and broke away to hurtle down a precipitous slope that no rider had ever braved.

'It was as though he had sensed our plan,' Mr Pierce said. 'As he flashed down that cliff – it was little less, anyhow – we didn't think any man could follow him down. But John Riley pulled his hat down over his ears, and with a wild yell charged down after the outlaw while his friends held their breath. Riley vanished from sight in a flurry of heels and a shower of dirt – and hardly a man among the hunters thought to find him alive.

More circumspectly, the others made their way down to the trap-yard across the creek trail. There, to their amazement, was the horse, yarded and winded, and there too was Riley – coming back up the slope. Riley was not very talkative about what had happened from the time he disappeared from view until the time he ended his chase. But he did vouchsafe the hint: 'See here, now,' he said. 'I went so fast down the slope the wind got in me eyes and the tears blinded me.' And, blind, he had ridden past the yard, into which the quarry had careered head long, and was unaware of the capture until his breeze-tortured eyes had cleared.

'It is difficult to imagine what Riley rode like down that slope,' Mr Pierce would say. 'The lash of branches, the menace of boulders, the clawing brush must have made it a nightmare . . . But John Riley enjoyed it.'

These were the tales told about Riley by others, in most cases years after Riley entertained his guest, the poet, on that cold night in 1890. However, some of them are remarkably similar to the story the poet himself told just a few months after his visit to Tom Groggin. The poet's name was A.B. 'Banjo' Paterson and the story was contained in the verses of his most famous poem, 'The Man from Snowy River', first published in the *Bulletin* magazine under that title on 26 April 1890.

The poem met with immediate success and it wasn't long before it had made Banjo Paterson a household name throughout Australia. It wasn't long, too, before horsemen from every corner of the land claimed they were the inspiration for the tale of the wild ride to catch a valuable colt that had joined the mountain brumbies. However, only one of them can be confirmed as ever having met Banjo Paterson – Jack Riley. In fact, the two met on two occasions. Jean Carmody writes:

> Walter Mitchell [Tom's father], then living at Bringenbrong [another upper Murray property], was the man instrumental in bringing together the stockman Jack Riley, and the poet Banjo Paterson, when Mitchell and Paterson went out into the mountains on a camping trip. The two men spent a night at Jack Riley's hut at Groggin, and during the evening Jack entertained the visitors with tales of his adventures in some of the wildest country in Australia. Next day, Jack guided the visitors up to the top of Kosciusko, then around the Great Divide towards the Tin Mine and on to The Pilot. It was at this time that Jack mentioned to his companions the days he had spent on the banks of the Snowy River, not very far ahead of where they were.

Noel Gough, in his centenary booklet, adds to this: 'Banjo Paterson visited Jack Riley, at Tom Groggin, on another occasion with Billy Lowden and his nephew, John Pierce Jr.'

Further confirmation of the connection comes from what would be regarded by most as a trustworthy source: a priest. Riley continued living at Tom Groggin, but by 1911 he was becoming old and frail. Finally he took a turn that looked like taking his life. A priest was called for, but reaching Tom Groggin was a huge ask. Nevertheless,

Father Patrick Hartigan, then an inspector of Catholic schools, made his way from Albury in search of the man seeking the last rites. In what would prove yet another literary connection, Hartigan was a poet, who under his pen-name of John O'Brien became known in 1921 for *Around the Boree Log and Other Verses*.

Driving a Renault 'eight-nine' that was more suited to a museum than the rugged tracks into the mountains, Father Hartigan made it as far as Jingellic, north-west of Corryong, when night fell. The locals warned him against trying to push on to the Mitchell property at Bringenbrong in a vehicle that had no windscreen and only oil lamps for headlights. As he wrote later:

> If you have to cross a swollen creek wherein the current will sweep your wardrobe out of the sulky, [a bushman] will tell you that 'it's not too bad'; if he knows that the water will be over your horse's back, he will warn you that 'it's not too good'; if you have a mountain before you which will necessitate your tying a tree on to the back of your trap to keep it from dashing headlong, he will admit that 'it's a bit rough'; but when he tells you without any qualification that 'you won't get through', believe him.

Heading on to the upper Murray the next day he found out why:

> Sometimes we were on the river's level, at other times we saw it a tiny thread of silver hundreds of feet below. Up the steep gradients the little 'eight-nine' struggled all out on low gear; down the almost perpendicular descents she felt her way, axle grease frying on her red-hot brakes.

That was just the beginning. At Khancoban, inquiries about the road ahead led to yet another tale. Had the priest not heard about Jack Cox of Mangoplah? No:

> Well, he had some sheep up here in the drought. They had a sulky with provisions, and coming down the Geehi Wall [the steepest part of the bush track leading to the Groggin flats], it started to push the horse before it in spite of everything; so a big 'pommy' they had with them reckoned he could hold it. They took the horse out, and the big bloke tried to wheel the trap like a wheelbarrow. It got away from him, and they haven't found it since.

Finally, 13 kilometres on from Khancoban, at the last property along the last thing that could be flattered with the term 'road', they found Jack Riley. Father Hartigan described him as:

> a little old man who had battled out his life in the hills. He was a guide on the mountain, and had not left it for two score years. His hut was at Tom Groggin, and his mates had carried him on a packhorse for 40 miles [64 kilometres] through that almost impassable country, so that he might be within reach of the priest and the doctor. The busy world was outside his orbit altogether. He had never been in a train, had never seen a motor car, and knew very little of his religion. At least he had the Faith and wanted to see the priest before he went over the mountain for the last time. He was so reverent about it all, and so anxious to do 'the right thing', that it was a privilege to gather in that sheep which had missed the mustering so long.

After tending to Riley's spiritual needs, that night Father Hartigan sat around the fire with the men who'd carried him out:

> We spoke of their lives, and of 'the mountain' of which they spoke with awe – of the dangers of it, of the lure of it, of the mists that rise without warning to blanket out the world, and a lost man camps for the night on the brink of Eternity.
>
> We spoke of the wild horses. Yes, there were still some on The Pilot.

> Good sorts, too; wasn't Snowdon loose for a time on 'the hills'? Too right he was. Did Morgan the bushranger 'lift' him from the Bowlers, and when hard pressed let him go with the clean-skins?

It was during their storytelling that Father Hartigan decided to risk his ability to recite verse. 'Uninvited, and self-announced,' he wrote:

> I rose and gave them 'The Man from Snowy River'. They bore it with patience, and when I had finished there was neither applause nor disapproval. Each man smoked in silence, and 'spat across the cat'. The gloom was heavy and disquieting, and to dispel it – also to elicit some opinion on the merits (if any) of the effort, I remarked: 'It was somewhere up here that the man from Snowy River did that ride, wasn't it?'
>
> 'That's him inside,' said one of the company.
>
> 'Who? Where?'
>
> 'The old cove you came up to see.'
>
> 'What, Riley?'
>
> 'Yes, he ran in that colt, and up till he got sick the other day, no one could hold him down the mountain. Go in and have a yarn with him.'

The next morning, when Riley was awake, Father Hartigan did so.

'We often had to do that sort of thing and had tougher goes than that,' Riley told Hartigan. 'I was taking a party to Kossy, and was telling them about it, and one of them put it in a book; but he brings in the names of a lot of men who weren't there. There was nobody named Clancy; there was me and So-and-so, and So-and-so.'

Riley later recovered and returned to his hut, but his employer, John Pierce, realised Riley was no longer able to look after the cattle. He appointed a new overseer, Fred Jarvis, with instructions to keep an eye on Riley as well. Then, in 1914, as winter approached and the cold around Tom Groggin grew more intense, Riley had another turn.

As the *Argus* reported on Friday, 17 July 1914: 'Word reached Corryong on Saturday [11 July] that his condition was serious, and some of his friends decided to bring him to Corryong to the hospital. With this object Mr W.H. Findlay, a well-known Kosciusko guide, went up to Groggin on Sunday last.'

Will Findlay told Tom Mitchell a slightly different story:

> He'd been pretty sick once before, and had been away with that disease where your legs all swell up, you know, dropsy – but he was cured and had come back to his hut in Groggin. I was out there mustering cattle all round those hills with three other men, and I called in to see old Jack and found him pretty bad. I said we would take him into Corryong to the doctor but he said no, he'd rather stay there. So we left him, and we went on with the mustering. A few days later we looked in again and here is the poor old fellow lying on the floor just about at the end of his tether. So we knocked together a bit of a stretcher out of a couple of saplings and some hessian that was kicking around the hut, and we set off to carry him in to the doctor.

The *Argus* listed the other men with Findlay as A. and J. McInnes, the overseer Fred Jarvis and Bob Butler:

> About half-past 9 o'clock on Tuesday the party left the Groggin Hut, carrying Riley on the stretcher, the men taking turn about at the handles and leading pack horses with provisions and blankets. The first 4 or 5 miles [6 to 8 kilometres] from the valley was covered without much difficulty, but when it became necessary to climb out of the gorge over the shoulder of the Hermit Hill [now known as Hermit Mountain] the real difficulties began. The track ascends through wild scrub and rocks over 2000 feet [610 metres], and the party soon found that the task was beyond them. To make matters worse, snow began to fall, and the cold became intense.

Tom Mitchell also described the scene:

> Jack Riley, his spirit hovering between this world and the one just a little beyond us all, lay silent, or shouted sporadic bursts of words mingled with queer sounds. Snatches of song, strange names, imprecations, sighs, terms of endearment, yells of encouragement, or warnings to unseen men, all came tumbling forth, sometimes with startling clarity, sometimes just a babble of incoherencies.

The men found they were unable to manoeuvre the laden stretcher up the steep and narrow track that ascended Hermit Mountain, which at that point flanks the Murray River with almost vertical slopes known as the Murray Gates. Almost at a loss as to what to do, the mountain men turned to their horses. Tom Mitchell takes up the story:

> Bob Butler was the smallest and lightest of the party, and he jumped up onto the quietest of the horses and poor old Jack was lifted up into the saddle. Bob held him there with his arms round the thin waist. The horse, panting and straining, was led and pushed inch by inch up the mountain. At the top the weather was blowing a bitter gale, with flurries of snow stinging down through the straining trunks of the forest. Jack Riley's head slumped and they thought that he had gone, but he rallied as they began to pick their way through the fallen timber on the descent.

Hermit's Creek was reached late in the afternoon. There, according to Tom Mitchell:

> They offered him a drink of his beloved whisky, but to their surprise he refused, saying that he could not swallow it. 'Cripes, he must be crook!' someone remarked.
>
> 'If we can get him to the hut at Surveyor's Creek, we can get him

into a bunk and warm him, and he'll be all right,' was the common opinion.

The *Argus* describes what happened next:

> The stretcher had then to be brought into use again, and just at dark the party reached Surveyor's Creek Junction, where a deserted mining hut provided a shelter for the night. Mr Jarvis went up the creek to the tin mine, and arranged for assistance in the morning, and the others made a fire and installed the patient as comfortable as possible in front of it. He seemed to rally a little, and spoke to his friends, but the weakness reasserted itself, and shortly afterwards he suddenly swayed and died.

Jack Riley's spirit stayed in his beloved mountains, but his body was carried out the next day, strapped to the back of a pack horse. He was taken to Corryong, where he was laid out on a billiard table in the Coffee Palace, a local emporium, before being buried in Corryong Cemetery on 16 July 1914.

Jack Riley may have gone to his rest, but the controversy over his identity as the man from Snowy River was only just getting started. Riley's death was reported in the *Argus* under the headline 'Man from Snowy River. Death of the original.' However, Banjo Paterson sowed the seeds of confusion himself in later life. In an article, 'Looking Backward', published on 21 December 1938 in the *Sydney Mail*, he wrote:

> 'The Man from Snowy River' was written to describe the cleaning-up of the wild horses in our own district, which was rough enough for most

> people, but not nearly as rough as they had it on the Snowy. To make any sort of a job of it, I had to create a character, to imagine a man who would ride better than anybody else, and where would he come from except the Snowy? And what sort of horse would he ride except a half-thoroughbred mountain pony?
>
> Kipling felt in his bones that there must have been a well in his medieval fortress [presumably a reference to the well in *Puck of Pook's Hill*], and I felt equally convinced that there must have been a man from the Snowy River. I was right. They have turned up from all the mountain districts – men who did exactly the same ride, and could give you the chapter and verse for every hill they descended and every creek they crossed. It was no small satisfaction to find that there really had been a man from Snowy River – more than one of them.

That wasn't good enough for young Tom Mitchell, who had been brought up believing that Jack Riley was the true man from Snowy River. And it seems he had good cause, as he spelt out in a letter to the Royal Australian Historical Society:

> There will be claimants to be The Man from Snowy River from now until kingdom come. At any moment I am expecting Don Bradman, Henry Bolte and Bob Hawke to lodge claims. I asked Banjo Paterson point blank, 'Who was the Man from Snowy River?' And he replied, 'Jack Riley.' That was at the Queen's Club, Sydney, in 1936, when my mother had a little party to farewell the Australian Ski Team (of which I was captain) en route to compete against New Zealand.

To the *Corryong Courier* he wrote: 'My mother had a small party in Sydney to farewell us and the team. Among her friends there was Banjo Paterson, and I asked Banjo exactly who was the Man from Snowy River. Banjo told me that the man was to a large extent imaginary – BUT WAS WOVEN AROUND JACK RILEY.' (Capitals are Mitchell's.)

Mitchell added: 'I am trying to find a letter at home that Banjo wrote me about this trip with my father, and of meeting the man from Snowy River and of how he (Banjo) was impressed by the way my father could kill snakes with his stockwhip without getting off his horse.'

In 1936, of course, Paterson was seventy-two, recalling events that had taken place when he was twenty-six. Unfortunately, the letter Tom Mitchell refers to appears to have been lost. And it's a great loss because written confirmation from the poet himself might have settled the matter once and for all. However, there is something that definitely proves Paterson at least knew Riley. There's another Paterson poem, and it names him. 'Johnny Riley's Cow – A Ballad of Federation' was written by Banjo Paterson in 1898, but not published until 1983, well after the poet's death in 1941. The text leaves no doubt that Paterson was quite familiar with Riley:

Come all you Federationists and hearken to me now –
I've a story will instruct you very highly.
'Tis about a free selector and his Federation cow
And the free selector's name was Johnny Riley.
He was farming forty acres on the Upper Murray side,
Where the river's very shallow and it isn't very wide.

– Extract from 'Johnny Riley's Cow – A Ballad of Federation'
by A.B. Paterson from *A Vision Splendid*, Collins/Angus & Robertson
Publishers, 1990, reprinted with permission of HarperCollins
Publishers Australia

It not only names Riley, it does a pretty good job of giving his address. In the meantime, the dispute has continued to bubble with, as Tom Mitchell observed, any number of contenders. In a short article, 'So "The Man from Snowy River" is a Myth!', that appeared in the September 1956 issue of the *Riverlander* and in the *Cooma–Monaro Express*, Donald Howard named some of the them:

> When roaming around the bush, I met a character on Wave Hill, in the Northern Territory, who claimed the honour for himself. In his seventies, grey bearded with legs permanently bent to the shape of the saddle, Old Owen Cummins had at least one thing in common with Riley – he disliked the poem too! 'It happened on the Dargo Plains,' he told me. 'But it was nothing like the way Paterson told it. He only saw part of it.'
>
> Still another claimant is a man from Delegate way, called Wright. Many of the old-timers there used to claim he was the original. Up around Jindabyne, Jim Spencer is the choice, but go to Adaminaby, and they'll tell you he was Charlie McKechnie. Wherever you go in cattle country, you'll meet someone who claims the honour for himself or another.

After Jack Riley's death, his grave went unmarked for forty years until, as Tom Mitchell wrote in the same issue of the *Riverlander*:

> I was Shire President, just after the war, and caused a head stone to be erected over it. I felt that a routine one would be entirely out of character with old Jack. So I got hold of a rough-hewn semi-circular piece of granite that had been intended for the new bridge at Jingellic years before, but not used; and I had a small plinth, suitably inscribed, mounted on this rough granite.

It read: 'In Memory of THE MAN FROM SNOWY RIVER/JACK RILEY/ BURIED HERE 16TH JULY 1914.'

These days, Riley is anything but forgotten. The Folk Museum in Corryong has a display on his life and times, and his pack-saddle, initialled JR. The museum also details the exploits of the local horsemen in World War I, where their abilities in the saddle were highly valued in the Australian Light Horse. Incidentally, Elyne Mitchell, Tom Mitchell's wife, was the daughter of Sir Harry Chauvel, commander of the fabled Desert Corps of 34000 horsemen and cameleers. The Coffee Palace is still there, as is the billiard table where Riley was laid out. The Coffee Palace now sells farm machinery and historic photos of the local district, including the Surveyor's Creek hut and Riley outside his hut at Tom Groggin. Both huts have long since succumbed to the elements.

Most importantly, though, The Man from Snowy River Bush Festival is held annually in and around Corryong during April. The festival commemorates Riley's last ride from Tom Groggin and includes bush poetry and music and a series of tests of horsemanship. Details can be found at www.manfromsnowyriverbushfestival.com.au. The festival draws large crowds from all over the district and further afield, including some of the best horsemen in the country. At one recent event, there was even a relative of Jack Riley, presumably a descendant of one of his siblings. However, no-one got this descendant's contact details before he left.

At other times, visitors to Corryong can visit Jack Riley's grave, in the cemetery on a hill just on the edge of town. There is also a display on his life and Banjo Paterson's. His grave is well tended, and often has flowers on it, left by people who are still moved by his story.

So was he or wasn't he the Man from Snowy River? The proof may be inconclusive, but on the balance of probabilities Riley was, at the very least, an inspiration for the poem. Without doubt, he was the kind of man Banjo had in mind. And just as Banjo wrote in his poem, years after Riley's death there were plenty of stockmen still telling stories of his rides. That Riley was one of the best was recognised by the *Argus* obituary:

> Familiar with every inch of 'Head of the River Country' he has given willing assistance to numbers of tourists passing through, and was better known than probably any other man on the mountains. A fearless and dashing horseman in his young days, a first-class hand among stock, and an Irishman, open-hearted and generous, he was liked and respected by all who knew him. In bushcraft, even among the experts of the Murray, Gippsland, and Monaro, he stood alone.

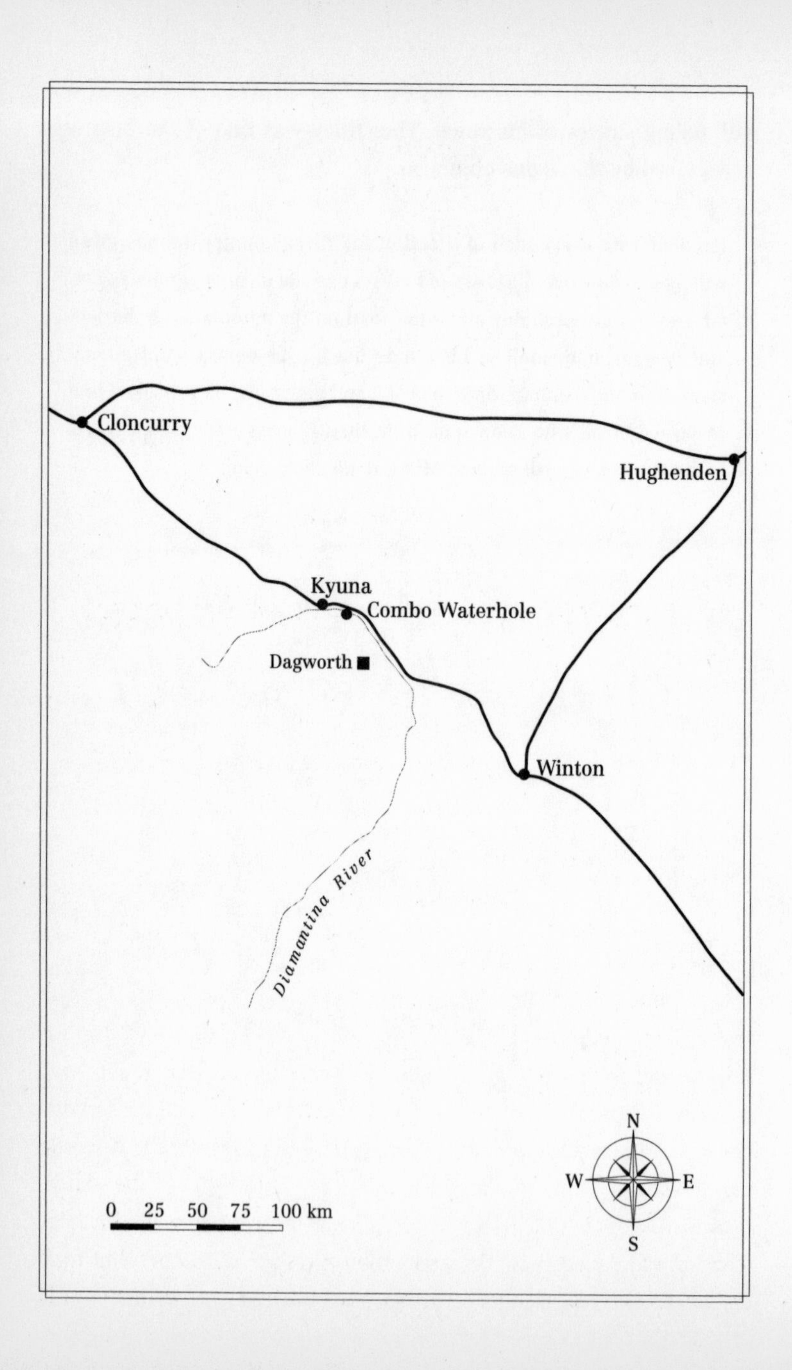

Cloncurry
Hughenden
Kyuna
Combo Waterhole
Dagworth
Winton
Diamantina River
N
W
E
S
0 25 50 75 100 km

Detail of the *Bulletin* cover, Saturday, 8 September 1894. There is no known image of Samuel Hoffmeister still in existence *(State Library of New South Wales)*

6

THE NOT SO JOLLY SWAGMAN, 1894: Samuel Hoffmeister (18??–1894)

On 1 September 1894, an extraordinary article appeared in the *Bulletin* magazine. It was titled 'The Anarchists of the Bush' and detailed the distribution of anarchist literature in Queensland, and the spread of anarchist symbols (including a woman pointing to a building in flames with the slogan 'Anarchy is Liberty') on the roads between Sydney and Melbourne. 'These things are probably the work of a few madmen,' the unattributed article explained, 'but that does not lessen the danger to the society which has made them mad.

The swagman's usual greeting, "Old man, it ain't far off," (a reference to Judgement Day) may yet possess a more dread significance than attaches to the voice of mere idle discontent.'

The magazine's publishers could not have known how close 'it' really was. For in the early hours of the day following publication, on Sunday, 2 September, a heavily guarded woolshed in the Queensland outback was attacked under cover of darkness by a group of armed men. After a fierce and prolonged exchange of gunfire, the building went up in flames. If the country wasn't teetering on the abyss, it had already begun the terrible descent.

The problem was globalism. A century before that term came into vogue, economic structures (aided by high-speed communications like the telegraph) had expanded to circle the planet. Where Australia was concerned, banking and land ownership were closely linked to Britain. Britain's financial system in turn was linked to the economies of Europe and the United States. In 1890, it all started to go pear-shaped. Australia's economy, dependent on mining and primary production, was squeezed by falling demand for its resources and lower prices, and consequently the banks started to restrict credit. Money sunk into speculative land booms evaporated overnight.

At the same time labour was becoming increasingly unionised, while pastoralists, in particular, were finding money getting tight. In the wool industry, the squattocracy was feeling the pinch and trying to find cheaper labour to bring in the clip. With the help of the maritime unions, which in August 1890 refused to handle wool shorn by non-union labour, the shearers resisted. In January 1891, the shearers struck. Amid growing unrest, non-union labour was brought in from other states, often under police guard. At one point even the army was deployed, armed with a machine gun. By mid-year the strike was broken when the union's executive was arrested at Barcaldine, charged with conspiracy, and imprisoned for terms of up to three years. Later that year, however, common sense prevailed

The First Settlers Discover Buckley, an oil by F.W. Woodhouse painted in 1861, depicts the moment in 1835 when convict William Buckley returned to civilisation after thirty-two years in the Australian bush. *(Image: La Trobe Picture Collection, State Library of Victoria)*

Detail from *The First Settlers Discover Buckley*. His accounts mention being given a possum-skin rug, for which he exchanged his by-then threadbare jacket. *(Image: La Trobe Picture Collection, State Library of Victoria)*

Memorial to Joseph Hawdon and Charles Bonney, the first overlanders, at Wentworth, near the Murray–Darling junction. *(Photo: Nikki Bond)*

Remants of the Overland Telegraph. Through country like this, John Ross and his exploration team were required to find water for the line's workers, timber for the line's poles and a route that was suitable for its support teams. *(Photo: JABA – Connecting the Continent Website Project)*

The MacDonnell Ranges, the major obstacle for the Overland Telegraph route's support teams of horses and bullocks. *(Photo: National Archives of Australia, A6135, K8/3/88/8)*

Droving on the Barkly. Duffer Harry Redford stole a herd of similar size in 1870. *(Photo courtesy Mark Coombe, www.outbackpics.com)*

Jack Riley's hut at Tom Groggin in the Snowy Mountains, circa 1900. Riley was visited by Banjo Paterson early in 1895, and *The Man From Snowy River* was written shortly afterwards. *(Reproduced by James Nicholas, Corryong. Photo: courtesy Corryong Historical Society)*

Tom Groggin (with the modern-day station in the middle distance), the only large area of level ground in the upper Murray. The original Riley hut has long since disintegrated. *(Photo: Michelle Havenstein)*

Jack Riley's grave in Corryong Cemetery. *(Photo: Michelle Havenstein)*

The buildings that remained at Dagworth after the burning of the woolshed were heavily defended, as the presence of three police at a stockade around one of the outbuildings reveals. Several of the men in this photo were present during the shootout that took place while the woolshed was being set alight. *(Photo: John Oxley Library Collection, State Library of Queensland, 15771)*

The Bulletin

Registered at the General Post Office, Sydney, for transmission by post as a Newspaper.

Vol. 14—No. 760. SATURDAY, SEPTEMBER 8, 1894. Price 6d.

THE FIRESTICK POLICY.

THE BULLETIN: "See here, my lad, a word in your ear. *That will not help you an atom.*"

The cover of the *Bulletin*, Saturday, 8 September 1894, was a response to the burning of Queensland's Dagworth woolshed by striking shearers on September 2. However, the 1 September issue of the *Bulletin* carried an unattributed article on the plight of unemployed swagmen in the midst of the great depression of the 1890s. It suggested incendiary attacks could be the last resort of desperate men. Then, early in 1895, *Bulletin* contributor Banjo Paterson visited Dagworth, where he wrote the anti-authoritarian swagman's song, *Waltzing Matilda*. *(Source: State Library of New South Wales)*

Desert islands in a sea of green. Queensland Channel Country floods, such as this one on South Galway Station, could turn parched floodplains into a vast swathe of cattle-fattening grass, leaving the higher ground bone dry. Kidman hoped a chain of such stations could 'drought-proof' his enormous operations. *(Photo: John Rickertt)*

and a national agreement was reached, one that set reasonable rates of pay while allowing the use of non-union labour.

The economy, meanwhile, went from bad to worse. In 1892, 14000 people registered when the government opened a labour bureau in Sydney. In July miners in Broken Hill struck when their pay deal was torn up and non-union labour employed. At one point a group of strikers' wives was confronted by police and troopers with fixed bayonets. Then came 1893. The banks, which had been faltering since the depression began, started to fail. At the beginning of April, the biggest bank in the country, the Commercial, suspended operations. Within days, twelve other banks had followed suit as people rushed to withdraw their savings. At the end of the month, the Victorian government closed all the banks in the state for a week, while it tried to deal with the crisis.

Small investors got hammered. Businesses closed, people lost their savings, and the unemployment queues grew ever longer. It was little wonder the anarchists were able to gain ground. Anarchy could hardly have been worse than the organised economy of the 1890s.

The *Bulletin*'s article, 'The Anarchists of the Bush', detailed some of the consequences:

> The swagmen of the past could be easily divided into two classes – good workmen, who promptly smashed their cheques at the nearest pub, and then humped 'bluey' in honest search of a fresh job; and professional 'sundowners,' [so-called as they usually came looking for a meal at sundown, when it was too late to do any work to earn it] who turned up, year in and year out, with automatic regularity. With neither of these have the unemployed of today anything in common. The old swagman had, in most cases, either innate laziness or inordinate love of rum to thank for his position, and the squatter was well repaid for rations when labour's own legs brought labour without cost to capital's door. Today all is changed. Thanks to their own land hunger and

> consequent slavery to the banks, nine-tenths of the squatters have no money to pay for labour; and farmers have even more than in the past to rely on their own unaided exertions for putting in and taking off their crops. Unfortunately the number of wage-earners has not decreased in proportion to the shrinkage in demand. This winter men, who, a few years ago, had never to ask twice for a job, are saying in the bitterness of their hearts, 'I've never begged before; and rather than live this dog's life I'll go to gaol.' When the legitimate bush-worker is thus tried, it is easy to understand the damnable despair of the hordes of artisans, labourers, clerks, larrikins, and social camp-followers who are now swarming out of the cities into the poverty-cursed country districts.

On the squatter's side, it was no picnic either. Many were not able to weather the financial storm, and in 1894 Charles Flower was compelled to write the song, 'The Broken-Down Squatter':

> When the country was cursed with the drought at its worst
> And the cattle were dying in scores
> Though down on my luck, I kept up my pluck
> Thinking justice might temper the laws
> But the farce has been played, and the Government aid
> Ain't extended to squatters, old son
> When my money was spent, they doubled the rent
> And resumed the best half of the run
>
> . . . For it's useless to squat when the rents are so hot
> That you can't save the price of your grub
> And there's not much to choose 'twixt the banks and the screws
> Once a fellow gets put up a tree

The tone reflects the *Bulletin* article, which went on to explain how a lot of properties had stopped providing food for passing swagmen, as they had traditionally done. Some, it said, took the excuse of hard times to assert their 'native meanness', while others, men like Flower, couldn't afford to feed themselves, let alone 'scores of hungry men for the pure love of the race'. And the reference to scores was no exaggeration. The article detailed a small southern New South Wales property that was feeding 100 travellers a month, another that was slaughtering two bullocks a week for travellers. It went on:

> At the present time hundreds of men are tramping across wind-swept plains and over mud-choked roads, without swags, and owning no earthly possession save the rags which hang about their half-starved carcases. Fathers are leaving their children to the tender mercies of strangers rather than see them die from exposure [there were cases of children being sold and babies murdered when homes couldn't be found for them]. Worse – delicate women and half-grown girls are wandering about without either food or shelter. In the huts that still remain, strange companies meet night after night – drawn together by a common wretchedness. They curse the hand that has doled them out their pint of flour, and, illogically it may be, speak of the approaching reign of chaos as a period which, if not bright with hope, is, at any rate, lurid with the fiercer fires of revenge. And this is the spectacle which Australia, with greater natural wealth than almost any other country in the world, offers after a hundred years of settlement!

Who wrote this unsigned harangue? Was it the *Bulletin*'s proprietor, J.F. Archibald? Perhaps it was one of the contributors, such as Henry Lawson, who was soon to be hired by the *Worker*, and wrote at length about labour's struggle, including a bizarre stream-of-consciousness rant entitled 'Death of an Anarchist'. A third candidate was someone who, due to the failure of an earlier political piece, went by the pseudonym 'The Banjo' – lawyer, land-holder and poet, Andrew Barton Paterson.

Whoever penned 'The Anarchists of the Bush' gives this clue to his identity: 'The writer was within the past fortnight implored by a strong young fellow to take him on at 5s. per week, while land which, five years ago, could not be grubbed for less than £1 to £2 is now being made ready for the plough at from 7s. to 17s. 6d. per acre.' Obviously the author of this article was a land-holder, like Paterson. The perennially cash-strapped Lawson can on these grounds be discounted. Of course, without clear evidence the suggestion is purely speculative. What is beyond doubt is that whoever the author was, Archibald, Lawson and Paterson were among the readers. And following the smoking gun, or in this case, the smoking woolshed, leads to some fascinating connections with Australia's most famous song, Banjo Paterson's lasting tribute to the swagman, 'Waltzing Matilda', penned just months later.

> In those hard times, nobody was satisfied [Paterson wrote of the 1890s in a *Sydney Morning Herald* article published on 11 March 1939], so I thought – like Hamlet – that it was up to me to set the world right. I read heavily in history and economics, and the outcome was my first literary effort – a pamphlet called 'Australia for the Australians'. I blush every time I think of it!
>
> When my pamphlet fell as flat as the great inland desert, I tried my hand at 'poetry', and strung together four flamboyant verses about the expedition against the Mahdi, who was going well and strong at the time. As the *Bulletin* was the most unsatisfied paper in Australia, I sent them to that paper. I had adopted the pen name of 'The Banjo', after a so-called racehorse, which we had on the station. I was afraid to use my own name lest the editor, identifying me with the author of the pamphlet, would dump my contribution, unread, into the waste paper basket.

If Paterson was the author of the *Bulletin* piece, this previous experience with a signed political article may explain why he was cautious about signing his name to it. The same couldn't be said for his hell-raising fellow contributor Lawson who'd had to flee Queensland after writing the poem published in the *Worker* in May 1891, 'Freedom on the Wallaby', which includes the incendiary lines: 'We'll make the bankers [in later versions, 'tyrants'] feel the sting o' those that they would throttle,/They needn't say the fault was ours if blood should stain the wattle.'

At the time the *Bulletin* piece was written, the union shearers were on strike again. The battling squatters had repudiated their 1891 agreement and tried to lower the rates of pay for shearing, whether union or non-union. Amid the desperate employment situation, there were still plenty of willing takers. Non-union shearers were again being moved to the woolsheds, under increasingly heavy police guard. Shearing sheds at Redcliffe, Manuka, Cambridge Downs, Ayrshire Downs, Casilis and elsewhere were torched.

On 26 August a paddle-steamer, the *Rodney*, carrying non-union labour up the Darling, tied up for the night and her cautious skipper set a guard around her. It made no difference. In the darkness 100 armed men boarded her, sent the non-union labourers running for their lives and set the vessel alight. It burned to the waterline, then went to the bottom.

Less than a week later, on 1 September, it was a quiet, slightly overcast night at Dagworth Woolshed, halfway between Winton and Kynuna in the north-west of Queensland. At 10.30 p.m. overseer Weldon Tomlin and police constable Michael Daly went on duty, keeping watch on the shed and the adjacent huts. Daly was armed with a carbine, a revolver, and fifty-nine rounds of ammunition. As Constable Daly later testified:

> About half past 12 I heard a volley of shots fired from the downs side about 50 yards [45 metres] from the shed. I was about 10 or 15 yards from the corner of the shed between it and the huts. I heard one shot strike the iron of a hut and several whistled past me. I fired in the direction of the flashes (2 shots). The attacking party returned the fire and one of the attacking party called out from I should say about 40 yards, 'Put up your arms you bastards or die.'

Station manager Bob Macpherson, also testified: 'I was aroused about midnight of the 1st by a volley of shots. I was in the hut nearest the shed, got up and procured a revolver from my brother after some time. Before that I heard a voice call out "Hold up your hands or die" and afterwards, "Hold up your hands you bastards or die."

Outside, Daly and Tomlin were in the midst of a firefight. The former reported:

> I went to a heap of earth close to the shed for cover and from there fired 3 or 4 shots in the direction of the attacking party. I then came to the nearest hut occupied by Messrs Macpherson brothers and Mr Dyer [another manager] to advise them of the position of affairs. I was joined by Mr Dyer and returned to the heap of earth. He was armed with a Winchester rifle.

Macpherson soon joined them: 'Dyer went away with Constable Daly and when I got a revolver I followed. When I saw a flash of 3 or 4 shots about 40 yards [37 metres] away from the attacking party I returned the fire and immediately heard a bullet whistle past me. I fired five more shots – the attacking party kept up a continuous fire.'

Dyer and Daly poured gunfire into the darkness, as the police constable recalled:

> We fired 7 or 8 shots each and then saw a match struck at the shed immediately followed by a blaze as if from kerosene. We both fired in the direction of the match. After some time the fire reached the roof of the shed, all this time the attacking party kept up continuous fire under which it was impossible to reach the shed. I heard the same voice say before the match was struck: 'Give it to the bastards. We have waited long enough for this and now we'll have it.'

Macpherson also saw the shed go up:

> I could see Dyer, Daly and Tomlin returning the fire. Before the shed was set fire to I heard the same voice say: 'Rally up boys and let them have it. You'll die or we'll die.' I saw the shed on fire. It was impossible to attempt to save it in consequence of the incessant firing of the attacking party. About 140 lambs and other property were burnt in the shed. The firing continued on and off for three-quarters of an hour and only ceased when the shed was fully at large.

The attackers were extremely close, as Daly testified:

> The voice appeared to be within 30 yards [27 metres] from the shed and about 40 yards from where we were . . . The shed was completely burnt except one corner. I could see none of the attacking party; it was a very dark night. When the shed blazed up the attacking party retired further back . . . [Macpherson] attempted to save the lambs and some wool but was fired on by the attacking party and retired.

The woolshed burned until about 2 a.m.

When daylight broke over the woolshed's smoking ruins, both Daly and Macpherson searched the area for evidence. As Daly testified:

> I examined the ground from where the attacking party was firing and found four discharged cartridges and two loaded ones, some were within 20 yards [18 metres] of the shed. I occupied that night, when not on watch, the hut nearest the shed. The next morning I found three bullet holes in it. One passed through the wall at the head of the bunk I occupy and lodged in the inner door. If I had been in that bunk when the shot was fired I must have been shot. I also saw fresh bullet marks in the walls of the other huts, one of which was occupied by a woman and two children.

Macpherson added:

> I examined the place at daylight and saw several empty and full cartridges picked up from 10 to 30 yards [9 to 27 metres] from the shed, 26 were found. I saw melted bullets in the shed, and one taken out of an inner door in the hut nearest the shed – 3 bullets were fired at that hut. If one man had been in his bunk, he would have been shot. In another hut fired at there were 14 men. In another hut fired at there was a woman and her two daughters. Neither I nor the other defenders could have fired the shots at the huts. The attacking party firing at the shed and its defenders could not have accidentally hit any of the huts especially the one containing the woman which was about 200 yards [183 metres] off the line of fire. The cartridge cases picked up were principally Winchester rifle and some Martini Henry and some revolver.

Hopes of pursuing the attackers were soon dashed, as Bob Macpherson explained: 'It rained before daylight sufficient to destroy all tracks which I searched for without success,' however, 'I found three gates open near the shed, one leading to the head-station and two towards the back country.'

Considering the hail of gunfire involved, it was a miracle that no-one was wounded or killed. Indeed, it came as no great surprise when, on Sunday afternoon, a man at a campsite beside a waterhole some 25 kilometres from Dagworth and 6 kilometres from Kynuna was reported dead from a gunshot wound. His name was Samuel 'Frenchy' Hoffmeister, and he has been variously described as a Bavarian anarchist, a prominent unionist, and 'a bit mad'.

By now, telegrams were flying between Winton's police magistrate, Ernest Eglinton, and the Colonial Secretary in Brisbane. On 3 September:

> There is no doubt same gang burning all sheds. I would urge native trackers be hurried into this district. Information just received that a man named Hoffmeister a unionist found shot dead about 2 miles [3 kilometres] from Kynuna. Police are of opinion he was one of the attacking mob at Dagworth and was wounded there. I think doctor should be sent to examine wound and see if bullet corresponds with those used by defenders at Dagworth. Seven unionists were with Hoffmeister when he died. They assert he suicided. Should I accompany doctor?

While Eglinton, police sub-inspector Dillon and Dr Wellford made their way to Kynuna on the 3rd and 4th, the media was already onto the story. In Brisbane's *Courier Mail* of 4 September, it was the chief topic of the editorial:

> Fortunately nobody was hit on the station side. Whether all the rioters escaped unscathed is not known, but it is a curious circumstance that the dead body of a well-known unionist was found about 12 miles [19 kilometres] from Dagworth. It was asserted by other men in the

> vicinity that he had committed suicide, but the matter is to be closely investigated. What appears certain is that he had been shot. Of course the shooting at Dagworth must under the circumstances have been of a random character. The crime was of the usual cowardly sort. Numbers and darkness were necessary to its committal. This makes the eighth of the woolshed series. Whether or not there are more than one gang engaged in this work of destruction is not known. But however few or many these scoundrels may be there is nothing for it now but to regard and treat them as bushrangers or outlaws. Mercy is worse than wasted on such ruffians while they are at large with their rifles and their fire-sticks. They have made war upon society and society must make war upon them. We understand that one of the police magistrates in the North-west has found it necessary to seek protection in the discharge of his duties because his fearlessness as an officer of the law has marked him out for revenge. Queensland cannot tolerate such a condition of things in the North-west. No man's life will be safe on those vast plains if this savagery is permitted to develop. Happily for the credit of the colony the Government is not at all disposed to trifle with its most solemn obligations. It will use its constitutional power to the uttermost.

In other reports of the incident, the newspaper detailed the government's response:

> Affairs in the west have taken a serious turn – so serious in fact to justify the statement recently made in the House by the Colonial Secretary that the strike had developed into an insurrection. At about 8 o'clock on Sunday night Mr. Tozer [Colonial Secretary] received a wire from the Police Magistrate at Winton stating that Dagworth shed had been burnt down by about sixteen armed men . . . In consequence of the seriousness of this last event the Government are taking active steps to deal with persons found armed. Every effort is being made to trace the insurrectionists by the police in the district. We understand that

> instructions have been given to the troopers not to separate, and that the seven men who were with Hoffmeister when he died have been detained pending enquiries.

It's at this point that the plot, as they say, thickens. On 5 September, Eglinton in Kynuna started his investigation of the death of Hoffmeister. The detained unionists were interviewed and, though their stories showed several inconsistencies, Neil Highland's gives the gist of what is supposed to have happened. In Highland's account the unionists are all tucked in bed that fateful night, sleeping like lambs – rather than immolating the lambs 20 kilometres down the road:

> When Frenchy came it looked like rain, he came about sundown [on Saturday, 1 September]. He appeared sober – I heard his voice but did not hear what he said. He came from the direction of the Kynuna Camp . . . Frenchy was mounted and leading a packhorse. He slept beneath a tree between me and another fly. I went to bed about 8 or 9. It was before 10. No-one occupied my tent but myself. Some of the others had gone to bed before me. I saw them all in bed that night about 2 . . . All the men were in the Camp in the morning and remained there in the forenoon including Frenchy who was walking up and down the Camp. We had dinner between 12 and 1. Frenchy had his dinner at the fire. Others were there. No strangers. After dinner Frenchy came to the fire and I saw him burning some papers and heard him mutter something like 'That done I am satisfied.' He walked away about 20 yards [18 metres] – I heard a report of firearms and went in that direction and saw Frenchy lying down partly on his left side near a fly occupied by Crimmins and his mate. I did not notice if anything was on it – some of my mates were at the body before I got there. They were looking on. I thought he was dead. There was a revolver pouch near his back and a revolver about his chest somewhere – I saw blood about his mouth. I went away, got my horses and reported it to Mr McCowan [manager at nearby Kynuna Station]. The first time I saw the

> revolver was when it was close to his body. I did not touch it or see anyone else do so. After seeing Mr McCowan I returned to the camp and covered up the body and left the camp the same evening and went to the Kynuna Union Camp . . . I was friendly towards him. So were the others. There was no quarrel or dispute between Frenchy and myself or any other man that I know of – I assume that he shot himself, but why I can't say. On the night it rained (Saturday night) no one called at the camp. It was a revolver and pouch like the one produced that I saw with Frenchy when he put his swag in my tent. He also put in a rifle, too. I don't know of any other rifles in the camp but Frenchy's.

Also in evidence Senior Constable Austin Cafferty testified that he examined Hoffmeister's body and found fresh blood coming from the dead man's mouth. Considering that at least two hours must have elapsed from the time of the gunshot to the time of his arrival, the definition of fresh must have been quite broad. There was one strong indicator of suicide though, as reported in the *Courier Mail* on 20 September: 'The enquiry into the death of Hoffmeister at a union camp at Kynuna resulted in a verdict of suicide, as medical testimony went to show that the wound being in the roof of the mouth the teeth would not have been intact had he been shot by another person.'

Hoffmeister was buried at Kynuna Homestead on the same day as his inquest, 5 September. The next day, Ernest Eglinton reported to the Colonial Secretary: 'Held inquiry yesterday at Kynuna re death Samuel Hoffmeister. Clear case of suicide by shooting himself with revolver through the mouth. Am now proceeding to Dagworth woolshed to hold inquiry re burning.'

However, as the *Courier Mail* reported, and the inquiry into the Dagworth fire learned the next day, Hoffmeister was taking a lot of unanswered questions to his grave. At the Dagworth inquiry on 6 September, Constable Daly testified:

> I was present when the police examined the body of a man named Hoffmeister 15 miles [24 kilometres] from here [Dagworth] Sunday last. He had a Martini sporting rifle with him and 68 rounds of ammunition for it. The rifle appeared to be recently used. He also had 29 exploded rifle cartridges, a revolver and 21 cartridges. I found a similar exploded cartridge case at the place where the men were firing on the shed. There might have been others I did not find. I found a bullet in the hut I occupied and also found one in one of the other huts. Hoffmeister was a unionist shearer and had his union tickets on his body which was found in a unionist camp.

This contradicts the evidence given at the inquiry into Hoffmeister's suicide. His mates said he was supposed to have had a good night's sleep, but Daly has him participating in a shooting rampage. Eglinton concluded in a telegram on 7 September: 'Hoffmeister suicided 14 miles [23 kilometres] from Dagworth woolshed morning after the fire and had a rifle and a large number of loaded and exploded cartridges corresponding with some exploded cartridges found at place from where unionists fired on shed.'

Curiouser and curiouser.

No motive for 'suicide' was suggested. Was he mad and had simply taken his life? Had he feared capture and decided that rather than go to jail, he preferred to die? Or had he been wounded during the firefight and made it back to camp, where he died, and his mates, realising that his gunshot wound would blow their alibi and send them to jail, made his death look like suicide?

On 12 September the *Courier* voiced its suspicions. 'The evidence in connection with the death of Hoffmeister is plain as to suicide,' it reported, 'but in several points the witnesses contradict each other, and the cause of the suicide was unaccounted for. Four of the twelve men who were with him have served sentences.'

On 8 September, the weekend after the burning of Dagworth, the incendiarists made the cover of the *Bulletin*. An illustration showed a bookish *Bulletin* character admonishing a bushie brandishing a fire-stick. 'See here, my lad,' the caption reads, 'a word in your ear. That will not help you an atom.'

The *Bulletin* was spot on once again. The burning of Dagworth prompted the government of Queensland to introduce one of the most appalling pieces of legislation ever seen in Australia, the *Peace Preservation Act*. Among its many extraordinary provisions, it could require the people of entire districts to relinquish all their weapons, and people could be subjected to detention without bail or charge for indefinite periods at the discretion of the police. Queenslanders may have been divided by the shearers' strike, but worker and landowner were united by what soon became known as the Coercion Act.

From the *Courier*, 11 September:

MEETING IN CENTENNIAL HALL

A public meeting 'to protest against the Coercion Bill' was held in the Centennial Hall, Adelaide Street, last night. The attendance was large, seating and standing room being wholly occupied. The chairman, the Hon W. Brookes, MLC, said he was greatly pleased at that large meeting . . . The Government seemed – and it was very important to bear this in mind – to have got into their head that the public would allow them to do whatever they like. That feeling ought to be nipped in the bud, but he thought the meeting would do more than that; he hoped and trusted it would lay the axe at the root of the tree. (*Cheers.*)

Mr D.R. McConnell read the following telegram received from Longreach : – 'Western people highly indignant against Government Coercion Act. Consider likely to cause bloodshed. Only a handful of men committing outrages. Winton statement re bodies of armed men parading bush utterly false and ridiculous. Unionists most desirous to uphold law. Many innocent men expect arrest under Star Chamber process for sympathy with unions. Government also condemned for sending black-trackers amongst high-spirited white men; would not dare to treat mining districts thus. If civil revolt, Government wholly responsible. Will hold meeting. – C. B. Fitzgerald.'

At a later period of the evening, the following telegram, received from Longreach, was read: – 'Resolution condemning Coercion Bill carried unanimously by public meeting; over 1000 persons present.'

[Former Premier and former Chief Justice] Sir Charles Lilley was received with prolonged cheers. When these had ceased, he said they were not there that evening as shearers, nor as members of an Opposition, and they were not there as supporters of the Government. (*Applause.*) They were there as citizens . . . They would all regret that they had lived to see the introduction of such an iniquitous Act. (*Applause.*) He had to move:

That this meeting of the citizens of Brisbane protests against the Coercion Act submitted to Parliament by the Government under the title of the 'Peace Preservation Bill', because – (1) it would be powerless to gain its stated object, the preservation of peace; and (2) It would be a tyrannical infringement of the liberty of the citizens of this colony, by giving the Government an arbitrary power of imprisonment, and by establishing a system of secret tribunals . . .

It had never been the policy of our country to give such authority to any man. Any man might try to get it by force, but for centuries we had resisted such endeavours to usurp our liberty, and we had won back our rights as citizens.

The language suggests a population teetering towards rebellion. The economy was a mess, unemployment soaring, men were literally taking up arms to fight for their livelihoods and protect their property, the Queensland government was drawing battlelines against the people it was supposed to represent, and just about everyone hated the banks. The next day the *Courier* was reporting from Winton: 'All the stations in this district have armed guards, and much uneasiness exists . . . Police reinforcements, including black trackers, arrived to-day.'

Incredibly, the Peace Preservation Bill was passed on 25 September. This despite the fact that the strike was officially ended the day before. The violence continued sporadically, but with stations negotiating contracts, and guards still posted, some sheds were attacked though none were burned down. However, right into December haystacks and pastures were still being set alight.

Throughout these events the *Bulletin*'s contributor, Banjo Paterson, had a close connection with the area in which they occurred. He'd been in the district as recently as August, just before the attack on Dagworth. He returned in January 1895, but while it's been suggested by some researchers that he was drawn by the violent events in Queensland's north-west there was another, more compelling, reason.

Her name was Sarah Riley, she lived at Winton, and Paterson was courting her. Some accounts suggest she and Paterson were already engaged, hence the frequent visits. As it happened, Sarah was friends with Christina Macpherson, whose mother had recently died in Melbourne, causing her to move up to her brothers' property at Dagworth. Paterson and his partner were invited to visit.

It's a shame Banjo didn't keep a diary. For, as with events surrounding Jack Riley in Chapter 5, the events of his 1895 visit are clearly muddied by inaccuracies, contradictions and faulty recollections. There have been several reconstructions, notably those of Sydney May in the 1940s and 1950s, and Richard Magoffin from the 1970s to the present day. Then there are the explanations of the key players, which only confuse matters more, but will be considered shortly.

First there's Sydney May's version. According to him, Paterson, Bob Macpherson and a black boy were riding along a channel of the

Diamantina River when they saw a sheep that appeared to have died of natural causes. Macpherson suspected otherwise and closer inspection revealed that it had been slaughtered, partially eaten, then made to look like it had died naturally. Macpherson suspected swagmen.

Another story Macpherson is supposed to have related during a picnic at the Combo waterhole on the Diamantina was of a swagman who leapt into a Dagworth waterhole and drowned when confronted by a contingent of police, who were in fact searching for an escaped murderer named Harry Wood. May deals with the large number of police by suggesting that the policeman on Wood's trail was Constable Patrick Duffy, that perhaps his police number was 123, and that in subsequently referring to 'troopers one, two, three' Paterson was using poetic license.

Meanwhile, when the men were back at the homestead, Christina Macpherson is said to have been playing an autoharp (a simplified form of a zither), picking out a tune that she'd heard in Victoria, at the Warrnambool races in April the year before. Liking the tune, Banjo Paterson asked to hear the words. Christina didn't know any, and Paterson decided to write some. The song was based on 'Thou Bonnie Wood of Craigielea'. May notes that it also bears similarities with 'The Bold Fusilier', especially in the chorus:

> Who'll be a sojer, who'll be a sojer, who'll be a sojer for Marlbro' with me?
> And he cried as he tramped through the dear streets of Rochester –
> Who'll be a sojer for Marlbro' with me?

Finally, one night over dinner, jackeroo Jack Carter mentioned that he'd seen a couple of men waltzing Matilda (a local expression for wandering about the countryside carrying a swag, or bedroll) down in a billabong. Shortly after the meaning of the phrase was given, the song was written, and subsequently brushed up at various locations around the district.

Richard Magoffin refutes much of this. Doggedly researching for many years, he's discounted the Harry Wood story for happening too long before and too far away. As for the drowning episode specifically by suicide, checking the Register of Deaths and Coroner's Inquests there was a drowning at Dagworth in the Scour Waterhole three years before Paterson's visit. It appears, however, to have been accidental as the victim, a wool-scourer named George Pope, was last seen drunk in his tent. No constabulary were involved.

The only other suicide was Hoffmeister, not at Combo Waterhole, but at another on an old coach road 25 kilometres from where Dagworth Homestead used to be and 6 kilometres from Kynuna.

Magoffin does relate, however, the story of the butchered sheep found while Paterson and Bob Macpherson were out riding.

It is worth noting that Sydney May makes absolutely no mention of the Hoffmeister suicide, the shearers' strike, or the burning of Dagworth Homestead, even though he advises that he's done painstaking research. It doesn't seem to have extended to flipping through some of the newspapers of the period to get some context for the song and its times. May does admit that he never met Paterson, but says that his version of events was checked with members of Paterson's family who said it agreed with what they'd been told about how the song came about. Another thing May doesn't mention is Paterson's fiancée, Sarah Riley. There are suggestions the couple split over this visit, because Paterson was spending more time with Christina, writing 'Waltzing Matilda'. Of course, it could just as easily have been because he spent too much of his time out riding with her brother.

As it happens, late in their lives Christina and Banjo provided details of what happened in 1895. Ladies first. In an undated letter, probably from the early 1930s, Christina Macpherson wrote:

> [Banjo Paterson] was on a visit to Winton, North Queensland, and I was staying with my brothers about 80 miles [130 kilometres] from Winton.

> We went in to Winton for a week or so & one day I played (from ear) a tune which I had heard played by a band at the Races in Warnambool [sic], a country town in the Western District of Victoria. Mr Patterson [sic] asked what it was – I could not tell him, & he then said he thought he could write some lines to it. He then and there wrote the first verse. We tried it and thought it went well, so he then wrote the other verses. I might add that in a short time everyone in the District was singing it . . . When Mr Patterson returned to Sydney he wrote and asked me to send him the tune. I am no musician but did my best: & later on he told me he had sent it on to a musical friend of his who thought it would make a good bush song.

The significant element here is that she doesn't mention Riley and Paterson coming to her. She went to them in Winton. There's no riding around the property, and no autoharp either.

As for Banjo, he alluded to the writing of the song in a radio talk he gave on the ABC in 1938. The talk was titled 'Golden Water', a reference to the finding of seemingly limitless amounts of artesian water beneath the arid country out west:

> I do not know that I have properly conveyed the feeling of excitability which possessed everybody in the early days of the bore water: people seemed to be looking out on to limitless horizons and except (very occasionally) in a mining camp I can remember nothing like it. The shearers staged a strike by way of expressing themselves, and Macpherson's woolshed at Dagworth was burnt down and a man was picked up dead. This engendered no malice and I have seen the Macphersons handing out champagne through a pub window to these very shearers. And here a personal reminiscence may be worth recording. While resting for lunch, or while changing horses on our four-in-hand journeys, Miss Macpherson, afterwards wife of the financial magnate, J. McCall McCowan, used to play a little Scottish tune on a zither and I put words

> to the tune and called it 'Waltzing Matilda'. Not a very great literary achievement, perhaps, but it has been sung in many parts of the world. It was the effect of the bore water.

So here he's not writing the song at Dagworth or Winton, but somewhere out on the road, like Combo Waterhole. However, he's in error about Christina. She, like Paterson's one-time fiancée, Sarah Riley, never married. In 1896 Christina's sister Jean married Sam McCall McCowan, the manager from adjoining Kynuna Station, who'd called the police to investigate Hoffmeister's death. Indeed, Jean and Sam's relationship may have been the reason for picnic trips in the direction of the Diamantina waterholes, which lay between the two properties. The comment about the attack at Dagworth engendering no malice is also strange. Yet despite the inconsistencies, this reference certainly shows that Banjo was well aware of the event and even late in life was still linking it, if tangentially, to 'Waltzing Matilda'.

Another reference to events at Dagworth during the strike appears in Paterson's essay 'The Dog', which previously published, appeared again in his 1917 collection, *Three Elephant Power and Other Stories*:

> Dogs, like horses, have very keen intuition. They know when the men around them are frightened, though they may not know the cause. In a great Queensland strike, when the shearers attacked and burnt Dagworth shed, some rifle-volleys were exchanged. The air was full of human electricity, each man giving out waves of fear and excitement. Mark now the effect it had on the dogs. They were not in the fighting; nobody fired at them, and nobody spoke to them; but every dog left his master, left the sheep, and went away to the homestead, about 6 miles [10 kilometres] off. There wasn't a dog about the shed next day after the fight. The noise of the rifles had not frightened them, because they were well-accustomed to that.

It can confidently be said that the evidence points to Paterson being well aware of what had happened up country from Winton, where he was visiting just a few months after the Shearers' Strike. Of all the versions of how 'Waltzing Matilda' came to be written, Magoffin's is now generally accepted, particularly with regard to dates and places. His discovery of the earliest versions of the song, written by both Christina and Banjo is also illuminating. In particular, the first line makes no mention of a 'jolly' swagman. Instead it runs: 'Oh, once there was a swagman.' Magoffin points out that both writers clearly use the plural in the line: 'Down came policemen – one, two, three.' And the line 'You'll never take me alive, said he' was originally 'Drowning himself by the coolibah tree.'

Magoffin goes on to explain how the politically sensitive Paterson, fearful of the consequences Lawson suffered in writing 'Freedom on the Wallaby', used the literary device of allegory to disguise the true meaning of 'Waltzing Matilda'. Thus 'swagman' refers to Hoffmeister, an itinerant swagman-shearer, 'waiting till his billy boiled' is a reference to the events relating to Hoffmeister having taken place after lunch, 'camped in a billabong' refers to Hoffmeister's camp, 'the jumbuk' refers to the sheep burned at Dagworth, 'the squatter' refers to the Macphersons, 'riding a thoroughbred' refers to the Macphersons' horses all being thoroughbreds, 'the policemen' refers to the search party for those involved in the attack, and 'drowning himself' refers to committing suicide to avoid the consequences of the attack, as Hoffmeister may have done.

It's a wide-ranging interpretation, but even if you believe the only place to search for allegories is in a billabong, the events surrounding the song still provide a context for its understanding. 'Waltzing Matilda' was written in the midst of one of the worst economic depressions in this country's history. It was written about a swagman at a time when the countryside was haunted by thousands of them, many in rags and starving, with many more Australians threatened by the same fate.

In referring to three policemen who accompany the squatter, it again refers directly to its times – when the Queensland countryside was gripped by the heaviest hand of authority it had ever known.

And the swagman's death in preference to capture? It harks back to the line in the *Bulletin* article, 'The Anarchists of the Bush': 'it is easy to understand the damnable despair of the hordes of artisans, labourers, clerks, larrikins, and social camp-followers who are now swarming out of the cities into the poverty-cursed country districts.' It also echoes the sentiment at the public meeting held in Brisbane when the Coercion Bill was being considered: 'for centuries we had resisted such endeavours to usurp our liberty . . .' Paterson's swagman would rather die than give up his.

Many people have noted hearing 'Waltzing Matilda' or getting copies of it from early 1895 onwards. Sydney May detailed how it was sung at the North Gregory Hotel in Winton and at the Winton races, and proved instantly popular. Why? It's all in the chorus of the original version, which asks 'Who'll come a-waltzing Matilda with me?' Who'll help shoulder the swagman's burden? Anyone who joins the chorus. When he'd rather die than submit to heavy-handed authority, the swagman's defiant spirit poses the question again. Who'll help him oppose injustice? Anyone who joins the chorus. In referring directly to the greatest social upheaval of its time, 'Waltzing Matilda' can be seen as a Depression-era song, and a very good one. It's about hard times, endurance and the desire for freedom, and both squatter and worker could immediately identify with all three.

The song was finally published in 1903, with music arranged by Marie Cowan and Paterson named as the author. This version refers to the 'jolly' swagman. And when he jumps into the billabong, mention of his suicide transforms into 'You'll never take me alive'.

Most purists lean to the original version of the song, but there is an interesting twist to the use of the word 'jolly'. In one of his more hyperbolic rants in the *Worker* of 6 October 1894, Henry Lawson was taking unionists to task for using such crude terms as 'scab' to refer to non-union labour. In conclusion he wrote:

> There are four words which will be fondly remembered by us when we are old men, and when the A.W.U. [Australian Workers' Union] will only remember with shame that so many of its members were foolish and ignorant to use and admire such words as 'scab' and 'Skitely Wing'. These four words – 'chum', 'jolly', 'mate' and 'sweetheart' – will never die.

As it turned out, most of them did die as far as Lawson's understanding of their meanings went. Yet there is a tantalising possibility. 'Jolly' was probably inserted in the first line of 'Waltzing Matilda' to help the flow, but Lawson's comment suggests the term may also have had a union connotation. Is another reading 'once a union swagman'?

In academic circles the song is often derided as a simplistic, cliché-ridden oddity. Yet until 1895, Australia had never known anything like it. It certainly spoke to people far more than 'God Save the King/Queen', and it has gone on to become the unofficial national anthem. It is the only song Australians break into spontaneously at moments of national celebration. It is the song that has united us, in good times and bad, from the sporting field to the battlefield.

'Waltzing Matilda' is the strongest expression of Australians' ability to unite and pull together through thick and thin, a quality firmly rooted in the experience of the hardships of the bush, but one that most Australians see in themselves. Banjo Paterson may not have intended it, but his idiosyncratic song embodies that spirit. In that context, it is our national anthem. It's not official yet, but perhaps as the swaggie in the *Bulletin* of September 1894 said, 'Old man, it ain't far off.'

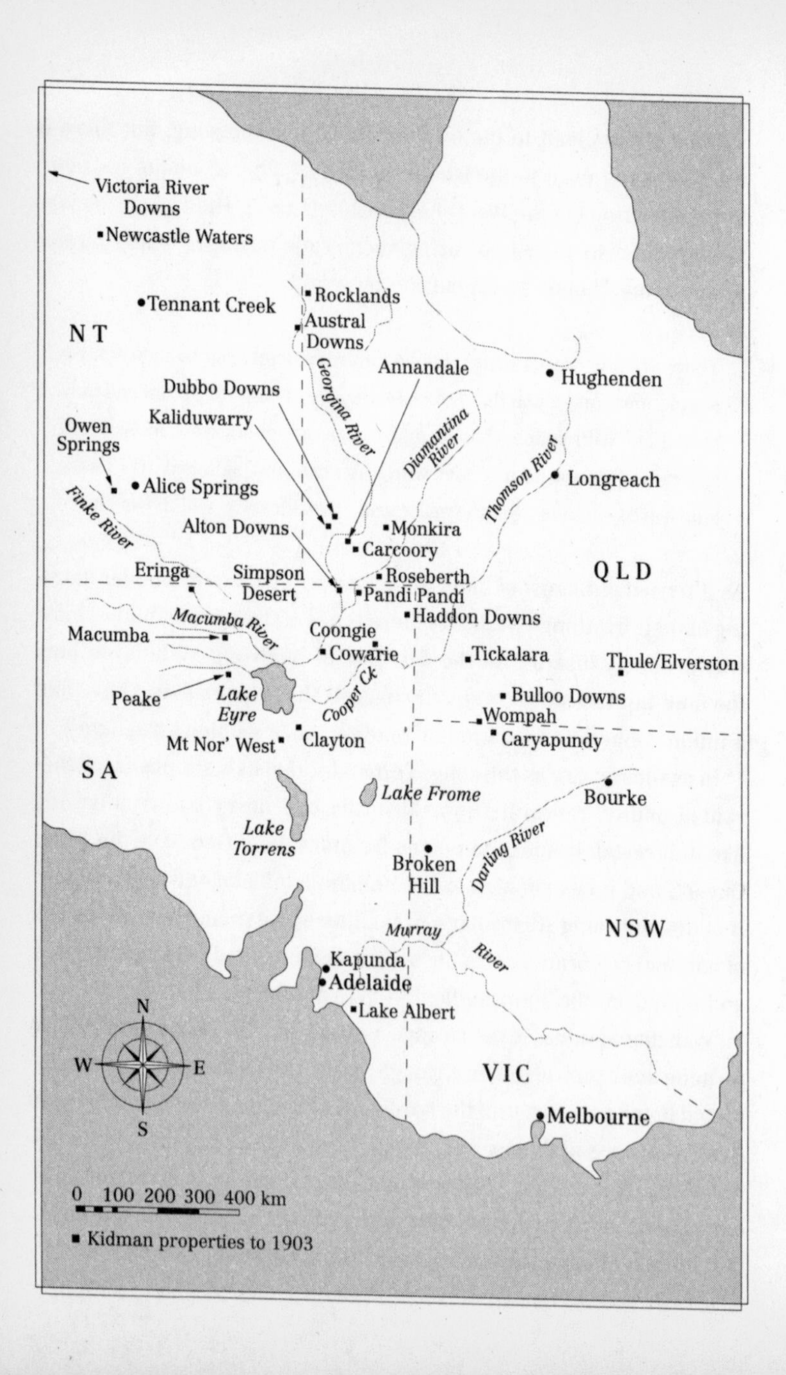
Victoria River Downs
Newcastle Waters
Tennant Creek
N T
Rocklands
Austral Downs
Georgina River
Annandale
Hughenden
Dubbo Downs
Kaliduwarry
Owen Springs
Alice Springs
Diamantina River
Thomson River
Longreach
Finke River
Alton Downs
Monkira
Carcoory
Eringa
Simpson Desert
Roseberth
Pandi Pandi
Q L D
Haddon Downs
Macumba River
Macumba
Coongie
Cowarie
Tickalara
Thule/Elverston
Peake
Lake Eyre
Cooper Ck
Bulloo Downs
Wompah
Caryapundy
Mt Nor' West
Clayton
S A
Lake Frome
Bourke
Lake Torrens
Broken Hill
Darling River
Murray River
N S W
Kapunda
Adelaide
Lake Albert
N
W
E
S
V I C
Melbourne
0 100 200 300 400 km
Kidman properties to 1903

Sir Sidney Kidman, date unknown
(State Library of South Australia, SLSA: B 6749)

7
BUSH GENIUS,
1895: Sir Sidney Kidman
(1857–1935)

As the depression of the 1890s dragged on (see previous chapter), squatters large and small went to the wall. With the banks hounding them, stock prices at abysmal levels, and no relief in sight, men who fancied themselves Australia's landed gentry could only watch as their grass castles were sold from under them. Yet not everyone suffered in the economic hard times. For one man, a bushie, the squatters' misfortunes were the chance he'd been waiting for. In fact, he'd been watching, planning and preparing for over two decades for the opportunities that only hard times could bring. And by 1895, the time was ripe.

Sidney Kidman had been born on a small land-holding in Adelaide in 1857. Only fourteen months after he, the fifth son, was born, his father had died of bronchitis, leaving his wife pregnant with the sixth Kidman boy. In 1863, the boys' mother remarried, to a farmhand named Starr, who spent most of his time drinking and fighting. As his older brothers had done, Sidney left as soon as he was able. As he told the *Adelaide Observer* of 5 September 1903:

> I think I was thirteen when I decided to clear out. I got hold of a cheap horse and bound for nowhere in particular, and with practically nothing on my back and no money in my pockets, away I went. I rode to Kapunda. I earned a few shillings there and then I went on to the Burra. If I remember rightly, it was there that I swapped my horse with a bit to boot. I gradually worked my way north until at last I struck the Barrier [Range, in western New South Wales].

This would have been in 1870, the same year Harry Redford (see Chapter 4) was heading south with his mob of cattle from Bowen Downs. Sid, meanwhile, was heading north looking for his older brothers – George, Fred, Tom and Sackville – and a job. When he found his brother George, he was told to go straight home, but refused. He eventually found work near Poolamacca homestead, doing odd jobs for room and board at a bush pub called German Charlie's. He chopped wood, and for a few pennies tended visitors' horses and equipment.

German Charlie's was a wild place, a frontier outpost on the edge of the arid heart of the country. German Charlie was pretty wild himself, a colourful character among the tough men on the fringe of civilisation. The young Kidman listened to them all and learned.

It was just a few months later that brother George found Kidman a job, with a 'squatter' named Harry Raines. Raines had no title to the land he was grazing stock on, but as the rightful owner hadn't taken up the land, Raines considered it fair game. As Kidman told a newspaper interviewer:

> I got a job with him at eight shillings a week to do as I was told. I used to sleep in the dugout, the coldest shop I was ever in. In those days people did not have big swags and a lot of bedding but just a rug. That was all I had. I had to get up early, as it was the only chance to get warm, and hunt up the saddle horses.
>
> Sometimes I would mind the goats and sheep and have a look for any stray cattle or sheep for Harry. He would say they were his; it was all open country. After the big drought broke in 1869 a lot of cattle came over from the Flinders Ranges and any that Harry could get belonged to him. I was sent away with a bit of a rug and a little tucker in my swag to look for them scores of miles away.

Like so many bushies before him, Kidman learned a lot about survival from an Aboriginal. Young Billy and Kidman shared the work around the camp and at night huddled together for warmth, with their rugs and Billy's dog. By day they supplemented their inadequate rations by catching possums and fish. As was his habit with others he met, Kidman absorbed every bit of knowledge Billy had to offer, improving his bushcraft all the time. Soon he was so skilful that Raines started to hire him out as a guide to the new settlers filtering into the area. Through the experience he gained as a guide and the information he gleaned from the settlers he met, Kidman's knowledge of the country for hundreds of kilometres around the Barrier was constantly increasing. Soon he was being described as 'the kid who knows his way about'. That alone was a skill people were prepared to pay for.

Kidman was a princely fifteen when, in 1872, the selector who owned Raines's land finally turned up and turfed them all out. Raines went looking for a selection of his own. Kidman went looking for his brothers. He found three of them – George, Fred and Sackville – on Mount Gipps Station, where he got work at 10 shillings a week. For eighteen months he got to see how a proper station operated, until another youngster turned up and asked for a job. He was employed at £1 a week, double Kidman's wages, to do the same work. Kidman didn't think he was being fairly treated but, as was reported years later in the *Argus* of 5 September 1935, 'when he sought an increase he was sacked.'

He returned to German Charlie's a little older and wiser, and landed a job tending Charlie's small herd of cattle for £1 a week. The herd was largely made up of strays and unbranded cattle that were wandering the bush. Some were wild as hawks, and Kidman gained valuable experience looking after up to a hundred cattle at a time. Soon he'd learned how to pick the herd's mood and to identify the leaders and the followers, the foragers and the bullies. He found he could maintain control by being alert and ready for the first sign of a break, and catching it before it started.

When he wasn't with the cattle or delivering beef to the drilling teams that were starting to tap into the vast artesian water supplies that Banjo Paterson referred to in his 'Golden Water' ABC radio talk (see previous chapter), Kidman still hired himself out to guide new settlers, but now his rate was £2 a week.

Around the campfire, Kidman heard the story of Harry Redford's audacious scheme to take a mob of cattle from Bowen Downs all the way to Adelaide, and how he'd not only succeeded, but been found not guilty in the subsequent trial of 1873 (see Chapter 4). For most of the people of the bush, it was one in the eye for the squatters and absentee landlords. Yet for a canny teenager like Kidman, it was much more. He knew Redford had travelled the stock through country that killed the explorers Burke and Wills, in the process pioneering a new stock route that connected the vast open spaces of central and western Queensland to the lucrative markets in Adelaide. The region was supposed to be a fearful desert, but obviously there was more to it than that.

By this time Kidman had already started trading in stock himself. On one of his trips he picked up a small mob of horses at rock-bottom prices. Back at the bush pub, German Charlie sold the horses for a solid profit, with a generous commission for Kidman. It was a much quicker way to make money than chasing cows.

In 1873 Kidman's mother died. The drunkard Starr had long since gone, leaving her with her son from her previous marriage, and three young daughters. The girls were eventually raised by a relative. Kidman's younger brother, Charles, now set out to make his fortune, as his brothers had done before him. However, his mother had not died penniless, and all her children benefited, as Kidman explained to a journalist in the *Adelaide Observer* of 28 July 1928.

> When my mother died I inherited about £1000, and got the interest on it for a few years. The trustee of her estate was a well-known Adelaide lawyer, and on one occasion I wanted £200 to £300 to pay George Miller for some horses I bought from him. I got the money, but had to pay 8 or 10 per cent for it. In later years I was going across to Melbourne on the express with my wife . . . and I introduced her to the lawyer. He said to me, 'I have always taken a great interest in you, Kidman.' 'Yes,' I replied, 'and you have always taken a lot of interest out of me, too.'

Not long after his mother's death, the outback gave Sidney Kidman yet another lesson about life in the arid west. A drought descended on the entire western New South Wales region, forcing German Charlie to sell off his increasingly blighted cattle, and lay off young Kidman. What caught Kidman's attention was how desperate things became on the surrounding stations. All they could do was hope for rain, while their cattle lost condition, and value. Soon, many faced financial ruin. The squatters were in reality sitting ducks – at the mercy of weather that too often could be merciless.

Meanwhile, Kidman had to make a living. Still in his teens, he'd had his fill of finding work only to lose it, and decided he knew enough to become his own boss. Copper had been found at Cobar and, mining being a hungry business, beef prices in Cobar were high. So in 1875, the eighteen-year-old Kidman went into the butchering business. He rode out to a station 130 kilometres from Cobar to buy cattle, then drove them back to Cobar for sale. Prices were good, but the 260-kilometre round trip took the gloss off. Not long after he started, he switched to trading in horses. He was soon ranging from South Australia up into Queensland, building a business and a reputation for having an impeccable eye for stock.

Kidman spent much of the next decade in the saddle, sometimes in partnership with other brokers or his brothers. In that time he saw and learned much about the far outback of New South Wales, Queensland and South Australia. Most impressions of this vast area are that it's as dry as a church tea party, but the canny Kidman saw things differently.

From time to time, as he rode through the arid country of the far west, he'd come across areas that were lush with feed for stock. This despite the fact that rain hadn't fallen in the area for months and the creekbeds were bone dry. How could this be? Kidman realised that it could only be the result of floods. Years later, in *Memoirs of a Stockman*, Harry Peck recalled that Kidman often said: 'Give me the country in western Queensland, where a bullock will fatten on herbage in three months, and after rain following a dry spell the soil will grow feed sweet and lasting.'

This was how Harry Redford had got his stolen cattle down to South Australia. He'd followed the floods down, and found good feed the whole way. In fact, great feed. When Burke and Wills had been there in 1860 it had been barren. In the late 1870s, as Kidman could see with his own eyes, it had every kind of luscious grass imaginable – pepper and button grass, Flinders, couch, wild sorghum, clover, cane grass and Mitchell grass. Much of it retained its nutrition even after it had dried. As for its quality, stockmen said cattle grew fat just looking at it. Wherever the floodwaters reached became flushed with green, while the land around it remained parched and brown.

Kidman grew to appreciate all these things thanks to years spent in the saddle. However, to really understand how the floodplains worked you needed an overview of the entire area. Unfortunately, satellite views from space were pretty scarce in the 1880s, so it fell to a woman to teach Kidman the fundamentals of outback geography.

Her name was Isabel Wright, and whereas Kidman had bolted from home at the first opportunity, she'd completed her schooling at her home in Kapunda, South Australia. Kidman had got to know her on his trips to the Kapunda horse markets, and it was Isabel who introduced the 'kid who could find his way about' to maps. What she revealed was profound.

First, the far west of Queensland and New South Wales was laced by a network of waterways – composed primarily of the Georgina and Diamantina rivers, and Cooper Creek, and their numerous tributaries. A lot of the time these rivers were bone-dry, but between them the area they covered was truly immense. It extended towards the Gulf of Carpentaria, across to the Queensland coast and down into north-eastern South Australia. A similar system covered the region between Central Australia and South Australia, involving the Finke, Hugh and Macumba Rivers, the water sources for the Overland Telegraph referred to in Chapter 3.

Second, not one of the rivers flowed to the sea. Bizarrely, they all sank into the sandy flood plains of the west, unless they made it as far as Lake Eyre, well into South Australia. As such, explorers searching for an inland sea had been looking in the wrong place. The sea was there, but it lay beneath the parched land, and the places where the waters spread before sinking beneath the ground, the flood plains, could be stupendously fertile.

Third, the sheer size of the inland water-system helped it to work. As Kidman had seen in the drought years, rainfall in the outback could be ruinously fickle. Yet the bigger the catchment area, the better the chances that rain would fall somewhere within it. If a cyclone blundered inland from the coast of Queensland, the Cooper would be set flowing by the vast waters dumped west of the Great Divide. When the wet season set in up at the Gulf, the Georgina and Diamantina rose. In either case, water would come snaking down the dry riverbeds, bringing life to the otherwise rain-deprived inland. Little wonder Aboriginal culture associates water with the Rainbow Serpent, one of the most powerful Dreamtime spirits. Without a drop of rain falling inland, the rivers could still inundate millions of hectares of land.

Yet fertile, well-watered land was completely useless if fat stock promptly starved to death or died of thirst trying to get to market through the hideously dry and barren country that surrounded it. And even if the surrounding land was good, it could be just as hostile if someone else owned it. Yet, peering at Isabel's maps, the young couple knew they were looking at a potentially grassy highway, a back corridor down which Kidman's horses and cattle could travel to South Australia's markets, and beyond. One station wasn't enough, though: you needed a chain of them all the way to Adelaide. Realising that potential, however, would require an operation so large that it appeared beyond their wildest dreams. Knowledge, though, is power, and on lonely nights around the campfires of remote stock routes, Kidman had time to plan ways to put his hard-won knowledge to use.

By the early 1880s Kidman was trading in any outback commodity that might turn a profit. At one point, in 1884, he almost became one of the richest men alive. As he later related in a newspaper article:

> About this time I was beginning to move along. After the drought I went to Cobham Lake Station and bought 900 cows and bullocks – all they could muster out of 10 000 – at £3 a head. I travelled the cattle via Broken Hill and sold them at the Burra [a South Australian mining town]. On the way I met Jim Poole, who was a partner with David James, sinking a tank at the Nine-Mile, which is a few miles from where Broken Hill now is. I gave Jim Poole ten of the culls [cattle culled from the herd] for a one-fourteenth share of the Broken Hill and also left ten bullocks to be broken in. The culls were worth about £60.

The deal was registered in July 1884. Not long after, Kidman met a sharebroker who agreed to try to sell his share for a price that would give Kidman a quick profit. Two months after he'd bought the share, though, it was realised that Broken Hill was basically a solid block of silver. And the bits of it that weren't silver were lead and zinc. Kidman desperately tried to contact the broker and stop him selling the share, only to get a valuable lesson in the tyranny of distance as his letter slowly made its way to the broker. It arrived just as Kidman got a letter saying the share had been sold, with Kidman profiting to the tune of £40. Yet within six years that share was to be worth over £1 million. Based on BHP's current market capitalisation, the share would now be worth over $2 billion, plus the company has paid some pretty handsome dividends in the last 120 years.

There was one consolation, though. In the same year, Kidman asked Isabel Wright if she'd marry him, and she agreed. As author Ion Idriess wrote of the marriage in the *Sydney Mail* of 11 September 1935, 'I asked [Kidman] only a few weeks ago, "What was the greatest bargain you ever made." His eyes lit up as he turned smilingly towards the garden. "My wife. She has been my best mate for fifty years".'

Soon, too, booming Broken Hill was good for business, and Kidman knew that where miners were concerned it was all about getting in first. Soon he partnered with his brother, Sackville, in a butchery at nearby Silverton. Sack was the more cautious and astute of the two, a curb on his younger brother's impetuosity, but together they thrived. Kidman bought and sold the cattle and also got into the coach business. In 1885, with former coach driver Jim Nicholas, he and Sack formed Kidman & Nicholas, which ended up rivalling Cobb & Co., and provided an outlet for the horses Kidman was trading. Kidman thoroughly enjoyed his life. He was to tell a journalist:

> I travelled the 'three rivers' in Queensland, selling and buying cattle and camping out and was content wherever I was. Many persons would have been miserable if they had been in the predicament I was once in on Cooper Creek, when I was going to take fifty camels to Nockatunga to go to Western Australia. I was travelling up the Cooper in flood time. The Afghan I had with the horses got lost and I was two days from Nappamerry to Tanapara on the Wilson. I had a horse and a pair of hobbles. I was two days and a night without anything to eat and no blankets. I rode through floodwater for about 100 miles [160 kilometres]. When I was within 6 miles [10 kilometres] of Nappa Merrie, a wild duck flew up from its nest and I found nine eggs. I hobbled the horse and lit a fire. As a rule, I never carried matches but as good luck would have it I had them on this occasion. I roasted the nine duck eggs and had a good feed. I never want to eat nine roast duck eggs again after fasting for two days! I often swam the Queensland rivers just by hanging on to a bullock's tail.

When gold was found in Western Australia in 1888, 1891 and 1892, in prodigious quantities, Kidman and Sack expanded their cattle, horse and transport operations with deliberate speed. Kidman & Nicholas bought out one mail run for £10 000 and made the money back in seven months. The diversification into Western Australia was a move that was to insulate the brothers during the economic depression that started to tear through the eastern states in the 1890s. It also put them into a position to take advantage of the many squatters who were soon facing economic hard times.

Prior to 1895, Sidney Kidman had only dabbled in property. He'd bought a home in Kapunda in 1884 when he married Isabel. Then, in 1887, at age thirty, he acquired Thule Station, a 184-square-kilometre unwatered run of open mulga flats and ridge country not far from Charleville, Queensland. He then took an interest in Cobbrum, a 215-square-kilometre adjoining run. The two properties were consolidated with a third, Oblong, to become Elverston in April 1890. However, he let the properties go in 1893.

Two years later, though, Kidman and Sackville's world changed greatly. By then, the banks were closing down properties and trying to sell them off. The Kidmans, on the other hand, were cashed up, and soon it was open season on the sitting ducks, the squatters. In 1895, with the prices of properties across the eastern states at rock bottom, the Kidman brothers started buying.

The first property the brothers bought was Cowarie, a small property in South Australia. It wasn't close to their main operations in Broken Hill, or their coaching business in the west, but it was on the way to the South Australian markets. The next year they bought Annandale, one of Queensland's remotest properties. The property, which would later be consolidated into a station covering 6700 square kilometres, cost the brothers £5000, but they estimated it was carrying 5000 cattle and hundreds of horses. Even with stock prices abysmally low, the property was carrying enough stock to cover the cost of buying it. Even better, it had extensive frontage on the Georgina River, and two floodwater lakes. In the same year, 1896, the brothers got Owen Springs, in the Northern Territory. It was a property heavily stocked with horses, located west of Alice Springs.

Then, in 1897, the buying started in earnest, and it didn't stop. By March 1898 they had bought a 160-square-kilometre property just north of Broken Hill, 386-square-kilometre Alton Downs on the South Australia–Queensland border, and 1813-square-kilometre Tickalara and Roseberth in Queensland. Then there were Haddon Downs, Pandi Pandi and Clayton Stations in South Australia. The Kidmans' stock exceeded 20000 cattle, 20000 sheep and 5000 horses. But it was just the beginning.

The brothers Kidman weren't randomly buying up every property in the flood-plain country that they could get their hands on. They were buying links in Kidman's long-dreamed-of chain that extended from Queensland (and Central Australia) down towards the markets in Broken Hill and on into South Australia.

Sackville was by now Broken Hill's biggest butcher. During the miners' strike in Broken Hill, he'd continued to supply the men, often helping feed their starving families. When the strike was over, all Broken Hill bought its meat from Sack. Business was booming.

By 1899 the brothers had also bought Kaliduwarry, 2000 square kilometres near Annandale in Queensland's south-east corner. Adjoining it and Annandale, they got Dubbo Downs for a song. The 2300-square-kilometre property they bought on the Georgina cost them just £2100. Caryapundy was 844 square kilometres near the Queensland–New South Wales border. Not far north of Adelaide they'd acquired 2070-square-kilometre Mount Nor' West.

By this stage, people were starting to realise what the Kidmans were up to. But any rumblings of discontent didn't come from the bush, they came from the city. As the high-living landholders who operated their properties from the comfort of Sydney and Melbourne fell prey to drought and debt, they came to resent the brash young men who swooped on their empires.

The banks, meanwhile, loved the Kidman boys. Stuck with worthless properties, oblivious and disinterested in whether they were stocked with scrawny animals or not, they saw salvation in the two brothers. And not only did Kidman and Sack get the properties cheaply, the terms of payment were often extraordinary. In many instances they paid a deposit (say, £300), took possession, then mustered the stock and used them to pay off the balance. In other words the cost to them might be a mere tenth of the already depressed value.

Perhaps if the Sydney property tycoons had spent half as much time in the saddle as Sidney Kidman did, they'd have known enough about their properties to realise they were giving them away. Yet fools and their money are soon parted, and a consummate bushman like Kidman was laughing all the way to the banks. He was also constructing an operation whose concept was, for sheer size, nothing short of stupendous. It required an intimate knowledge of the outback that only a bushie could hope to achieve, and a set of phenomenal bush skills to bring it about.

Suddenly, though, the Kidman operation was dealt two devastating blows. The first came early in 1899. In March Sackville Kidman contracted peritonitis, and within a few short days, the infection killed him, aged forty-three. Broken Hill stopped for the funeral. An obituary in the *Critic* of 8 July 1899 quoted a Mr Wallace, owner of Sturt's Meadows: 'If there was one man in the world to whom I would have given my last drop of heart's blood it was to Sack Kidman. His men say they have not lost a master, but a brother or father.'

Kidman felt the loss keenly. In 1903 he told the *Adelaide Observer*, 'Sack was a wonderful judge, and terribly shrewd. I own a few cattle and a few stations now, but if poor Sack had lived we would have owned more cattle in Australia than anyone else.'

Despite Sack's death, Kidman continued to build the already formidable Kidman empire. During 1900 he acquired the 5500-square-kilometre Eringa on the South Australia–Northern Territory border; the 2070-square-kilometre Austral Downs on the Herbert River, further north on the Queensland–Northern Territory border; and the 2600-square-kilometre Carcoory, between the Diamantina and Georgina rivers, north of Birdsville.

Then came the second blow. As Australia entered the new century, drought took hold of almost the entire continent on a scale beyond any previous experience. In building his chain of stations, Kidman had hoped to make his operation virtually drought-proof. The plan was that if one place was stricken, he could move the stock to a station where the feed was good. And throughout their buying spree, Kidman and Sack had always hired the best men they could find. To be able to stage cattle down between properties or to markets required great skill if the cattle were to maintain condition.

Kidman had also learned his lesson from the disastrous sale of his share in BHP. He insisted his managers use the Overland Telegraph system, pioneered by John Ross (see Chapter 3) in 1870 and by 1900 networked across the outback, to report on the condition of his properties. That way he hoped to better manage the extremes of drought and flood.

Yet this was no ordinary drought. It had been dry since the brothers had started buying in 1895, but between 1900 and 1903 almost no rain fell in the vast catchment that fed what was becoming known as the Channel Country. On his many stations, Kidman's stock couldn't be moved. It was too dry even to get them from one place to another. Yet his men had to try. The losses were terrible: when 1000 breeding cows were sent in hope of feed and water at Pandi Pandi, every one of them died; 2000 bullocks were sent from Carcoory, and they all died.

In the *Adelaide Observer* of 28 July 1928, Kidman described the disaster:

> I lost my inheritance, and more besides, in about two months at Carcoory after the terrible drought of 1901. It only had about 4000

> cattle on it when I bought it. I went up the Birdsville Track, and when I landed at Carcoory, I asked, 'How many cattle have you got.' They said, 'Only two; we have killed one, and the other one is not yours.'

Another herd of 500 bullocks tried to get through a 190-kilometre dry stretch in Queensland when clouds rolled towards them. Within minutes the men found themselves in the most terrible dust storm they had ever seen. The dust was so thick that it grew dark. The cattle and packhorses, their red-rimmed eyes almost glowing in the gloom, huddled with their backs to the wind, but by dusk seventy cattle had smothered. Where the packhorses had been unloaded, equipment was quickly buried and lost. As night fell the men tried to get the cattle moving, to take advantage of the cooler temperatures, but the storm was too intense.

Many of the cattle became separated from the herd during the night. The dust storm finally broke after sunrise the next day, but the remaining cattle were still 30 kilometres from water. There was no choice but to push them on through the heat, their tongues lolling badly, the weaker animals dropping from exhaustion. Of the herd of 500, only seventy-two survived.

In the *Sydney Mail* in 1935, Ion Idriess put Kidman's total losses in the drought of 1901 at 70000. And yet, Kidman survived. He was forced to sell his interest in the Western Australian coaching business, and Owen Springs in the Northern Territory. Still he clung tenaciously to every one of the properties that formed the basis of his enormous chain-of-supply strategy.

By 1903, the worst was over. In an interview given that year, he listed the properties he had bought or still held:

> Today I own or have an interest in the following: In the Northern Territory – Victoria Downs, with its 45 000 head of cattle, Newcastle Waters, Austral Downs; South Australia – Lake Albert, Eringa, Peake,

> Macumba, Mount Nor' West, Clayton, Coongy [Coongie], on the Cooper, Pandi Pandi on the Diamantina, Alton Downs; Queensland – Annandale, Collegwairi, Dubbo, Cartrey, Rocklands, Monkira, Bulla [Bulloo] Downs; in New South Wales – Wompah and Tickalara.

Yet there was no rest for the 46-year-old. He was still in the saddle, riding thousands of kilometres to visit his properties and to buy and sell anything with four legs – cattle, sheep, horses, even goats. The invention of the motor car saw him driving wherever there were roads. Deeply tanned after years of outdoor life, the man increasingly referred to as 'The Cattle King' was also the subject of speculation: might he have some Aboriginal parentage? He didn't, but he had certainly acquired many bush skills, along with an admiration of those who had them, too. He described one of his early partners, Bill Emmett, in an article that appeared in the *Adelaide Observer* on July 14 1928:

> When we were at Wilcannia he used to live in a dugout, and I lived in a tin hut. He would get up at daylight, make a fire, boil a pannikin of tea, cut a piece off a pig's jaw, grill it, and eat it with a piece of damper. When he finished he would smack his lips, and say, 'Well, I call that a nice meal.' He lived like a blackfellow, and yet he was thankful for anything he got. That taught me to be thankful, too.

As for the Aboriginals on some of his properties, the article continued: 'Sir Sidney expressed the opinion that he thought the people on the Cooper, Diamantina and Bulloo Downs did not appreciate what the blackfellows ever did for them. "You would hear the horses come up at daylight, and they would be there with them at sunrise," he went on. "They had some of the finest blackfellows on Bulloo Downs that you would ever see in Australia".'

In 1903, the *Adelaide Observer* asked the secret of his success. His answer at first made no reference to the real secret:

> I don't know. I was always dealing in horses. I have always taken care of little things and I don't think anyone can go far wrong who does. When I ride on to one of my stations I look at all the small things. If the trifles are strewn all about, then I know why that station is not paying its way. If the small things are let go amiss, so will the big things.

The story is often told that he sacked men for lighting a cigarette with a match if there was a campfire handy. 'A man who won't look after his own interests won't look after mine,' he is quoted as saying. It may sound harsh, even miserly, but in the bush matches can be precious. The ability to light a fire can save a life hanging in the balance, so wasting matches would raise questions about the quality of a person's bushmanship. And Kidman needed the best.

There are also numerous tales of Kidman's generosity. At saleyards he was notorious for stopping the bidding once he was satisfied with the price an animal had achieved. Buyers often got bargains, as did their customers. Far from using his dominance as 'The Cattle King' to force prices up, there is ample evidence that he preferred a decent profit to profiteering. In *Memoirs of a Stockman*, Harry Peck, noted: 'Though invariably keen in a deal, Kidman was always fair to the other fellow . . . A helping hand to the struggler was always his motto, and many a man was helped to his feet, or to a new start, by Sidney Kidman.'

Kidman never publicly outlined his chain-of-supply strategy, though it was evident to the people of the bush, who realised it had potential benefits for them all. However in an answer to the *Adelaide Observer* in 1903, Kidman did skirt the topic:

> People think I have been making money for years. They must remember that I had stations before the drought, and held them all through. I, however, took the precaution to handle my stock; to send those from the bad places to my stations that were better off. I like the bush

> country, and am more pleased to talk to a man carrying a swag than to your politicians . . . I would just as soon have a good square meal on a station as sit down to the best spread at an hotel.

The sentiment was echoed in the book *All about Australians* in 1904:

> Success, however, has not spoiled him. He will always remain Sidney Kidman – a sort of rough diamond, but, after all, a delightful son of nature, free as the air, sound and substantial, honest to the core, with a masterful will, but a heart full of sympathy and kindness. His men swear by him; they admire his unconventionality, his plainness of manner and speech and his entire absence of superiority. They know he is the soul of honour. While they respect him as master they trust him as friend. He is a typical bushman, and yet he is not, for while he has the virtues of a man who has roughed it out back for many years he does not possess his vices.

The men who worked for him were in turn fiercely loyal, and proud to call themselves Kidman men. A Kidman drover was regarded as being of the same calibre as another station's manager. Many went on to establish their own reputations in the cattle industry, among them bushman's outfitter the late R.M. Williams, who started out as a Kidman saddler.

Kidman's empire, meanwhile, grew until 'the kid who knew his way about' had interests in properties that covered an area larger than England, Scotland and Wales combined. On his seventy-fifth birthday, in 1932, his employees put on a rodeo in Adelaide. It was attended by 50000 friends and well-wishers. It is still Australia's largest birthday party for a private individual.

After the drought of 1901, there were other setbacks for The Cattle King. According to Ion Idriess, he lost 85000 cattle in the south-west Queensland drought of 1914, and in 1927–1930, 120000 cattle,

100 000 sheep and 6000 horses. Yet Kidman's efforts to 'drought-proof' his empire paid off. As the *Argus* wrote in an obituary the day after his death on 2 September 1935:

> At the time of this death he controlled or had interests in 68 stations, embracing about 85 000 square miles [220 207 square kilometres] of country, and carrying about 176 000 cattle and 125 000 sheep . . . Sir Sidney Kidman's properties stretch intermittently from the Gulf of Carpentaria to Adelaide. His largest holding was probably Innamincka, in northern South Australia, which covers 7500 square miles [19 430 square kilometres]. In some parts, it is said, Sir Sidney Kidman could ride for 600 miles [965 kilometres] without trespassing.

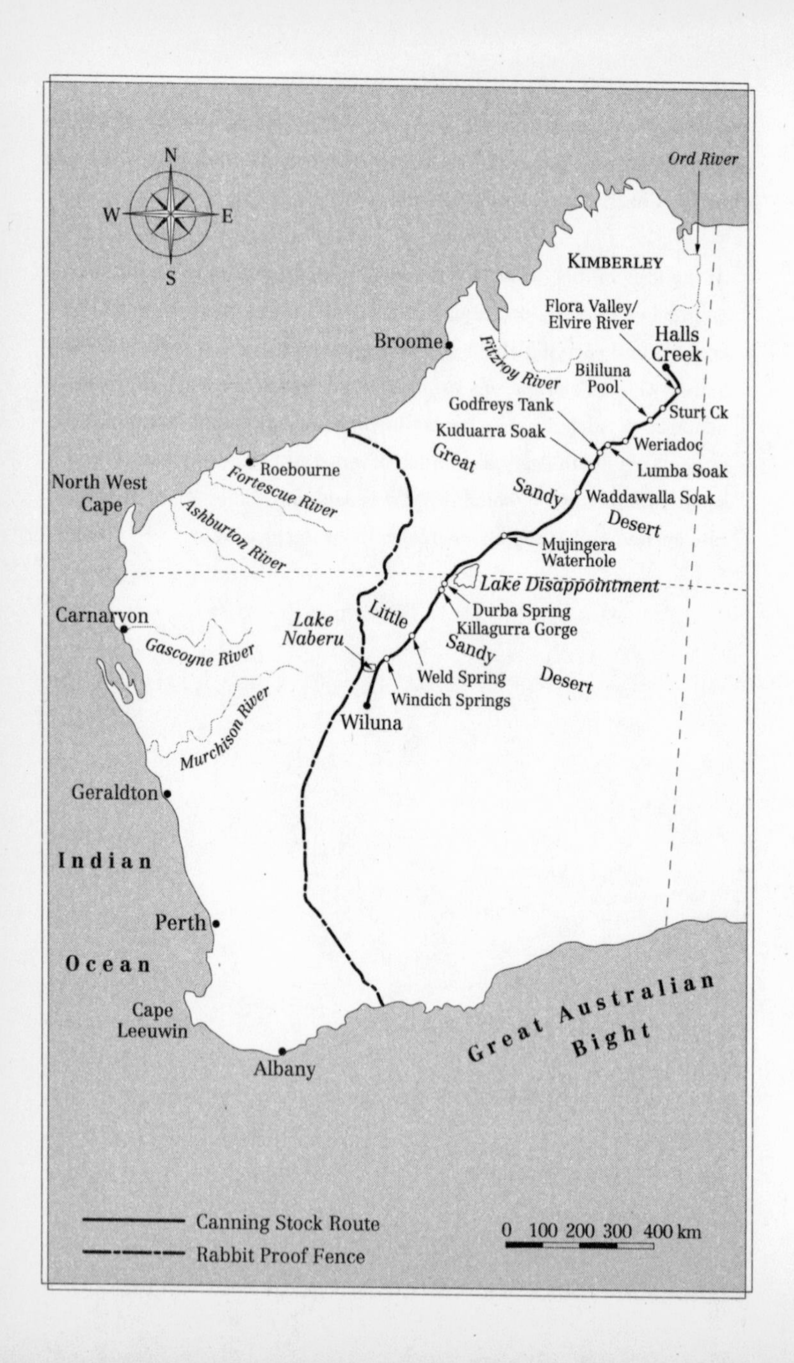
N
S
W
E
Ord River
KIMBERLEY
Flora Valley/
Elvire River
Halls
Creek
Broome
Fitzroy River
Bililuna
Pool
Godfreys Tank
Sturt Ck
Kuduarra Soak
Weriadoc
Great
Lumba Soak
Roebourne
North West
Cape
Fortescue River
Sandy
Waddawalla Soak
Ashburton River
Desert
Mujingera
Waterhole
Lake Disappointment
Durba Spring
Killagurra Gorge
Carnarvon
Lake
Naberu
Little
Sandy
Desert
Gascoyne River
Weld Spring
Windich Springs
Murchison River
Wiluna
Geraldton
Indian
Ocean
Perth
Cape
Leeuwin
Albany
Great Australian
Bight
Canning Stock Route
Rabbit Proof Fence
0 100 200 300 400 km

Alfred Canning, date unknown
(Reproduced courtesy the West Australian*)*

8

MISSION IMPOSSIBLE, 1906–1910: Alfred Canning (1860–1936)

In 1906, when the Western Australian government decided it needed a stock route linking the enormous pastoral interests in the state's East Kimberley region with the goldfields of Kalgoorlie and Coolgardie in the south, it had two options. It could take seriously the conclusion about the proposed route that explorer David Carnegie had arrived at in 1896: 'At least we have demonstrated the uselessness of any persons wasting their time and money in further investigations of that desolate region.' Alternatively, it could ignore

Carnegie and the other explorers who had died, or come close to perishing, amid the sandhills, searing heat and parched spinifex, and send someone else to have another go.

'I have the honour to inform you that you have been appointed in charge of an expedition . . .,' the Western Australian Under-Secretary for Mines Henry Sandford King wrote to forty-six-year-old surveyor Alfred Canning on 27 April 1906.

Canning, who was born and raised in Victoria, had already proved himself in the challenging interior of Western Australia, having surveyed the route for the 1800-kilometre rabbit-proof fence from near Esperance in the south to just east of Port Hedland in the north. Finding the route for a fence to contain the approaching menace that was devastating the eastern states was no picnic. As W.T. Fyfe testified in 1939, writing as Surveyor-General: 'Long stretches of waterless country, extending in some cases up to 120 miles [193 kilometres], greatly increased the difficulties encountered in this work, but they were all successfully overcome, and in 1905 the survey was completed.'

Only a year later, the Western Australian government wanted Canning to go one better. His brief was to establish the feasibility of a 1440-kilometre stock route from Wiluna to Hall's Creek through 'vast areas of sand ridges and desert'. The route would allow East Kimberly cattle, which suffered from cattle ticks and consequently couldn't be moved to coastal ports through the tick-free cattle country of the West Kimberley, to find markets to the south.

The expedition party was given a good send-off by the locals when it set out from Wiluna on 29 May 1906. The party consisted of: Canning; his second-in-command, Hubert Trotman, who'd been with Canning on the rabbit-proof fence survey; Mick and Joe Tobin (water borers); Tom Bourke (or Burke) and Otto Baumgarten (cameleers); Rob Moody (rouseabout); and Edward Blake (cook); plus twenty-three camels and two ponies. For man and beast they carried 1455 litres of water (each camel readily able to drink 45 litres at a time).

Most of the men were toughened from years in the bush. One, however, appears to have found religion, and hoped to improve his colleagues by using the nightly camps as an opportunity to recount biblical tales. 'And Jesus wandered in the desert for forty days and forty nights,' he informed the men one night.

'What a poor bloody bushman he must have been,' a member of his audience observed.

They first passed Lake Naberu, 120 kilometres from Wiluna, then Windich Springs 155 kilometres out, finding good sources of water and plenty of grazing for cattle at each. Then they went on to Weld Springs, 257 kilometres from Wiluna, where they crossed the tracks of explorer John Forrest, who had crossed Western Australia from west to east in 1874.

As the party pressed on to the north-east, into the Little Sandy Desert, they slipped into a daily pattern: either Canning or Trotman would reconnoitre for water and they'd shift the camp only when water had been found. Then the men would work to improve the source wherever possible: by digging, boring, or simply removing any debris that tainted it.

One of the key ways of finding water was to tap the knowledge of the local Aboriginal population. As Fyfe described it many years later: 'Useful guidance was obtained from natives, most of whom were so well rewarded that they did not want to leave the expedition, but Mr Canning, as far as possible, avoided taking them out of their own country.' However, Fyfe wasn't telling the whole story. As Hubert Trotman recollected, aged ninety, in Eleanor Smith's *The Beckoning West*:

> Burke and I set out one morning from Goodwin, taking chains supplied by the Police Department with which we hoped to secure a native and bring him back to camp. This sounds brutal and I did not relish the idea but it was imperative that we find water. I hoped by persuasion to allay the native's fears and this I was later able to do when I became accustomed to them and when I had learned to communicate with them.

Along the first part of the route, Goodwin Soak was a water source the expedition had been led to by their first native guide, Gabbi. Goodwin marked the limits of his tribal area, and so there Gabbi left the party. After Goodwin Soak, Canning decided to give preference to the native names for waterholes, hoping that drovers using the stock route would be understood by the locals when they were asking for directions.

The next native that Trotman caught was named Nappa (meaning 'water'), though for a time Nappa was suspected of leading the party astray, rather than to water. He directed them to one soak that was bone-dry, and Trotman was all for turning back, but Nappa insisted on going on. They'd been several days without water, but then Nappa stamped in the sand and announced, 'Mundi gabbi' (stone water).

The men started digging. Into the night they worked, until they noticed their shovels were striking damp earth – then, water. By 11 a.m. on Sunday, 6 July, the men finished sinking what they ended up calling Sunday Well. At 4 metres depth it was full of clear fresh water. It wasn't clear how Nappa knew about it, but he had introduced them to a vast artesian supply later found to cover thousands of square kilometres extending from the coast for some 700 kilometres inland. A couple of days later Nappa met a fellow tribesman who showed the men how to catch the outback frog *Cyclorana platycephala*, which fills its body with water and burrows deep into the earth to wait for the next rains. In desperate times, this water-holding frog can save a man's life.

Alfred Canning sets out in 1907 on the first expedition to build the Canning Stock Route, from Wiluna to Hall's Creek. The camels could navigate sandhills and survive the long desert stretches without water. *(Photo: reproduced courtesy the* West Australian*)*

Possibly the world's first offroad pram, modified in 1931 by conservationist Myles Dunphy, to take his son, Milo Kanangra, to see the peak in the Blue Mountains after which he'd been named. The pram was dubbed the Kanangra Limited Express, 'Limited' referring to its speed and lack of springs. The pram is now a museum piece. *(Photo: George Serras, National Museum of Australia)*

Detail from Myles Dunphy's map of Kowmung, including Mount Kanangra, to which he took his son in the 'Kanangra Express'. The map also has tips for walkers and shows features named after Myles and his wife, Margaret. *(Image: courtesy the Colong Foundation for Wilderness)*

The Stinson airliner VH-UHH in flight over rugged bushland. In 1937 it crashed in the mountain ranges on the NSW–Queensland border.
(Photo: courtesy the O'Reilly family)

All that remained of the Stinson airliner after it had crashed and burned.
(Photo: courtesy the O'Reilly family)

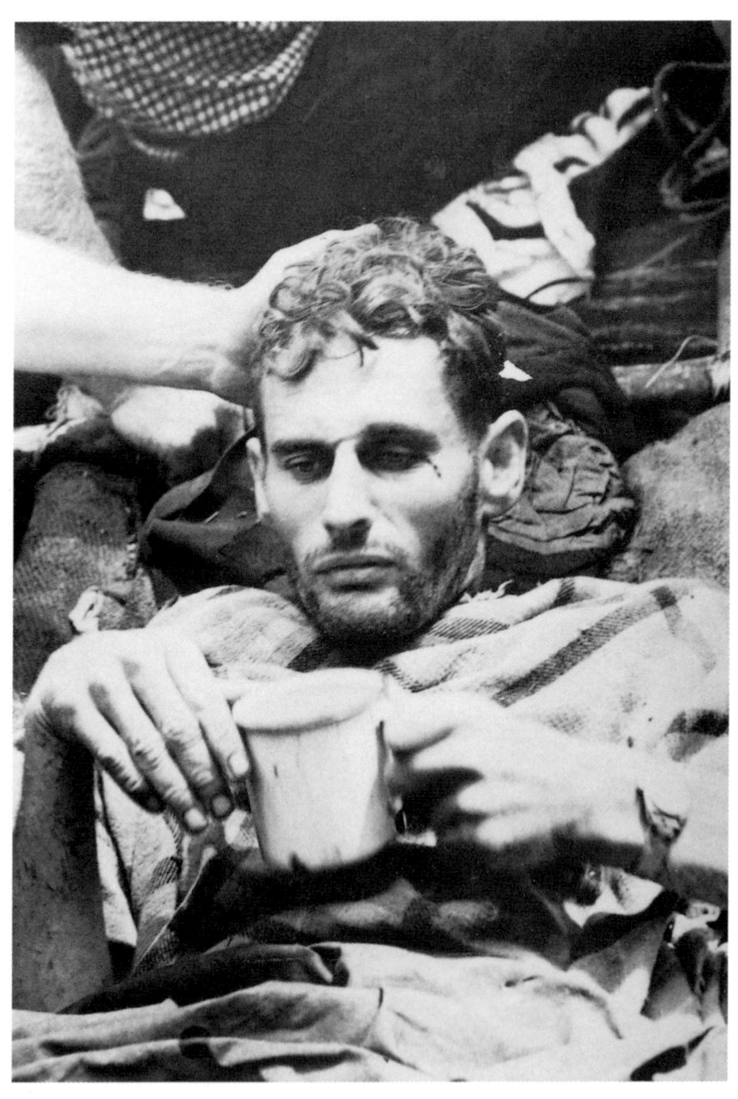

His head supported by one of the bushmen who helped rescue him, Stinson crash survivor John Proud shows the strain of ten days lying with a broken leg in the thick jungle of the Macpherson Range in 1937. *(Photo: courtesy the O'Reilly family)*

Bernard O'Reilly enjoys a well-earned cuppa after his rescue effort for the Stinson survivors. Exhausted emotionally and physically, he still had to deal with becoming an overnight hero. *(Photo: courtesy the O'Reilly family)*

After being chided about the winding roads at Woomera, wherever possible, Central Australian road builder Len Beadell made roads like the famed Gunbarrel Highway ramrod straight. *(Photo: courtesy the Beadell family)*

The waterhole that saved Len Beadell's life in 1958. By the time he'd reached it, en route to the Warburton Aboriginal Mission in searing temperatures, his water had run out and his fuel was almost exhausted. *(Photo: courtesy the Beadell family)*

Len Beadell the road builder, surveyor and bushie, was also a talented illustrator. This postcard drawn by Beadell makes witty use of the meaning of Woomera – throwing stick – and features the little lizard that was a trademark of his work. *(Image: courtesy Anne Beadell)*

The moment that marked the beginning of the Sydney 2000 Olympics. Steve Jefferys rears Ammo, giving Opening Ceremony organisers the iconic image of Australia that would seize the world's attention. *(Photo: Gregg Porteous, Newspix)*

For the next few weeks water sources and cattle feed were abundant, despite the fact Canning's party was among the dunes of the Little Sandy Desert. They dragooned another Aboriginal, whom they named Bandicoot – because he'd just caught one and promptly offered to share his bounty when he was captured by Trotman. However, Trotman declined, not being as desperately hungry as John Ross's party of 1870 (see Chapter 3). Bandicoot led the party to Killagurra Gorge, which had both good water and feed for cattle. Durba Spring was just 5 kilometres away. The abundance of water led Canning to a growing confidence that things might turn out all right after all. They were nearly halfway to Hall's Creek and were travelling well. Indeed, for the next 300 kilometres, during which they passed just west of Lake Disappointment (so named because it was a salt lake), they were well provided with water and food for the camels.

To the north-east they found Karrara Soak full of fresh water and lined with large white gums. Some 50 kilometres on they stumbled upon a dead camel that they suspected came from explorer Albert Calvert's expedition of 1896. They also came to Separation Well, which had been where two of Calvert's men had gone looking for water and subsequently perished. Having crossed the Little Sandy Desert, they were now in the Great Sandy, crossing endless ranges of sandhills. As Canning described them: 'I got out to the highest sandhills I could find, and in every direction the outlook was wretched, nothing but sandhill after sandhill.' This was the area that could make or break the feasibility of the stock route.

However, guided by Aboriginal people, they continued to find water. Probing deeper into the arid landscape, the party's local guide, Bungarra, expressed reluctance at leading Canning to water sources – they were, after all, scarce enough for his own people. At one point he warned Canning and Trotman of trouble from the Mujingera people they were then seeking. (The Mujingera were not a listed tribe, but a people referred to by the name of the waterhole they lived around.) While Bungarra refused to help Canning's team find the waterhole, fearing retribution if he did, the bushies located the water anyway. As Canning later reported:

> There is an opening about 12 feet [3.7 metres] by 10 feet [3 metres] on top and 10 feet [3 metres] deep at the bottom of which on the south side there is a narrow tunnel running towards the west about 40 feet [12 metres], gradually sloping downwards till at the end there is a fine pool of water. When I first went down, I could not see the size of the pool, but on our return journey we went down it with lanterns, and found it to be about 30 feet [9 metres] long, 5 or 6 feet [1.5 to 1.8 metres] deep and 10 feet [3 metres] wide, with a roof of opaline and limestone, 2 feet [0.6 metres] above the surface of the water.

The Mujingera weren't at all pleased by the white men's discovery, as Trotman recalled:

> But for the tell-tale footprints leading into it we would never have found Muningerra [sic]. The approach lay at the foot of a dead tree, the small entrance to the water 10 feet [3 metres] down, access to which was made by a dead gum. While we were inspecting the area, some twenty blacks appeared and although they showed no open hostility it was clear they were not happy at our intrusion.

Soon the daylight started to fade, but Canning's men couldn't leave as they still had to water their stock. The locals, meanwhile, were muttering among themselves. Trotman records:

> We were in a dilemma until, with Bungarra interpreting, Canning coaxed the tribe down the tree one by one into the cave, which they did without a murmur. When the last man had descended we removed the

> access tree and that night slept peacefully. In the morning we returned the tree to its place and released our captives, who, naturally enough, were not too pleased, and fled the scene.

Moving on the next day, Canning and the others encountered the Mujingera again. They were armed with spears and fighting sticks. It looked ominous, until the camels started to bellow, at which the tribe retreated to a safe distance. Canning, though, attempted to make peace and as a flock of cockatoos wheeled overhead, he fired a shotgun into the midst of the birds. Several fell, which he took and presented to the tribe, who immediately became friendly.

The Mujingera offered a man to replace Bungarra, but there was soon no doubt that he was leading the Europeans away from water, rather than to it. When the tribe reappeared at another waterhole, things looked like they might turn ugly until the camels, scenting water, bellowed at the delay in getting to it and thereby put the Mujingera to flight.

Despite his need for water, Trotman could sympathise with the traditional owners: 'I can understand the blacks' fierce indignation for apparently they thought we deliberately trailed them with the object of depleting their waterholes which, of course, had to carry them over many rainless years.'

Sure enough, the country ahead grew much tougher on them all. They were in the midst of the dunes, and worse, the land was gripped by drought and many of the wells they found, such as Ural Soak and Libral, were dry or very poor. As Trotman described it: 'Now followed days of incredible hardship as we made our way slowly over the largest sandridges on the route. Day followed day, the heat almost unbearable. Stupefied, we continue[d] on, feet moving because they must. Our throats were parched and although we forced ourselves to eat, we could barely swallow the food.'

And these were the winter months. They saw no Aboriginal people, a sure sign they were in extremely tough country. By 12 September, the party was 900 kilometres from Wiluna, with some 500 kilometres to go before the first sign of civilisation in the Kimberleys. They'd been overlanding for nearly three-and-a-half months. Finally they located Waddawalla Soak, cleaned it out, and were rewarded with a quick-flowing supply of clean water. It was the exception to the deadly rule of this thirsty country.

As the expedition pushed on, the men became increasingly fractious, mainly thanks to the cook, who'd turned out to be a whinger about everything, shortening the tempers of everyone else as they tried to endure their privations. Trotman noted that: 'At times a man could go no farther, and dropping exhausted in his tracks was not missed until all were in camp at night. It was always Canning who returned with a flask of brandy to get him on his feet and coax him back to camp.'

A group of Aboriginal people camped at Kanjamanilba Soak told them there was water at the rockholes ahead, but, when the men reached Kuduarra Soak, they found it so fouled by dead animals it was undrinkable. Desperate, they continued on, hoping to reach Godfreys Tank, named after Godfrey Massie, of David Carnegie's 1896 expedition, and marked on their maps as 'permanent water'. It was 50 kilometres away. As night fell, they kept going, guided by an Aboriginal they didn't trust, until they reached the tank.

It was dry.

The thirsty, exhausted men slumped, while Trotman started digging nearby, hoping to find water. To no avail. Alfred Canning looked around at his men and said, 'We'll bunk down now and decide what to do in the morning.'

At first light Trotman was up and searching. Near Godfreys Tank he found tracks heading to another deep depression that should normally hold water, but that was also dry. He lit a fire to attract attention and started digging. After hours of work they got just enough water for their horses. There was a little for them, but nothing for the camels.

'We'll get an early start in the morning back to Kuduarra and try to clean it out,' Canning decided.

Survival was now the only priority. The camels were unloaded and the greatly diminished supplies were left behind, booby trapped with a gun that was set up so it would frighten anyone tempted to tamper with the food. Then the party started the 50-kilometre march back to Kuduarra.

As the men dragged themselves forward, Trotman and water borer Joe Tobin forged ahead to the soak, hoping to get a start on cleaning it out so the others and the stock might have water as soon as they arrived. When they got there, they were so thirsty that they decided to risk the ghastly broth as they found it. Their stomachs instantly and violently rebelled.

Between convulsions Joe Tobin laconically observed, 'It's got quite a kick, hasn't it?'

When they'd recovered, they started cleaning out the soak. The expedition took a break to recover at Kuduarra, then loaded as much water as they could and returned to Godfreys Tank. They tracked down another guide but the only water they found beyond Godfreys Tank was salty. During this dry stage, Trotman noted:

> We rested through the hottest period in the shade of a tent fly thrown over anything that would support it. The camels, too, tried to escape from the sun and if there were not trees under which to shelter, poked their heads under our coverings. At times they would fight desperately for the most miserable shadow and if not separated they would fight desperately to the death for it.

At last their guide found Lumba Soak, which gave a decent supply of water. Canning chose a point not far south of the soak; the men bored there and got an excellent flow of water for their efforts. From there the country gradually improved. At Weriaddo there was more good water and, not far away, a line of river gums in a dry riverbed. It was the head of Sturt Creek, a watercourse they could follow into the Kimberley. Apart from the fact that the effort had nearly killed them, they'd made it.

They camped at Billiluna Pool, where they shot so much game they made themselves sick as they gorged on their first decent meal in months. The only problem they experienced on the Sturt was the mosquitoes. As Mick Tobin observed: 'They sound like a bloody stringed orchestra.'

The ragged men reached Flora Downs Station, situated on the Elvire River amid towering verdant trees, on 29 October 1906. The next day Canning rode into Hall's Creek and sent a telegraphic message to his boss, the honourable Mr King:

> Arrived camp Flora Valley. Got through without loss of camels or horses. Water assured between Lake Auld and 60 miles [97 kilometres] Godfreys Tank about every 10 miles [16 kilometres]. Deeper towards Wiluna. Sandhills avoided where possible. Long stretches without any. Other places short distances but generally broken and low. Party well. Will have to wait till summer rain. Camels could not face sand without rain and a spell. Many wells. Good supply 7 to 10 feet [2 to 3 metres] water rising 4 feet [1.2 metres] from surface. Anticipate wells 25 feet [8 metres] give ample supply of good water. Have to bore in places going back either end.

While he resupplied and waited for some rain to fall along his potential stock route, Canning wrote up his report, sent from Flora Valley on 10 January 1907. It noted: 'If wells stand drawing as I anticipate, route ought when finished to be about best watering stock route in the colony' – though by then Australia was a nation and Western Australia a state. His report concluded:

> In addition, I may add, that the different members of the party worked well and helped me in every particular. Also I found the natives invaluable. They appeared perfectly willing to show us their waters, and this saved us probably months of searching and perhaps severe hardship.
>
> I will have a number of bores to put down on my return trip, but I feel certain when completed a well-watered stock route will be opened up, thus giving an outlet, much needed, to East Kimberley, where they [pastoralists] are rapidly becoming fully stocked not being able to get rid of anything but prime bullocks and even then at poor price.

Amid the preparations for the return trip, Hubert Trotman managed to skewer his foot on a stake of wood. The wound became infected and Canning insisted his trusted lieutenant take a steamer back to Perth to recover. On 27 February 1907, Canning left Flora Valley with the remaining men, twenty camels, three horses and twenty goats, which they intended to use for meat and milk. The goats proved a great success, and a hit with Aboriginal people along the way. One Aboriginal, Nipper, soon became a capable goat shepherd and was kept with the party for the whole of the trip.

Canning returned by the same route he had come, improving the water supplies and mapping the country as he went. Once again, though, the scarcity of water in the arid central stretch was the source of serious trouble. Canning was the first to reach Waddawalla Soak on the afternoon of 5 April. He made camp, but was soon joined by Mick Tobin, who told him he'd seen an Aboriginal at the soak.

'Can I go and speak to him?' Tobin asked.

'Take Nipper with you to interpret,' Canning replied. 'And be careful.'

Tobin and Nipper went over to the soak and approached the man.

They had got to talking when cameleer Tom Burke appeared with his line of giant beasts, which typically started to bellow when they smelled water. Just as Tobin glanced away to look at the disturbance, the terrified Aboriginal let loose a spear. Tobin never saw it coming and was caught in the shoulder.

The Aboriginal ran and Tobin took off after him, firing his rifle.

'Let him go!' Canning shouted. Tobin took no notice.

Then the Aboriginal turned and prepared to throw another spear. Tobin dropped to one knee and aimed. Both weapons were discharged simultaneously, both with deadly effect. The Aboriginal man died instantly; Tobin never saw another sunrise.

Reflecting on the incident, Hubert Trotman noted that: 'There is no doubt that both men had been the victims of fear. Such a tragedy should never have happened . . . the black protected himself in the only way he knew.'

Canning was shocked by what had happened, writing of Tobin: 'He was a splendid man. He took a most intelligent interest in the work and was always willing to perform any necessary task. His loss was a great blow to me personally and of course to the whole camp, his brother feeling his death keenly.'

Mick Tobin's body was buried on the stock route and his grave can still be seen today. What happened to the body of the shot Aborigine is not recorded.

Meanwhile, the diminished party continued on, improving the water supplies and boring wells. By the time they returned to Wiluna, fourteen months after they'd left, they'd sunk twenty bores and opened up thirty-seven Aboriginal waterholes, with the longest distance between any two being only 26 kilometres. The length of the route was just under 1500 kilometres – although the distance covered in determining it was more like 3200 kilometres, with most of the search conducted on foot, since the stock were reserved for carrying supplies, rather than riders.

On his return to Perth, Alfred Canning was hailed a hero. A reception in his honour was held by both Houses of Parliament, and he was soon asked to prepare plans for an expedition to finish the establishment of the stock route. The wells had to be lined, more had to be sunk, various means of raising water from the wells in large enough volumes to water stock had to be provided, and so on.

Most of the original party was rehired for the expedition, along with many more men. However, Canning declined to hire the cook, Edward Blake, the reason being he was a troublemaker. And this didn't end with the expedition. Not long after, Canning was appalled to read allegations in the *West Australian* newspaper that he had mistreated Aborigines during the first expedition, and allowed his men to engage in improper relations with Aboriginal women. The accusations came from a disgruntled Blake.

'I have asked the Government for an Inquiry,' Canning told Trotman, who had recovered from his injured foot and was to join him on the well-construction expedition, 'I want you and the men to testify.'

The Royal Commission to Inquire into the Treatment of Natives by the Canning Exploration Party started on 15 January 1908. Among the witnesses was the local police commissioner. He'd given the stock-route party the chains that were at the heart of the allegations of mistreatment.

'The lives of the men depended on the blacks,' the police commissioner said. 'I know through experience that if left free at night, they would run away, with perhaps tragic results to the expedition.'

'Canning did stupid things,' the cook said in evidence. 'Like giving the natives guns.'

It was one of many contradictions that undermined the cook's flimsy case. Why would a man who was mistreating people and abusing their women give them arms? And why didn't the armed Aboriginals promptly shoot their persecutor?

As Hubert Trotman pointed out in evidence, had the charges been true, and they'd acted as suggested during their many years in the outback, they'd have been speared (or shot) well before now.

Eventually the cook's reputation was reduced to such tatters, his charges revealed as being so obviously motivated by malice that he finally capitulated and withdrew them all. Commissioner Sir Walter James, K.C., summed up by saying the main motive for the cook's wild charges was spite:

> It was not the natives the accuser was concerned about, it was Trotman against whom he had personal animus. I think the members of the Commission will see that these charges arose in the first place owing to personal ill-feeling of the cook towards Trotman and were widened for the purpose of throwing a slur upon the testimony of the persons concerned.

Alfred Canning and his men were exonerated by the Commission, but that said, the cook had a point. It's inconceivable that detaining innocent people by chaining them would be tolerated for an instant today. As for luring a group of people down a well and leaving them there for the night, it was indeed a lucky thing Canning and his men weren't speared when they released them. Today, of course, building a stock route through Aboriginal land would require permission from, consultation with and respect for the cultural sensitivities of the traditional owners. It could still be done, but it would be done very differently.

Hubert Trotman reflected on these issues many years later, when he said: 'After months of close contact with the blacks, I learnt that the chaining was not necessary; but, like most early explorers, we were as scared of them as they were of us. I would now, with the knowledge I have through experience, act in a different manner, but sixty years ago was another matter.'

Progress in Aboriginal affairs may have had some way to go, but progress in organising the coming expedition was swift. It set out from Wiluna in April 1908, a team of thirty-one, comprising bore experts, bush carpenters, cooks, cameleers and blacksmiths. They carried supplies to last twelve months.

The work progressed efficiently, month after month, despite temperatures that often reached 50 degrees Celsius. All went well until they again reached the halfway point, some 700 kilometres from Wiluna. There Trotman did the maths and realised they'd gone through more than half their supplies, which meant they were going to run out some time before they got to Halls Creek. Canning decided to go on ahead and bring supplies back down the route, meeting the men at Billiluna Pool on Sturt Creek.

After he left, the construction party shot birds, including duck, to supplement their rations. The new cook, however, soon tired of dressing the birds, so he devised an ingenious plan: duck-plucking competitions, with him as the judge. Surplus plucked ducks were salted for use on the coming dry section where game would be scarce. Eventually, though, the ducks ran out, and just about everything else. All they had left was flour, just over a cup per man, per day. As the saying goes, 'Man cannot live by bread alone' and, sure enough, at Weriaddo Well, the men on the construction team mutinied.

'We're not going anywhere,' they said, 'until we get meat.'

It was more than a little unreasonable, since staying where they were meant they'd all perish, but they'd surely had enough of damper for breakfast, lunch and dinner. Without supplies, though, there was nothing Hubert Trotman could do. So, while the men sat around, he set about building the well on his own. Eventually a cameleer, Gus Langham, who was suffering from a hernia, came over and gave his dogged leader a hand.

'How's the hernia?' Trotman asked.

'Bloody marvellous,' Langham replied.

One by one, over the next few days, the others returned to work.

They'd been shamed into it, perhaps, but they were no longer just doing a job; it was a matter of honour. Tired, hungry and weak, they worked on.

Canning, meanwhile, had reached Hall's Creek only to find that water was again presenting a major problem for the stock route. This time, though, the supplies were held up by floods. He set about organising cattle and goats for his men, and sent a telegram to his boss, the Minister for Mines:

> Completed thirty-one wells and shifted everything this end owing to meat supply giving out. Working back. Distributed well material for another twenty wells and completed boring with exception of four bores. Getting some livestock this end. Hope complete wells on return trip in five months. Health of party generally good. Please reply today. Leaving immediately (to rejoin men) no use sending mail which would not arrive before leaving.

Trotman, meanwhile, finished the well at Weriaddo and moved on to Billiluna, where they found a note from Canning explaining the situation. They shot more duck, and ate their first meat for several weeks. Even though the change in diet was hard on their stomachs, they thought it was worth it. The party reached Hall's Creek in November 1909, after more than eighteen months of well construction.

On the return trip, starting in February 1910, their supplies again failed to arrive. This time, Canning set off for Wiluna for stores with most of the men. Those who remained were asked to volunteer.

'It's up to you,' Trotman told them. 'We're just about out of tucker but we've got to finish the wells. We could starve or do a perish but apart from that we'll have a good time!'

Six men agreed to stay on, even though Trotman warned them that it could get worse than it had been at Weriaddo. As Gus Langham put it: 'If we're going to leave our carcasses in the desert, it's up to us to supply water for the poor bastards who'll come searching for us.'

The men worked on, their rations reduced to tea, sugar and flour. Then they worked on flour alone. After it ran out, the men worked for two days more on nothing at all. All the time Trotman was scanning the horizon towards Wiluna, desperately hoping for some sign of the supplies. At Windich Springs, 155 kilometres from Wiluna, he and Nipper were on look-out – Trotman with binoculars – when he thought he saw a cloud of dust.

'Looks like a willy-willy,' he said.

'That's no willy-willy,' Nipper replied. 'That's [camel handler] Bill Matheson. He'll come up along sundown.'

To Trotman's astonishment, sure enough, Matheson rode in at sundown with some supplies.

Again the men gorged until they were sick. 'That's gratitude for you,' Matheson joked. 'Here I travel my guts out to bring you food and you chuck it up.'

Matheson told them that their drays of supplies had been bogged on the road to Wiluna, along with those for the town. Yet the Wiluna townsfolk had rallied around to gather some supplies for the well team, even though they were in much the same boat. Matheson had brought all that could be spared, while Canning had gone in search of the bogged drays.

The construction party pressed on, blasted a huge water tank out of the rock at the Granites, and then got ready for a foodless dash to Wiluna. Two days later, Canning arrived. He'd found the drays, loaded his camels, returned to Wiluna with supplies for the townsfolk, then continued with supplies for his own men. His journey was in excess of 700 kilometres, plus the thousands he'd already walked on the stock route. But the wells were done. The men tidied themselves up for the return to civilisation.

The news of their coming preceded them, and Wiluna turned out in force to give them a hero's welcome. In May 1910, just over four years after the first exploration party had set out, a cheering crowd pressed in to offer congratulations as the dishevelled bearded men limped in. Once again, Hubert Trotman provided a sense of the occasion: 'It was a moving moment and none of us could speak.'

Ever the proper professional, when the party stopped at the post office, Alfred Canning went in and sent a telegram as brief as the achievement was great: 'Work completed. Canning.'

In 1939, W.T. Fyfe encapsulated Alfred Canning's realisation of the Canning Stock Route when he wrote:

> His remarkable organising ability and bush knowledge brought this effort to a successful conclusion, and about two years after leaving Wiluna the party reached Hall's Creek, having completed the task set by the Government, and established a stock route with fifty-two equipped wells, an average of 17 miles [27 kilometres] apart, each giving a good supply of water.

The route was first used in 1909, when Joseph McGee brought stock down from Flora Valley, even before the route was officially completed. However, problems with Aboriginal people along the route persisted. These were, after all, tribal lands, and still well populated with people who resented the European presence, especially when it included large numbers of stock drinking their water.

In April 1911, drovers George Shoesmith and James Thomson, and an Aboriginal stockman, were fatally speared in the dry section north of Lake Disappointment. Two months later, drover Tom Cole found stray cattle wandering north along the route and eventually located the bodies of the men. They were buried on the route, but later the bodies of the Europeans were exhumed and buried in Perth.

Fatalities continued, with John McLernon, a member of an oil exploration party, clubbed to death in 1922, and dingo trapper Joe Wilkins killed in 1936.

In 1929, Alfred Canning, who had already given decades of service to the development of Western Australia, was asked to lead a party to recondition the wells along the stock route, despite the fact that he was nearly seventy years old. He agreed to do so, making his third round trip of the route, again covering much of the gruelling terrain on foot. He completed the work eighteen months later, in 1930. He died in Perth on 22 May 1936, aged seventy-five.

The Canning Stock Route was used to overland stock until 1959, with Aboriginal stockmen frequently employed in droving the cattle. Eventually, it had become so run-down that many of the wells caved in and were dry. And by then, transporting cattle by rail and truck was starting to prove more economical and kept the stock in better condition.

Today, some of the wells have been reconditioned by volunteers intent on preserving the heritage of one of Australia's great stock routes. Several of the properties associated with the route, especially at the northern end, are now Aboriginal-owned. The route itself is still open, now a dusty, bumpy, four-wheel-drive track that is considered one of the world's great off-road adventures. It passes through some of the most spectacular desert scenery the country has to offer. It also gives an appreciation of just how close to impossible was the task undertaken by Alfred Canning. As with many of the bushies in this volume, Canning's success was due to combining the help of local Aborigines with his own extraordinary bush skills – and then adding a big dose of sheer determination.

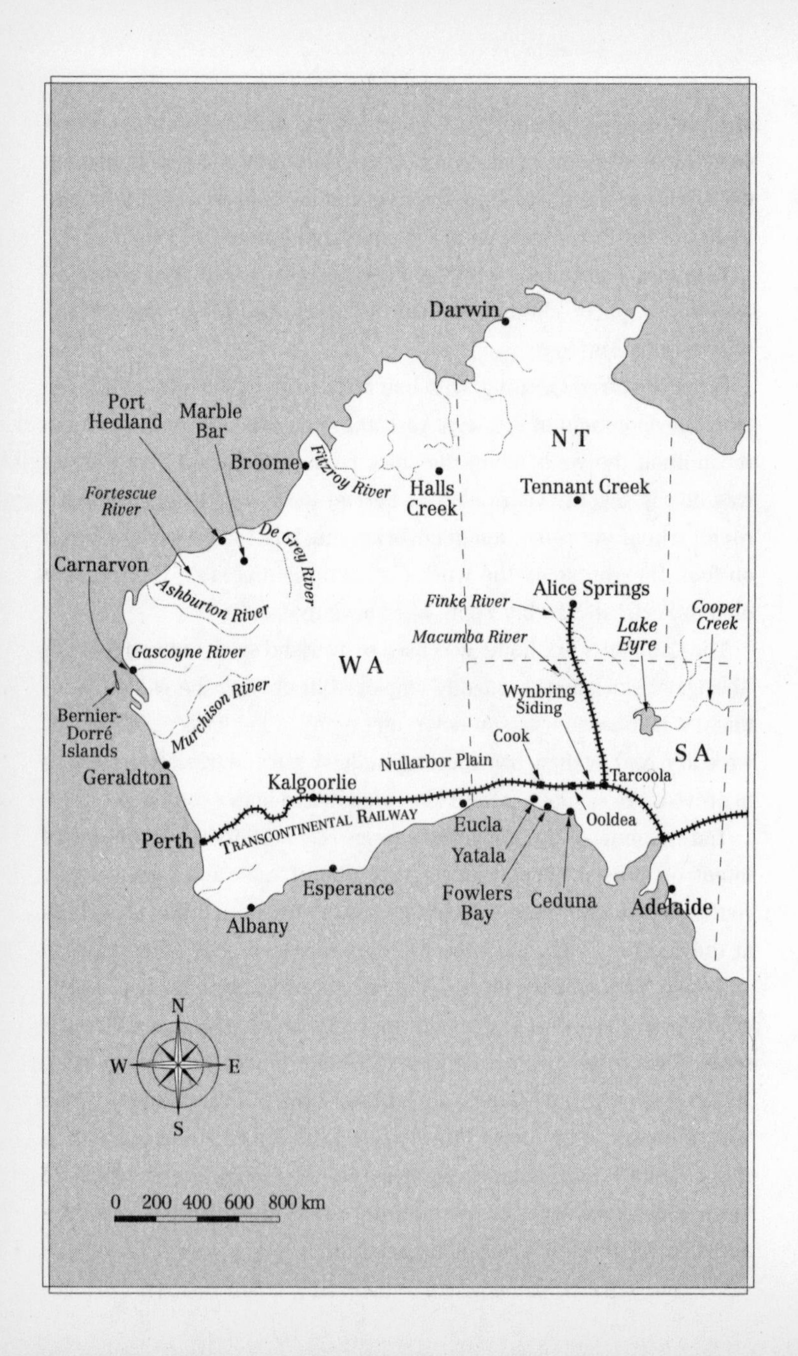

Darwin
Port Hedland
Marble Bar
Broome
Fitzroy River
Halls Creek
NT
Tennant Creek
Fortescue River
De Grey River
Carnarvon
Ashburton River
Alice Springs
Finke River
Cooper Creek
Lake Eyre
Macumba River
Gascoyne River
WA
Murchison River
Wynbring Siding
Bernier-Dorré Islands
Cook
SA
Nullarbor Plain
Geraldton
Kalgoorlie
Tarcoola
Eucla
Ooldea
Transcontinental Railway
Perth
Yatala
Esperance
Fowlers Bay
Ceduna
Adelaide
Albany
N
W
E
S
0 200 400 600 800 km

Daisy Bates, 1936
(State Library of South Australia, SLSA: B 6799)

9

THE DYING PILLOW, 1910–1945: Daisy Bates (1863–1951)

During the 1920s and 1930s, travellers on the recently completed (1917) Transcontinental Railway Line at times witnessed one of Australia's most extraordinary sights. At one of the many railway sidings where trains stopped to replenish the water for their steam engines, passengers might see an impeccably dressed white woman surrounded by heavily armed tribal Aborigines. The travellers, who included in their number future kings of England and Australian prime ministers, all knew the name of the white woman and the details of her remarkable story.

In her lifetime, Daisy May Bates was famous for her untiring work among the Aboriginal people of Western Australia and South Australia. For many Europeans, she helped unravel some of the enduring enigmas of Aboriginal culture and customs, while championing the cause of Aboriginal welfare. However, during her lifetime, she also managed to polarise opinion about her work. Even friends and collaborators took issue with her intransigent position on certain Aboriginal customs and the future of their race.

In contemporary times, little has changed. Many writers on her life end up either damning or defending her, rather than simply giving an account of her contribution. The more that we discover about her, the more inconsistencies in her life-story are revealed, as well as the gaps in her story. Indeed, Bates emerges as an enigma and any account of her life becomes a weaving together of threads, the veracity of which is uncertain and the understanding of which is open to wide interpretation. Yet she was a key player in one of the chapters in the ongoing tragedy of Western culture's impact on Aboriginal Australia, and she became so by going bush for almost half of her life.

Bates was born Daisy May O'Dwyer in Tipperary, Ireland, probably on 16 October 1863. Some accounts suggest she was perhaps born in 1861, while the author of a 'personal memoir' of Bates (published in the 1970s), Ernestine Hill, suggests she was in her nineties when she died in 1951. Bates may have had a small personal fortune; she may have come from a family that had fallen on hard times; she may have come from a family with close associations to the British Royal Family for several generations.

In 1884, at the age of twenty (based on the birth date of 1863) she travelled to Australia, ostensibly to cure a spot on her lung. She became a governess on a Western Queensland property, an area which at the time had a ratio of nine European men to each woman. That same year (possibly in March), she appears to have married Edwin Murrant, considered actually to have been Harry 'Breaker' Morant, who was later executed for shooting prisoners in the Boer War. The marriage quickly failed due to the strong-willed natures of both partners, or possibly due to Morant's profligate lifestyle. Bates may then have become engaged to Philip Gipps, who appears to have died suddenly. Soon after this, in February 1885, she married drover John Bates, possibly bigamously, in New South Wales.

In 1886 the couple had a son, Arthur (or Arnold) Hamilton, but this didn't prevent the marriage from failing some time later. Exactly when isn't clear, but Daisy reputedly travelled widely around the states of Australia before returning to England in 1894. There have been suggestions that the failing economy, the debts of her husband, and the need to support her then eight-year-old son prompted the move. It has also been suggested by Hill that Bates's return to Australia in 1899 was due to economic conditions improving or her husband finding work on a station (or finding a property) in the north-west of Western Australia. Bates was then thirty-five.

In her autobiographical work, *The Passing of the Aborigines: A Lifetime Spent among the Natives of Australia*, published in 1938 when she was nearing seventy-five, Bates explains that a letter had been published in the *Times* alleging cruelty to the Aborigines in Western Australia's north-west. As she was about to set sail for the same locality, she visited the editor and offered to investigate and report further on the true condition of the Aborigines. There is no mention of husbands, sons and north-west properties, although Ernestine Hill suggests that Bates paid for her son's schooling in Perth, and his accommodation. She also invested in property, and when she travelled the north-west for six months from March 1900, Hill believes she must have done so with her husband, even though they were probably by then estranged.

Both Bates and Hill refer to her north-west trip and similarly describe the tour as starting at Port Hedland, where her toes were nibbled by soldier crabs whenever she put them on the ground. Bates wrote in 1938: 'I then traversed in my buggy 800 miles [1287 kilometres] of country, taking six months to accomplish it. I could not prove one charge of cruelty, except that of "giving offal to natives instead of good meat", and "sending them away from the stations without food when work was slack".'

However, Bates gives a rather different account in 1901, shortly after the trip of the previous year. On this occasion, she wasn't writing for the *Times* of London, rather the substantially less glamorous *Journal of the Department of Agriculture in Western Australia*. In 'From Port Hedland to Carnarvon by Buggy' she wrote nothing about soldier crabs, and states an objective other than reporting on the conditions of Aborigines:

> In travelling through the Nor'West one must be prepared to rough it in the extreme sense of the word, leaving one's squeamishness and fastidiousness in the matter of foods and household comforts of every kind safely stowed away in one's Perth hotel.
>
> When I first mooted the idea of a journey through the bush in order to observe the country, and see for myself the capabilities – pastoral, agronomical, and mineral – of West Australia, that portion of the Nor'West which I selected for my first trip was painted in anything but attractive colouring. I would be harassed by flies – sand flies and house flies, big ants and little ants, and all sorts of horrid creeping insects – by day, and at night my peaceful slumbers would be prevented by various species of mosquito, the 'Scot's Grey' amongst them, with a trunk of the capacity of an elephant and a bloodthirstiness incomparable – the names of the other species of mosquito are only spoken aloud under the shadow of the bullock dray. Fresh water tea would be unobtainable; baths *quite* [her emphasis] out of the question in the inland country.

> Centipedes, with a curious predilection for playing hide and seek in the toes of one's shoes, were quite common occurrences; myriads of flying grasshoppers cannoned against your face as you drove through them, leaving stinging blotches from the force of the impact. Even in the winter the thermometer registered something like 120 degrees during the day; the renovation of one's wardrobe would be confined to Turkey twill and hobnailed boots. Yet, not withstanding all these and numerous other doleful forebodings, Friday, the 2nd of March, 1900 saw me on board the SS *Sultan* bound for Cossack.

There was also no mention of travelling companions, such as her family. However, she did write of her encounters with Aboriginal people, as a sidelight to the main reporting into the conditions for pastoral, agricultural and mineral exploitation of the region:

> The natives in Roebourne number about 200, some of them very fine looking men; the women are very inferior looking. They make several articles from the spinifex grass, which grows so abundantly about here. Netted bags, which they manipulate with a small kangaroo bone, beads, rope, and a splendid glue, which they use to fasten their spear heads on the end of the wooden spears. This spinifex, though very spiky, makes excellent bedding when camping out.
>
> The natives, in cases of sickness, take a sharp-pointed wooden carved flat stick, one point of which they stick into their stomachs and leave it there to fester; I believe they generally recover under this treatment. I do not know if it is only used in special cases of illness, or whether it is used in all cases. They have no Deity, but many devils, and to frighten the evil spirits they have a long carved stick with a hole in one rounded end through which a string made of human hair is passed, and they twirl this round and round, making a booming and most depressing noise sufficient to send any poor devil flying from the sound of it. There are about twenty kinds of food plants which they use, amongst them the 'beach bean' and

> the Australian millet, the seeds of which they collect in large quantities, grind them between stones, and bake them. They have also various methods of burying their dead – on trees, in a hollow log, or doubled up underground. They have, too, a very curious instrument which I could not find the use of. It is a rod about nine or ten feet in length, and towards the top they place crosswise two carved flat sticks about a foot apart, and from the points of these they make a kind of hexagon of human hair.

Near Port Hedland she viewed some rock carvings, but wrote of them rather indifferently: 'I found, on inspection, a rude attempt at a kylie, a turtle, a faint likeness to a shark, a bird, and sundry other nondescript indents, but the little belt upon which the carvings were is now the main road to the causeway, and the tracings are being rapidly obliterated.'

Her report also included what was to be one of the first of many detailed descriptions of Aboriginal burials:

> I have heard the following account of the burial of a De Grey woman, witnessed by the man from whom I got the story: – Bark was placed round the body, and a very shallow, oval grave was then dug, and the body put into the cavity, and immediately as many jumped on the body as the grave would hold, and set up a most unmerciful howling in chorus; meanwhile those of the women who couldn't get in threw sand into the grave from tiny cockle shells. The mourners on the grave had to be dragged away, and afterwards the grave was covered. In the case of a child dying, the mother takes the elbow bone of the deceased, and carries it about with her for a long time.

It was one of the first oblique references to a theme that would become almost endemic in her later work – cannibalism. And Bates followed it with further details that included self-mutilation:

> The return of the 'prodigal son' is also rather interesting. Suppose a blackfellow goes away for some time, either droving or with another tribe. When he returns his mother goes to him, folds him in her arms, and howls loudly over him. Then she gets a good sharp conch, and proceeds to cut herself with it, all the while howling for all she's worth. When much blood issues from the cut she subsides, and her place is taken by a male relative, who forthwith cuts himself with a jagged tomahawk, drawing much blood, and so on, till they all have an innings in the auto-bloodletting business, when the rejoicings at the return of the prodigal son are over. A Government official told me today of his having seen a native woman gather the roots of a certain tree, pound them into a kind of flour, open a vein in her arm, letting the blood fall on the flour, mix, bake and eat it.

Hill mentions in *A Personal Memoir* that Bates saw the old and destitute crawling sick and untended in and out of their windbreaks, and prisoners herded into Roebourne jail. None of these incidents were mentioned in Bates's 1901 article. In her autobiography, *The Passing of the Aborigines*, Bates mentions being allocated a kin relationship in the Aboriginal culture of Sherlock River Station. Again, there is no mention of this in the earlier article.

Instead, there appears to be an observant and intelligent mind at work behind Bates's early writings. Hearsay is reported as such. She tends to write from the position of a detached observer, seldom strays from her topic, and her writing is uncoloured by any prescient sense of a great life mission. There are only occasional excursions into anecdote.

Yet it was her interest in Aboriginal life (and perhaps her demonstrated willingness to undergo great hardship far from civilisation) that led, in 1904, to her appointment by the Western Australia Registrar-General to report on Aboriginal customs, languages and dialects. This was despite the fact that she had no formal training as an anthropologist, itself a fledgling discipline. It was an appointment that in the ensuing eight years was to take the then forty-year-old from one end of Western Australia to the other – into the north-west, central west, Perth and south-west.

Much of what she found was the rapid annihilation of the races that once prospered. The pioneering of many of the bushies referred to throughout this book was the vanguard of an exploitation of the land that left no place for Aboriginal people. Opposition to white aspirations was routinely crushed, the scarcity of European women led to cohabitation with the indigenous population, which had the effect of breaking down traditional marriage structures, while spreading venereal disease. The beaten people were forced off their land and away from their waterholes.

Bates lamented the passing of great cultures, such as the groups around Perth and the south-west's once populous Bibbulmun, even as she strove to salvage every available piece of cultural information. Yet her primary interest was academic, as she wrote in *The Passing of the Aborigines*:

> I realised that the Australian native was not so much deliberately secretive as inarticulate. He looked upon his 'black life' as a life apart from his association with the whites, few of whom had shown any interest in it . . .
>
> The natives I found at first amused, and then stimulated to further confidence by my obviously eager and sustained interest. I pretended that my native name was Kallower, and that I was a mirruroo-jandu, or magic woman who had been one of the twenty-two wives of Leeberr, a patriarchal or 'dreamtime' father. After that, the way was clear. They accepted me as a kindred spirit, and with the utmost patience elucidated the seeming tangle of relationships and class-groups, the marriage laws, the tribal tabus, the traditional songs and dances. They even allowed me free access to the sacred places and the sacred

> ceremonies of the initiations of men, which their own women must never see under penalty of death.
>
> The abstruse 'matronymics' and 'patronymics' of native marriage laws as expounded in the hieroglyphics of the anthropologists, through which I have vainly floundered many times before and since with no clear conception of their exact meaning, the natives could simplify for me – a definition of the four group classes, and the cross-cousin marriage of paternal aunt's children to the maternal uncles' children, the only lawful marriage between the groups.

However, it was the West Australian visit of two groups of anthropologists in 1910 that may have provided the catalyst for a significant change in Bates's outlook. One was a Cambridge University expedition, lead by Professor A.R. Radcliffe-Brown, assisted by E.L. Grant Watson. The other party, led by a Mr Laurell, was from Sweden. Bates met both parties, although the Swedes spoke no English. It was eventually decided that Bates would accompany the Englishmen, appointed to the capacity of travelling protector of Aborigines by the Western Australia government. The party headed north to the Geraldton region, where, according to Bates: 'It took some time to convince the natives that my companions were not policemen, of whom, for their own reasons, they lived in an unholy fear at that time. After some vain endeavours at explanation, I found it easier to introduce them as my two sons!'

The group eventually moved on to Dorré and Bernier islands. Even for Bates, at age forty-six and well-experienced in Aboriginal welfare, it was a shock. In the most eloquent chapter of *The Passing of the Aborigines*, she wrote:

> Dorré and Bernier Islands: there is not, in all my sad sojourn among the last sad people of the primitive Australian race, a memory one-half so tragic or so harrowing, or a name that conjures up such a deplorable

picture of misery and horror unalleviated, as these two grim and barren islands of the West Australian coast that for a period, mercifully brief, were the tombs of the living dead.

In accordance with its policy of safeguarding the aborigines, the West Australian Government, in 1904, had authorized Dr Roth, a Queensland anthropologist, to inquire into native conditions. After intensive study of the problem, Dr Roth made the suggestion, among others, that all diseased natives from the whole of the north-west should be isolated for treatment. The Government immediately adopted the suggestion, the unhappiest decision ever arrived at by a humane administration, a ghastly failure in the attempt to arrest the ravages of disease, and an infliction of physical and mental torture that it could not perhaps have been expected to foresee.

At the cost of many thousands of pounds, the authorities established an isolation hospital on two islands bordering Shark Bay, some 30 miles [48 kilometres] from Carnarvon . . .

Diseased natives were gathered in, by policemen and other appointed officers, over an area of hundreds of thousands of square miles. Regardless of tribe and custom and country and relationship, they were herded together – the women on Dorré and the men on Bernier. Many had never seen the sea before, and lived and died in terror of it . . .

When I landed on Bernier Island in November 1910, there were only fifteen men left alive there, but I counted thirty-eight graves . . . Deaths were frequent – appallingly frequent, sometimes three in a day – for most of the natives were obviously in the last stages of venereal disease and tuberculosis. Nothing could save them, and they had been transported, some of them thousands of miles, to strange and unnatural surrounds and solitude. They were afraid of the hospital, its ceaseless probings and dressings and injections were a daily torture. They were afraid of each other, living and dead. They were afraid of the ever-moaning sea . . .

There were seventy-seven women on Dorré Island, many of them bed-ridden. I dared not count the graves there. A frightful sight it was to see grey-headed women, their faces and limbs repulsive in disease, but an ever more frightful sight to see the young – and there were children among them . . .

Companionship in misery was impossible to them, for there were so many spiritual and totemic differences. Some of them were alone of their group, and they could not give food or a firestick to a possible enemy or a stranger for fear of evil magic. A woman would be called upon to bath and feed or bury another woman whose spirit she knew was certain to haunt her.

Restlessly they roamed the islands in all weather, avoiding each other as strangers. Some of them cried all day and all night in a listless and terrible monotony of grief. There were others who stood silently for hours on a headland, straining their hollow, hopeless eyes across the narrow strait for the glimpse of a loved wife or husband or a far lost country, and far too often the smoke signal of death went up from the islands. In death itself they could find no sanctuary, for they believed that their souls, when they left the poor broken bodies, would be orphaned in a strange ground, among enemies more evil and vindictive than those on earth . . .

To question the poor shuddering souls of these doomed exiles was slow work and saddening, but as I sat with them in the darkness of their mias [shelters that they preferred to the hospital] at night, the torture of hospital routine was forgotten, and harking back to thoughts of home, they were, for an hour or so, happy. Of all the tribes there so dismally represented, from Halls Creek to Broome and Nullagine, from the Fitzroy River to Winning Pool and Marble Bar and Lake Way, I learned much of infinite value in vocabularies and customs and pedigrees and legends. The scientists, I think, made intermittent headway . . .

I did what I could among them with little errands of mercy; distributing rations and blankets from my own government stores when boats were delayed; bringing sweets and dainties for young and old,

> extra blankets in the rain, and where I could a word of love and understanding.

Her account demonstrates an intimate knowledge of Aboriginal social structure and relationship to land. It was also on Dorré and Bernier, Bates claims, that she earned the Aboriginal name Kabbarli, meaning grandmother. It was a name by which she was to become known throughout Australia. It was not a name she pretended to in order to gain information from dying people; it was given to her in recognition of her care for those who knew that death was near. At a time when it was widely believed that Aborigines were a dying race, Bates, the detached observer, was shifting to a new role, that of 'smoothing the dying pillow' – an expression that first appeared in the *Age* (28 October 1858), but was made famous by Bates.

As for the scientists, Bates parted company with them in March 1911. Bates maintains that she toured Aboriginal camps at the heads of the Ashburton, Gascoyne, Murchison and Fortescue rivers. Radcliffe-Brown continued north. Grant Watson returned to England where he wrote a novel, *Where Bonds Are Loosed*, based on his experiences at Dorré and Bernier. The islands were shut down not long after the anthropologists' visit.

There are some suggestions that there was considerable conflict between the expedition members, and that Radcliffe-Brown published some of Bates's work as his own. There is one story that he once spoke at a scientific conference and was followed to the podium by Bates. Instead of presenting her findings, she is supposed to have thanked Radcliffe-Brown for his excellent presentation of her work, and then sat down. However, in *The Passing of the Aborigines* she simply wrote:

> In dealing with the Australian aborigines, it is only too easy for the anthropologist to elaborate a fantasy based on theories and the

> foreign logics of other native races, and then proceed to build it up in his field work . . . The first lessons that I learned were never to intrude my own intelligence upon him, and to have patience, the patience that waits for hours and years for the links in the long chain to be pieced together . . . Most of my data is the gradual compiling of many, many years.

Many of those years were spent camped out in the bush, often isolated from civilisation, detailing tribal lands, customs and ceremonies. In 1912 Bates submitted her reports on her findings to the Western Australian government's Registrar-General. They were submitted to Dr Andrew Lang, in England, for revision and annotation, but the Western Australian government didn't publish them. They returned Bates's reports to her, saying she was free to do with them what she wanted. There'd been a change of government, but effectively, after eight years of field work, Bates had been snubbed.

However, she was made an Honorary Protector (unpaid) of Aborigines at Eucla in the same year. She stayed at Eucla, near the South Australian border, until 1914 then, aged fifty, moved to South Australia, where she found the same pattern of a people in decline. In *The Passing of the Aborigines*, she wrote:

> I rigged my first little tent home in South Australia on the hills west of Fowlers Bay in 1914. Koolbarri and Beenbong built my breakwind and settled down beside it with remnants of groups of the eastern, western and northern edge of the [Nullarbor] Plain. Among them were three who were blind and helpless, Dowie of the Boundary Dam mallee-hen; Jinjabulla, last of the emu men of Ooldea; and Binily, a *wirongu* – rain or cloud woman of Tarcoola . . . I delighted them by striking camp and taking them with me to a little haven of their own, a place called Wirilya, 26 miles [42 kilometres] from Yalata.

The same year, 1914, she was invited to the eastern states to speak to the Science Congress of the Association for the Advancement of Science. There Bates's significant contribution to the understanding of Aboriginal culture was recognised, but there was little by way of financial or academic support for her continued efforts. Soon, though, she was based in South Australia, researching connections with the Western Australian Aboriginal groups that literally spanned deserts and half a continent. As Hill put it, her applications to the South Australian government for support received little notice. Camped on the far western border of the state, she was simply too far away to be heard.

Yet Bates was happy, and eloquently so. As she wrote of her life, 'A glorious thing it is to live in a tent in the infinite – to awaken in the grey of dawn, a good hour before the sun outlines the low ridges of the horizon.'

It was in 1919, when she was in her mid-fifties, that she first pitched her camp at the Ooldea siding, one of many train stops to which Aboriginal people came looking for food and handouts in return for trinkets sold to passing rail travellers. Bates continued researching Aboriginal culture, still working without pay, but supporting herself and her Aboriginals with the income from the articles she wrote, the sale of her property and donations from welfare groups.

One of her earliest articles from her new camp was 'Ooldea Water', published in the *Royal Geographic Society of Australia – SA Branch Proceedings*, 1919–20. In it she described the site, and its significance:

> Ooldea Water, an old native camping ground, lies 3½ miles [6 kilometres] direct north from Ooldea railway siding . . . The country round about the soak might be called undulating upland. The highest hill on the line to the soak is only about 60 feet [18 metres], from which a large portion of the great plain may be seen . . . a more unpromising area could not be imagined. Before the white men came the natives

> had opened up but two soaks, one sweet and one bitter, but apart from these the natives, with their scoops, hollowed out little temporary soaks in the sand, which were covered over by natural processes as soon as the natives left the district . . .
>
> Evidences of a large local tribe having existed hereabouts are numerous. They had such a tremendous asset in their unfailing water supply in these dry areas that tribes came from all parts in drought times, bringing gifts for barter or exchange with them, and for many miles around Ooldea was the place chosen for initiation and other ceremonies in which large numbers necessarily took part . . .
>
> The native legends in connection with Ooldea Water and Ooldea Range, the blow-holes in the vicinity, and other peculiar features, are many and interesting. I am slowly securing many of these for publication. The task of translating them is rather difficult as the 'dramatisation' occurring in their recital has to be separately interpreted . . . For instance, one of these blowholes, only a few hundred yards from the siding, sends forth a 'boo-boo' when a big south wind is blowing, and in others the suction is inward, the natives saying that the sounds are the inhaling and exhaling of the huge magic snake that owned the plain. It is possible that when the plain is fully explored many interesting discoveries will be made, for the natives have left the central portion of the great plain to the ganba (magic snake) for time immemorial.

She also noted the decline of its traditional owners: 'Every native belonging to Ooldea water is dead. I nursed and tended the last "owner", Jinjabula, who was blind for some years, and who died at Fowlers Bay, some 100 miles [160 kilometres] from his own district, in 1919.'

Then came a remarkable assertion: 'The Ooldea men call themselves Koogurda-meat-eaters, and indulged in human flesh whenever they were able to get it. Women killed and cooked many of their new-born babies, sharing the food with the next youngest to the little baby.'

It is a sensational observation, even though Bates admits she only met one of Ooldea's traditional owners, Jinjabula, when he was old and dying. Yet she doesn't attribute the information to him. As for the women's customs, it was hearsay, unable to be substantiated, not to mention inconsistent with the less scholarly assertions of William Buckley in Chapter 1. It was, however, attention grabbing and was to become a recurring theme in her journalism of years to come, not to mention the source of enduring controversy and criticism.

Unfortunately, it wasn't the only aspect of Bates that has tarnished her reputation. For example, in *The Passing of the Aborigines*, we meet Bates the staunch royalist:

> In February 1920, I was appointed a Justice of the Peace for South Australia. A few weeks later I was asked by the authorities to arrange a display of aborigines at Ooldea, in honour of his Royal Highness, the Prince of Wales, who was to pass on the east–west railway on his tour of Australia . . .
>
> In the afternoon of April 26, I was enjoying a cup of tea when one of the women, Comajee, sitting outside my breakwind, called a word of warning and, to my surprise, ran and hid among the trees. Down through the sandhills came an angry mob of about eighty men, not walking in single file, native fashion, but in a body, not a woman or child among them . . . Ranging themselves according to their totems – kangaroo, dingo, eagle-hawk and mallee-hen – they took four fire-sticks from my fire, sign of blood-relationship. I then addressed myself to Nyimbana, one of the ring-leaders.
>
> 'Naa?'
>
> 'Black-fella king belong to this country!' shouted Nyimbana in English. 'We don't want waijela [corruption of white-fella] here. This gabbi [water] our gabbi. Chasem waijela long way.

> 'White-fellows have frightened all our game away and taken our waters. The Kooga [game] will come back when the white men goes. This is our country. White-fellows took it away, and brought their sheep, bullocky and pony to hunt our totem meat away. You send paper to Gubmint and tell them we don't want white-fellow king. We want our own king and our own country.'

Years before native title claims were recognised, Nyimbana was making a strong case, which Bates completely missed. Instead, she gradually talked the men out of their plan, by suggesting they might get a king, a native named Nabbari, but that would mean they'd also become subjects and servants to his queen. And Nabbari wasn't then married. Bates wrote of the exchange: '"Very well. King must have wife. You give Nabbari one of your own women, which ever one he wants." There was a loud outburst. I turned aside to hide a smile, then "Nabbari king?" I asked again pleasantly. This time there was silence. They were thinking it out.'

This is the opposite of what might be expected from a true 'protector' of Aborigines. Amused by her ability to outwit the war party, she gave full rein to her self-interest:

> The display was to take place on July 10 at Cook, 86 miles [138 kilometres] west of Ooldea siding . . . I superintended the preparations with much anxiety. I was afraid that a sudden outburst of hostility, personal or tribal, at any moment would result in chaos. Carefully choosing my words, I explained the position to the natives in that, as they sent their sons to their people, so our great and good white King had sent his son to us all as we are his people. Some of them may have had the idea that the Prince of Wales was on his way to our initiation ceremony. Loyalty and enthusiasm ran high, and by keeping them busy, and stressing the importance of their best and brightest, I looked forward to success.

She got her triumph, and a fawning Bates was presented to the prince amid a great media glare. After the fanfare, though, it was back to grim reality:

> One morning, there arrived at my camp, naked and innocent, a contingent of twenty-six men, women and children from the Mann Ranges, nearly 1000 miles [1609 kilometres] north-west. They stood trembling and shrinking at their first sight of a white woman, but when I took the hand of the old man, and told him in his dialect that he could sit down without fear, the tension relaxed, and it became a question of clothing my new family.
>
> Just as I was buttoning the men into their first trousers, a thunder came from the Plain. All rose in terror to watch, wild-eyed, the monster of Nullarbor, the ganba (snake) coming to devour them. I needed all my tact and wisdom to prevent their flight. Two of the women were heavily pregnant. One of these, in spite of the abundant food bestowed on her, later gave birth to a girl baby in a hidden spot in the bush, and killed and ate the little creature. The other woman reared her child for a year or so, and then, giving birth to a half-caste at some siding, took both along the line and disposed of them either by neglect or design. One of the men survived civilization for a brief period of seven months. He had been taken by the 'magic snake' train to Kalgoorlie, where he contracted venereal disease, and returned to Ooldea only to die. On the day following his return we buried him near my tent, with Inyiga, a woman who, after killing her diseased half-caste child, succumbed to pneumonia.

Again the references to cannibalism are extraordinary. In the first reference to the mother eating her new-born child, Bates didn't witness and doesn't know what happened in childbirth, but assumes the child was eaten. The assertion that the second mother lost her children by 'neglect or design' ascribes a dark motive that also cannot be proven. It was Bates, of course, who had long since abandoned her own child, and who seems ready to ascribe far more heinous behaviour to other women who abandoned or lost theirs.

Amid this sensationalism, Bates's researches continued. During the 1920s, her articles were published in newspapers across the country. In 1923, for example, she revealed the Aboriginal conception of the cosmos to readers of Melbourne's *Argus* in an article titled 'Quaint Legends':

> Long before the story of the heavens had been interpreted by Asiatic, Egyptian or Greek, the Australian Aborigine had marked out a starry track of their own – a winding course through the heavens – inhabited by humans, animals, fabulous monsters, birds, and other creatures from some of which various groups believed they were descended. Almost every tribe had formed a constellation of one or other of its local totems, and the legend or myth attached to those was told by the elders to the young novitiates in the firelight of soft dark evenings, or in the midnight intervals between the initiation ceremonies. Amongst these constellations that of the kallaia or emu must be given first place, for it is the only 'black' constellation in the heavens. The dark spot in the Milky Way, which begins at the Southern Cross and stretches far beyond Aquila, towards the north-east, represents the emu totem of two once numerous and powerful groups who inhabited large areas within and north-east of the Central Australian ranges.
>
> The 'Coalsack' forms the head of the bird, its long neck, wings, legs and tail being formed out of the dark lanes which pass through portions of the Greek Zodiac and between Aquila and Lyra, where the nebulous lighter end of the opaque lanes constitutes the wispy tail of the bird.

All of this is readily verifiable in the Australian night sky away from the glare of city lights.

Bates also considered the issue of Aboriginal welfare, albeit in the almost obligatory context of unsubstantiated cannibalism, in an other-wise insightful article for the *Adelaide Register* in 1924:

> In the official dispatch case of every British officer sent out to administer the new-found colony that is now Australia, were special instructions relative to the welfare of the aborigines; and old state records show that these instructions were fully carried out. Missionaries came out with the first fleeters, and missionary endeavour began with their arrival; yet we are still debating over the methods for the preservation of the Aborigines, while the remnants continue to move steadily towards extinction . . .
>
> Today there are some six Boundary Dam men alive, and as many dingoes, emus, etc, all derelicts wandering along the East–West line and the west coast of South Australia, and between the Western Australian goldfields and Tarcoola areas. The central ranges and the ranges and the splendid waters within the aboriginal reserve have given up most of their inhabitants to civilization and death. There are earnest missionaries today as there were in Australia's early days, but many of the early missionaries died, broken-hearted over the failure of their efforts.

By age sixty, Bates had, to a great extent, become a missionary herself, although unique in her objectives. She opposed the civilisation of full-blood Aboriginal people, beyond 'buttoning the men into their first pair of trousers'. She was instead convinced that they were going to die out, and based on her experience, there was nothing anyone could do about it.

From her perspective, she was right. Traditional tribal life was being extinguished. However, the Aboriginal people weren't. Around her were many Aboriginal people making contact with white civilisation, adopting elements of it to greater or lesser degrees. An entire generation of part-Aboriginal people was growing up around her, but she steadfastly refused to recognise it. She refused to acknowledge or care for half-caste children, and boasted that none were born in any of her camps. For this, even her eventual friend and collaborator, Ernestine Hill, criticised her. Her accusation that full-blood Aborigines neglected their half-caste children also doesn't stand up to scrutiny. In this writer's experience (in particular while collaborating with Borroloola-born John Moriarty in writing his autobiography, *Saltwater Fella*) the opposite was the case.

Meanwhile, much of Bates's research was becoming a matter of documenting burial rites. In *The Passing of the Aborigines*, she described the scene when a twenty-five-year-old man, Jaijala, was 'pointed' with a magic stone:

> His little group of relatives had sat in darkness, wailing loudly and continually: but when they heard the brother's sudden cry, all ran to his breakwind, and a great keen went up from every member of the group for their newly dead. The men threw themselves flat on the ground, the women flinging themselves on top. Out of the struggling mass of mourners a man or woman would rise, only to fall back again on the living heap or on the bare ground in wild abandon. Men rising would clasp one another, and embrace, crying and screaming. 'Juniyuril' (bowels moving) is their sole expression of sorrow. Women would rise and lay their foot upon the head, back or shoulder of a father or brother of the dead youth, or would clasp one another and press their stomachs together to feel each other's sorrow. All the relations were naked. The deep voices of them mingled with the clear, long-sustained note of the women, and wailing and movement, movement and wailing, went on until the violence of the first grief was spent.

In all, Bates spent sixteen years at Ooldea, studying the remnants of Aboriginal tribal life, asserting her own moral code, smoothing the dying pillow as best she could. Yet she was growing old herself.

In 1933 she was invited to Canberra to advise the Commonwealth on Aboriginal Affairs. The following year, approaching seventy, she received the Order of Commander of the British Empire. Meanwhile, the flow of articles had reduced to a trickle, in part due to the effort of writing them, but as much because the market for her stories was declining (and many newspapers were finding her increasingly difficult to deal with).

In 1935, Bates suffered a series of setbacks that saw her leave Ooldea. She had been struggling with brush fires and recurring bouts of blindness. She wrote of these difficulties to her friend, Ernestine Hill, who then approached the managing director of the *Adelaide Advertiser*, Sir Lloyd Dumas, about the possibility of a series of articles, essentially telling Bates's life story, which would help Bates over the current crisis. Despite his editor's misgivings, Dumas made Bates a generous offer of £500 for the articles, plus transport to Adelaide and work facilities.

Bates refused the offer. She wrote that she had been in communication with the Commonwealth Government and believed she was about to be offered a position effectively as High Commissioner representing all the Aboriginal people of Australia, empowered to determine what was best for them in matters administrative and judicial. She anticipated a meeting with Prime Minister Joseph Lyons during a forthcoming trip on the Transcontinental Railway that would bring him through Ooldea. This meeting would enable them to seal their 'gentleman's agreement' and lead to Bates's initial appointment as Protector-in-General. It would be a huge accolade for the woman who had given thirty years of her life to the study of the Aboriginal people, but an enormous undertaking for the then seventy-year-old.

The meeting never took place. In a letter to Hill, she explained that Lyons' train had stopped at the siding, but his staff declared Lyons asleep and refused to wake him. Bates had stood beside the train in her finest clothing, beneath an umbrella that Hill maintains had once been handled by English royalty, and been utterly humiliated.

Soon after, Bates left Ooldea – her Aborigines consigned to the care of the police at Cook and Tarcoola – and moved to Adelaide. There she asked Hill to book her into the South Australian Hotel and rent offices in the Commonwealth Bank. After roughing it for so long, she demanded 'only the best'. 'My Natives and I', largely written by Hill, was serialised in the *Advertiser* from 4 January 1936, and was subsequently syndicated in the Melbourne *Herald*, Sydney *Sun*, Brisbane *Courier Mail* and *West Australian*. It reignited Bates's fame, but also fuelled strident criticism from the growing number of anthropologists around the country. Looking back on the publication, Hill disowned much of Bates's generalisations about cannibalism and her prejudice towards half-caste Aborigines. She also criticised Bates's sweeping statements. Yet the public lapped it up.

To Hill's dismay, the income from the series, which should have set Bates up for several years, was spent shortly after the articles appeared. Bates maintained that she had sent much-needed supplies to her Aborigines, but her high-living and the gifts she lavished on her assistants at the *Advertiser* accounted for a great deal. Again with Hill's support, Bates now embarked on the work that defined the later years of her life: *The Passing of the Aborigines*.

Published in 1938, it was sensational in places, searingly poignant in others, and secured an international reputation for its author. It is believed to have prompted actress Katharine Hepburn to commission research for a script that would enable her to play the role of Bates.

The author, meanwhile, returned to Ooldea. There, she found that her prophesy about the passing of the Aborigines had largely come true. None of the Aboriginal people she knew could be found. Those who were there were strangers, and they resented the intrusion of an old woman intent on imposing her values on them.

The last years of Bates's life mirrored those of the broken-hearted missionaries that had gone before her. In 1941, aged seventy-seven, she eventually settled at Wynbring Siding, east of Ooldea. By then World War II had begun, and belief in the 'dying pillow' had been replaced with the policy of assimilation. Half-caste children were forcibly removed from their mothers to be raised 'white' by religious societies and state and Commonwealth governments. The consequences were every bit as harrowing as the removal of Aborigines to Dorré and Bernier islands years before. Had Bates fully understood (as she had done at Dorré and Bernier) the powerful ties that bound Aboriginal people, including part-Aboriginal people, she may have been able to mount an articulate opposition to the policy that led to what is now known as the Stolen Generation.

Instead, she remained at Wynbring Siding until 1945, when, aged eighty-one, police became concerned about her welfare and removed her to Adelaide. She survived on a government allowance and the generosity of admirers until she died in an Adelaide nursing home on 18 April 1951, aged eighty-seven. Hill described her burial rite as 'virtually' a state funeral. That honour was not forthcoming, but the funeral was attended by politicians, academics, missionaries and a large public. Hill mentions that a grandson was also there.

After her death a memorial to Daisy Bates was erected at Ooldea Siding. Viewing the memorial isn't easy, though, as the diesel locomotives of the Transcontinental Railway no longer stop there. Bates's legacy is just as problematic. Much of her work has been discredited, but a good deal of it has also been recognised as an invaluable record of cultural information that would have been lost forever. Separating the fact from the fiction is part of the enigma that Bates has become. Yet her legacy has endured in ways she could never have imagined. For example, her research into the last of the Western Australian groups is routinely referred to in support of a number of Native Title claims. Bates's documentation of the Aborigines she was sure were passing from the earth forever has instead become one of the elements in ensuring they have a lasting future.

(Images of Daisy Bates with the Aboriginal people at Ooldea have not been reproduced in this volume out of respect for Aboriginal sensitivities. Some can be viewed at www.pictureaustralia.org)

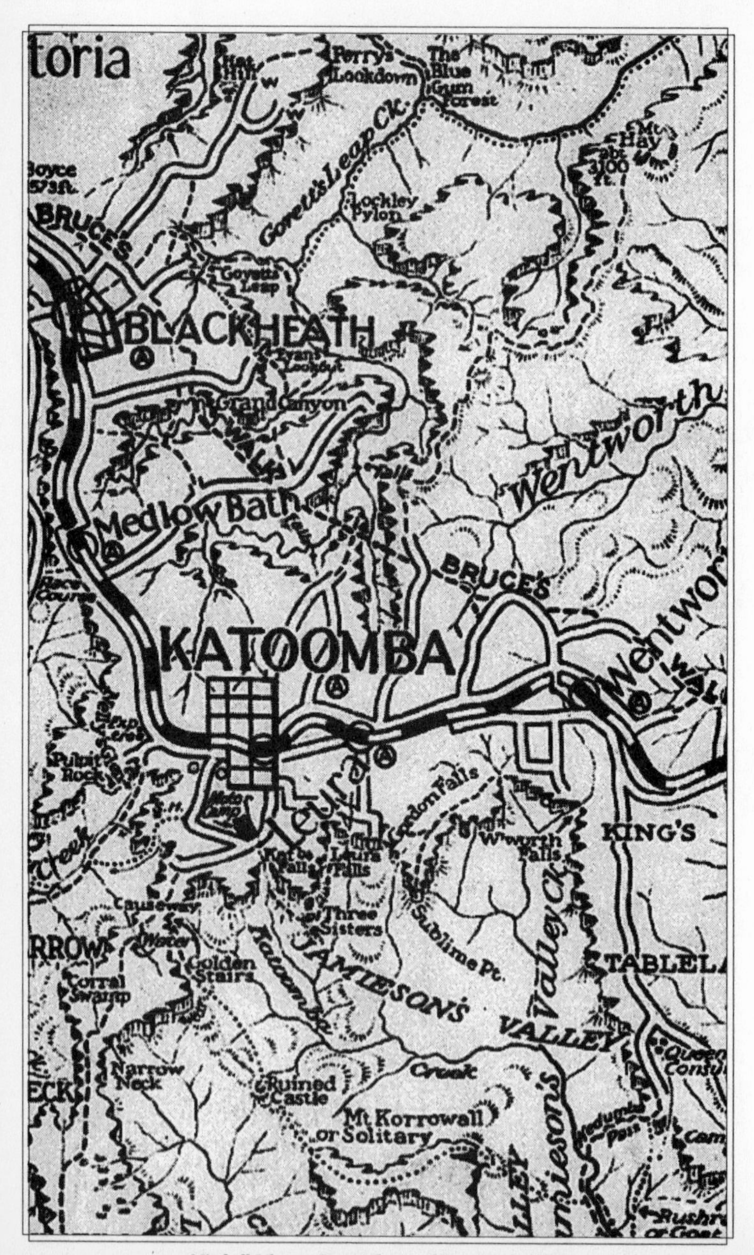

Mitchell Library, State Library of New South Wales

Myles Dunphy, circa 1930
(Colong Foundation Archive)

10

THE BLUE GUM FOREST, 1931: Myles Dunphy (1891–1985)

There's really only one qualification necessary for becoming a bushie. You need bush. Land that's been tamed or provided with creature comforts ceases to be the domain of a true bushie. Progress, it's called, and often it is a good thing, but sometimes what is gained is worth far less than what was lost. Often it takes wisdom to know the difference. And even then, wisdom sometimes isn't enough. Sooner or later someone has to act.

Millions of hectares of some of the most spectacular bushland in

Australia survives today in part because a young boy named Myles Dunphy paid attention in class at Kiama Public School. Early last century, the newly appointed Director-General of Public Education in New South Wales, Peter Board, introduced natural science to the state's school curriculum. As explained by Professor Dexter Dunphy, Myles's son, at a graduation ceremony address in 2001, his father 'was captivated by the new subject that encouraged him and his friends to seek out fossils, identify plants and insects' (extract reproduced by kind permission of Dexter Dunphy). From such simple initiatives, Dexter Dunphy pointed out, great things can come.

The young Dunphy, born in Melbourne on 19 October 1891, retained his interest in the natural world after leaving school. With his friends in his new home of Sydney he organised the Orizaba Tourist Club, named after the highest peak in Mexico (5610 metres). They played cricket and went on hikes, and though the club had folded by 1911, Dunphy and a couple of former members (Bert Larter and Frank McKeown) were still keen on the outdoors. That year they went to visit the scenic beauty spots around Katoomba, in the Blue Mountains, a two-hour train journey west of Sydney.

In the first of many journals he wrote throughout his life (now held in the Mitchell Library and by the Colong Foundation in Sydney), the twenty-year-old Dunphy wrote of what happened when they arrived at Echo Point, just in time to catch the sunset:

> On each side I saw the mighty walls and huge battlements of the Jamieson [sic] Valley . . . I had never seen such a scene before. Consequently the scene left a vivid impression on my mind . . . And the sky – I am immensely interested in natural phenomena, and have seen some very beautiful cloud effects, but I do not think, nay, I am certain, I have never seen one to excel the sunset I saw this night . . . It is hard to grasp the

> stupendous immensity connected with all things relating to the scenic part of the Mountains.
>
> – All quotations from Myles Dunphy's writings reproduced by kind permission of the Dunphy Estate

It is a spectacle that generations before and since have beheld, coming from all over the world to gaze in wonder. Most, however, are content to take a photo and clamber back onto their tour coaches, bound for the next scenic viewpoint. Not Dunphy. The next day he and his mates plunged into the wilderness, and so began a passion that was to last a lifetime: exploring the labyrinth of gorges and mountain ranges, with their thousand-metre cliffs of ancient sandstone.

Within three years he had discovered enough like-minded individuals to found a new club, and in 1914, the Mountain Trails Club (MTC) was formed. It was no ordinary recreational walking club. Membership was by invitation only and was limited exclusively to men who were prepared to probe deep into the Blue Mountains and explore their still vast wilderness areas. Over the next decade, World War I notwithstanding, the club prospered, its members devoting most of the holidays they got from their jobs in the nearby metropolis of Sydney (where Dunphy trained as an architect, qualifying in 1923) to discover the many natural wonders literally on the city's doorstep.

What they also found was how fragile the bush could be. Delicate ecosystems were suffering from pollution from the streams that passed through developed regions. Areas of great beauty were being scarred by forestry and land clearing. The only national park, with which the MTC was very familiar, was the Royal, south of the city. Meanwhile, it seemed incredible that there was no protection for the very things that drew tourists in droves to the small mountain towns dotting the east–west route first officially 'discovered' in 1813 (probably by following an ancient Aboriginal track) through the labyrinth of cliffs and canyons.

As early as 1922, Dunphy was starting to sketch out the area of the Blue Mountains he thought should be declared a national park. His scheme seemed vast at the time, almost 100 kilometres long, covering areas both to the north and south of the mountain towns. He also had a plan for turning Jack Riley's old stamping ground around Tom Groggin (see Chapter 5) into a national park – its area spanning the Snowy–Indi (the local name for the upper Murray) area and the New South Wales–Victoria border. But though Dunphy didn't lack vision when it came to grand plans for large areas of bush, much of which he'd trekked through ('trailed' being the term then used), he was a babe in the woods when it came to the bureaucratic manoeuvring needed to turn his dreams into reality.

He got a painful lesson in its workings in the mid 1920s. As he wrote in the *National Parks Journal* in December 1976, the Couridjah Corridor, in the south-eastern Blue Mountains, was an ideal introduction to the bush 'considering its length, canyon beauty, camping facilities, aloofness, wildlife content, wildflower garden, and the fact that walkers could step out of the train and into the bush at Picton Lakes and Buxton'.

Dunphy made a submission to the Forestry Commission extolling these and many other virtues that he thought underlined the value of turning the area into a public reserve. The Commission looked seriously at Dunphy's proposal, especially the details of the flora gleaned from his extensive exploration of the area. After a site inspection, the Commission could only agree that it was one of the finest forests they'd ever seen. And yes, it was right by the rail line – all of which made it ideal for logging. The Forestry Commission set up a sawmill and ripped the heart out of the Couridjah Corridor over the next ten years. It was a bitter lesson that Dunphy never forgot.

Meanwhile, the great outdoors was luring more and more people. In 1922 the Bush Tracks Club, Sydney Technical College Camping Club and the Bushlanders Club were formed, the latter admitting both men and women. Then, on 2 August 1927, a walker named Jack Debert wrote to the *Sun* newspaper: 'I would like to see in Sydney, a hikers' club, where hikers could meet and discuss routes, places of interest and so fill a long-felt want for those who go on walking trips.' Two days later a Miss Jess Scott responded to the newspaper: 'With some friends I periodically go out on walking tours and find it a very healthful and interesting pastime . . . It is one which, were it easier to get information re routes and conveniences for camping, would be unsurpassed.'

In fact, women were increasingly demonstrating that they were just as capable as men when it came to hiking and appreciating the bush. As Peter Meredith wrote in his biography of Dunphy and his son Milo:

> Women would sometimes go into the bush in single-sex groups . . . One such 'girl' was Marie Byles, who was among Australia's first female solicitors and who, even as a youngster, had covered more than 30 kilometres a day through rough country. A diminutive dynamo of 1.57 metres and 44 kilograms, Marie had travelled around the world on a cargo steamer, mountaineering en route, and would later become a committed conservationist. In the mid 1920s she organised all-women walking parties whose members carried revolvers to discourage importunate human males and other disagreeable life forms. Dot Butler (née English), another contemporary walker, recalled that one of Marie's companions used to carry a huge Colt stuck conspicuously in her belt.
>
> – Meredith extracts reproduced by kind permission of Peter Meredith

So even if you thought women were too soft for adventure, you'd be wise not to say so within earshot. Despite this, the conservative Mountain Trails Club stuck to its exclusively male guns. Inviting interested parties to the MTC's next meeting, Dunphy wrote in *the Sun*, the day after Jess Scott's letter: 'The club [the MTC] is an amateur exploring one, its members preferring rough country right away from settlement, and for that reason membership is by invitation only and ladies are not eligible for membership, although on some easier trips they have been included in parties carrying their own packs.'

Seven men accepted the invitation and a relatively easy walk was organised for later in the month. Then, in November, changes to the MTC's constitution were mooted. Some members wanted to make it easier to join. However, rather than water down the club's lofty and rugged ideals, it was decided to start a new club, under the auspices of the old. In the minutes of the MTC, Dunphy noted:

> All members present agreed that the MTC could not do less than render a public service by forming a new walking club; free and easy, open to all who cared to walk in the open. The club would have a liberal constitution and easy conditions of membership with definite objects of being a recreational walker's club, purely and simply, and be open to members of both sexes.

It was initially called the Waratah Walking Club, and a letter to the *Sun* on 5 November announced its formation and the date for its next meeting: 11 November 1927. At that meeting, the name was changed. According to Dunphy: 'It was at the next meeting that Charles Kilpatrick was elected honorary secretary and treasurer and that the name Sydney Bush Walkers was adopted.'

This is the first use of the term that quickly became 'bushwalker', which Peter Meredith notes was coined by club members Maurice Berry and Bert Gallop ('trailer' being the common term before then). It soon caught on (it's now part of the Australian language). Indeed, it proved so popular that later in 1927 the club decided to define the term, to differentiate it from recreational outdoor walking that could include, say, a stroll along a beach or down a suburban street. Dunphy explains:

> The club defined a 'bushwalker' as a walker, man or woman, who seeks social recreation and education in roadless wilderness or primitive areas or rugged country, and carries his or her own personal gear, food rations, and share of camp gear; who uses a tent for accommodation in order to stay in the bushland environment for as long as possible, and who practises bushcraft. A bushwalker is an exploring, camping walker who never ceases to learn something of the outdoors environment.

Most of the individuals in this book, from William Buckley onwards, would have qualified easily.

It may seem odd to point out, but the definition didn't include any mention of baby carriages. However, just a few years later, Dunphy and his young wife, Margaret, set about redefining outdoor activity to include the very young, to wit their toddler son, Milo Kanangra Dunphy. Milo was born on 13 May 1929, his curious middle name being that of one of the Blue Mountains that Dunphy had come to love so much (his first name was also the name of a mountain, named by Dunphy). Little wonder then, that just twenty months after the boy was born, Dunphy decided it was time the two should meet. And since the mountain wouldn't come to Milo . . .

Dunphy's writing style was normally quite formal, due to a working life filled with reports and submissions, but he allowed his bush wit full rein in 1962 in *The Sydney Bushwalker* when he described the 1931 trip. Of course, he could laugh about it later, but it was a different story at the time. First, Dunphy decided that little Milo would need to be carried in a pram:

> Satan, for my sins, guided me to a second-hand dump at Rockdale, and introduced me to the only pram for the job ever pupped and the nice

> mild-mannered man who had charge of it put it through its paces. That pram could do everything but eat and propel itself. It had nice red tassels around it, but I found a pair of scissors and gave it a jazz-cut later. I suspect that mild-mannered man saw me coming. He thought me a goat and pitied my child, and wished he could see the works when the child's mother's eyes lit on that antiquated Pharaoh's chariot.

First, though, Dunphy had to get it home:

> I bought the springless, squat, long-handled, wide, boxlike betasselled, heavy iron-framed, 40-pound [18-kilogram] insult to the pram family . . . and pitched it into the train where a lot of people looked at it so earnestly that it folded itself up in a new way that neither the mild-mannered man nor myself knew about. Having paid good money for it I felt inclined to pity the resurrected atrocity, but after carrying it home on my shoulder in the form of a hamper (one of its Jekyll and Hyde phases) I gave it a private, unmentionable and blistering cognomen [nickname].

The 'mild-mannered man' who'd sold it to him wasn't wrong about the reception it got chez Dunphy:

> Margaret (that's the wife) laughed quite rudely. I did the works for her, and this time the contraption folded up into a baby's cradle on rockers. We straightened it out again and changed it to a pram. Young Milo (our twenty-months' old curiosity box), climbed on top while I held it firmly to prevent it biting or kicking or folding up some other way, then we went for a preliminary tour round the yard. Milo was delighted. I had not the heart to tell him he would probably have to walk.

Dunphy turned the thing into what could be the world's first off-road pram, complete with numerous storage compartments, which brought its fighting weight up to a solid 28 kilograms. 'Then blimey! There stood the Kanangra Limited (speed and springs) Express, nearly as wide as a sulky replete with awning, stays, billycan box, side-tucker and gear boxes, foot-rest for the passenger, rifle-carrier and new tyres.'

Another name could have been Albatross. They discovered what they'd burdened themselves with as they toiled up the bushwalk's first ascent, Margaret roped to it and hauling from the front, while Dunphy pushed from behind. Both parents were also carrying packs:

> No parents ever slaved for their offspring as we did for our little Question Box sitting comfortably behind his green mosquito-netting fly screen. Then came half a mile [1 kilometre] of sharp loose ballast that chewed chunks of rubber from the little half-inch [1-centimetre] tyres and rattled Milo's teeth. About the middle of the afternoon we had to stop and give Milo a rest from the constant shaking.
>
> Next day while we lunched we had Edith Hill in sight before us. It is a boomer for everything on wheels or feet, so we had to consider a plan of action. First I went a mile [1.6 kilometres] onward up the hill with all I could carry, including rifle, water and Marg's swag. Returning, Marg was put on to the tow-rope, the brat made comfortable, then I set my hobnails firmly into Australia and pushed and pushed. An old lady we got some milk from reckoned it was the hardest kind of holiday she ever heard of.
>
> At length, on the fourth day, allowing one day in camp on account of rain, the big prospect south lifted into sight, and there stood the perambulator at Kanangra. Young Milo Kanangra had reached the place he was named after. No doubt ours is the first perambulator to be shoved to Kanangra and back and I think it will be the last until a better road is made – and I hope that never happens anyway. Next time we walk!

The pram is now one of the treasures, if that's the right word, of the National Museum of Australia, Canberra.

As they stood on mighty Kanangra, Dunphy may have also pointed out or named other features with family associations – Dunphy's Lookout, Margaret Falls and Myles Chasm. For while Dunphy walked the wilderness, he also started mapping and naming it. In his early walking days he'd found the maps that were available to him woefully inadequate, so he made his own. And as many of the features he found were nameless, he and his bushwalking companions took the task upon themselves. Some names had associations with walkers or their families, others were classical allusions, while others respected Aboriginal descriptions.

However, naming the wilderness had another purpose. As Dunphy wrote, 'The distribution of sketch maps, with place names – where none existed before – and track and trail information, definitely was a long-range method for establishing a favourable atmosphere for future national parks and primitive areas.'

The maps were extraordinarily detailed, with little messages such as 'Waste no fuel, think of others'. Drawn with, as biographer Peter Meredith put it, an architect–bushwalker's eye for detail rather than a cartographer's eye for comprehension, the maps 'to later generations accustomed to more user-friendly products, could be off-putting. As maps for bushwalkers, however, they quickly become the ultimate tool for navigating the wild areas of New South Wales.'

Indeed, they have an intimacy of style that tells its user that its creator has been to the places shown. More than any other maps of the mountains, they convey a sense of place. They're almost Aboriginal in their pointillist two-dimensional representation of a multidimensional world. And best of all, the maps can take you on a journey just by looking at them.

As part of his continuing campaign to have the Blue Mountains declared a national park, in 1930 Dunphy convinced New South Wales Surveyor-General H.B. Matthews to publish a comprehensive Department of Lands map of the Greater Blue Mountains. Dunphy wanted a map for walkers; Matthews wanted one for tourists. Realising that any map was better than none, Dunphy agreed to consult on the project on a voluntary basis.

Then, as the base map neared completion (drawn by a cartographer, with Dunphy providing the detail), he came up with another suggestion. Why not two maps: a small one for the general public and a larger one for the walkers and scouts? He called it the 'Bushwalkers' Edition'.

Matthews was reluctant, but Dunphy offered to organise a collection among the various outdoors clubs to cover the expense. The bushwalker was learning. Good ideas were all very well, but money talked. Matthews agreed to Dunphy's suggestion, but he came up with his own name for the full-sized set: *Tourist Map. Special Walking Clubs' Issue.*

In 1931, while Dunphy was toiling over the Blue Mountains map, a group from the Sydney Bushwalkers and Mountain Trails Club, led by Sydney artist Alan Rigby, was making a frightening discovery in the heart of the area the map covered. Taking advantage of the Easter long weekend, they'd headed into the Grose Valley to camp at one of it most treasured places.

The Blue Gum Forest was a magnificent stand of trees at the junction of the Grose River and Govetts Creek. The junction is at the centre of a gigantic natural amphitheatre formed by a ring of massive cliffs and stone buttresses. At the time, at several points around the rim, scenic lookouts were regularly thronged by visitors, awed by the scene. Yet in the middle of it farmer Clarrie Hungerford had been granted a lease to the Blue Gum Forest. It was a condition of his lease that he improve his 16-hectare allotment within a year, so he and another man were starting to fell trees. Their plan for the block was to grow walnuts.

To the bushwalkers, this was an outrage. To the tourism industry in nearby Blackheath, it must have been a nightmare. As far as cost versus benefit was concerned, it was like bulldozing the Sydney Opera House to build a fish cannery.

'It was unbelievable; it was the last straw!' Dunphy would write later in *The Bushwalker*:

> Being intelligent people the members of the party were well aware of the continual onset of agricultural, industrial and commercial activities against the bushland environment of recreation, wildlife habitat and natural scenic beauty. They knew that a lot of it was reasonable and inevitable in a young country. But also they were aware that a lot of activity was one-sided, indiscriminate destruction of natural values that should be preserved for the good of the nation . . .
>
> Here indiscriminate destruction was imminent in a major scenic area: action must be taken to delay it or put a stop to it. This was a classic instance where the extent of the damage to be done was appalling.

The principles were sound, but from previous experience the bushwalkers knew that much more was needed. So, it appears, did the leaseholder. There are many different versions of what actually happened during that Easter weekend, but it appears that Hungerford was well aware of the heritage value of the forest he was starting to clear – to the dollar.

There are suggestions that he agreed to stop ringbarking trees based on a proposal made at the time that he would be paid compensation for the lease. It may be that he hadn't started, but had stated his intentions, which spurred the bushwalkers to subsequent action. However, as Dunphy wrote in Volume 19 of his journal: 'There were no flies on Hungerford. He had an alert business mind and immediately saw his chance to make money.'

At a meeting of the Mountain Trails Club on 17 April 1931, Alan Rigby reported on the events at the Blue Gum Forest. It was decided that the club 'try to initiate and sustain action to save the magnificent trees from the lessee's axe'. If necessary, they were prepared to buy Hungerford out. Thus the Mountain Trails Club (and through its association, the Sydney Bushwalkers) took the first step towards actively campaigning to conserve wilderness. It was a decision whose significance was partially recognised at the time. As Dunphy later wrote: 'It was agreed . . . that the case could well be used as a starting point for action to indicate an important principle "that the best scenery should be dedicated or reserved for public use and benefit".'

Dunphy started negotiations with the government, other clubs and the lessee on behalf of the MTC and on 20 June wrote formally to Hungerford: 'The lessees stated the price required to purchase his right and title to the conditional Purchase Lease, confirmed only the previous December, and agreed to stay the ringbarking for the sum of £150.'

It was the equivalent of about $10000 in modern terms – loose change for some, a fortune to others. In the depths of the Depression years, it was fearfully high for the bushwalkers, especially considering the lease had been granted to Hungerford for next to nothing. Nevertheless, the bushwalking clubs started trying to raise the money. A Blue Gum Committee was formed by the MTC and the Sydney Bushwalkers to organise fundraising. Alan Rigby was on this committee, as was Dunphy, who as secretary of the MTC continued to handle the correspondence with Hungerford.

Meanwhile, Hungerford kept up the pressure. As Dunphy explained:

> On 17th August, he wrote saying the price was not too high; to lose the place for £150 would be a big sacrifice. Could postpone part payment for a time. On 16th October the Committee asked what time limit he would allow. He answered 18th October [the following year], that the offer was still open, and no further ringbarking had been done. His terms were: £50 deposit by end of November, and balance spread over twelve months.

Dunphy was also talking to the Department of Lands. All would be to no avail if the bushwalking clubs got Hungerford to transfer the lease, only to have the Department refuse to ratify the deal. Fortunately, the Department saw wisdom. All the clubs had to do was find the money.

It was time to get down to brass tacks. Dunphy wrote to Hungerford on 10 November, proposing a meeting of interested parties on the site. He agreed and the showdown at the Blue Gum Forest was arranged for Sunday, 15 November 1931.

On that Sunday, as Dunphy put it, 'Some time was spent in looking about the sylvan paradise.' Among the party was *Sydney Morning Herald* journalist and keen hiker, J.C. Lockley, pen-name Redgum, who described the scene for readers a few days later (19 November):

> The area is situated at about the junction of the Grose River and Govetts Leap Creek, where the two volumes of rumbling, rushing waters come together, and where for years the backwash from the streams has deposited acres of silt and sand, and built up a homeland in which thousands of silvery-stemmed grey and blue gums stand like giant columns in an outdoor cathedral as if to hold up the roof of green leaves and sky.
>
> Nowhere else in the Valley of the Grose are the gum trees more beautiful, or more worth preserving. In many instances their polished, colourful trunks, stripped of every shred of brown or amber bark, rise

> 80 feet [24 metres] without a suggestion of a lateral limb, and then begin to mingle with the headpieces of the neighbours just as green and attractive as their own top growths, which have won their way through to see the sun and the stars.

Over the years there have been question marks over whether Hungerford actually intended to grow walnuts. Some accounts suggest he was going to raise cattle. However, Redgum, in the article published just four days after he'd been there, also noted:

> Ringbarking had been begun and the first of the trees had fallen before the blows of the axemen before the hiking party dropped unexpectedly on the area. Irreparable damage would have been done had not the present lessee been asked to stay his hand to give the men who are seeking to save the trees a chance to buy back the 40-acre [16-hectare] section he had intended clearing for planting with walnuts. Several young nut trees are already making good stems and foliage *on the holding*. [my italics]

Others who were also at the meeting dispute this point, but assuming journalists can sometimes get it right, the walnut farming had already begun.

The meeting started around midday, in pouring rain, with about a dozen representatives of various walking and conservation groups wrapped in capes, sitting in a circle among the trees. The mood wasn't helped by Hungerford, as Dunphy noted: 'The weather was unkind, but the great trees standing up all around appeared magnificent — except one fine specimen which lay stretched out close to the river bank, a victim of the lessee's salesmanship. No doubt it was felled to give point to the necessity for saving the trees.'

It was a spur the bushwalkers couldn't ignore. They had great difficulties with the price, but only managed to beat Hungerford down to £130. However, he demanded £25 up-front, and the balance, £105, by 31 December, just six weeks away. The deal was done.

Now the clock was really ticking. Fortunately, the deposit was made easy by a donation from another interested group, The Wild Life Preservation Society, which immediately put forward the amount. The Sydney Bushwalkers donated £10, the Mountain Trails Club £8. So they were still looking for £87. No effort was spared in getting it. As Dunphy wrote:

> The Committee launched a campaign of advertisement and solicited further contributions from club members and friends. Committeemen Rigby, Turner and Bennett compiled an interesting pamphlet, of which 2000 were distributed . . . However, the Committee found the going very hard; the time, towards the end of the Depression [sic], was bad for this sort of thing: there was no money to spare.

Balls, socials, booklets of walking tours – they all raised some of the money, and given enough time they would eventually raise all of it, but there are only so many dances you can attend in six weeks before your legs get tired, even if they're used to climbing rugged mountain ranges. There are only so many lamingtons you can buy. As the deadline neared, it became obvious that the bushwalkers would have to borrow the bulk of the money. In the Depression, though, what bank would lend them the necessary funds? The answer was: none of them. As Dunphy put it:

> [A] real friend of the walking and conservation movement was required, now to assist in a practical way. The committee viewed the perspectives; one gentleman in particular was known to be a walking enthusiast, idealist and conservator. His senior business executive position indicated it was possible his financial stability would be able to stand the strain of a loan for a very good cause. Committeemen visited

> Mr. W.J. Cleary [the retired Chief Commissioner for Railways] and explained the position. Without any ado he made the Committee a loan of £80 for a term of two years, free of interest, but on condition that anonymity be maintained.

The Blue Gum Forest was saved.

The battle may have been won, but there was no rest for the bush-walkers. Dunphy, in particular, realised that large areas of significant national heritage were also under threat. Indeed, when Alan Rigby had first reported on the felling of the forest, back in April 1931, his news had overshadowed a proposal by Dunphy at the same meeting for a Snowy–Indi National Park. Now the priority was clearly the Blue Mountains, right on Sydney's doorstep, especially as a great deal of attention had been focused on it as a result of the Blue Gum campaign.

Indeed, much had changed since Easter 1931. Dunphy and his friends had waged a successful campaign, having learned from their mistakes in the past. They had built a network of contacts they could either recruit to help them or lobby for support. When it came to the future Blue Mountains National Park, they had the first building block in place. They even had a map, courtesy of the Lands Department and Dunphy's seemingly innocent suggestion to its Surveyor-General. It was published in 1932, just as the bushwalking clubs were forming the Blue Mountains National Park Committee, soon to become the National Parks and Primitive Areas Council (NPPAC). Dunphy wrote of the Council in the National Parks and Wildlife Service publication *Australia's 100 Years of National Parks*:

> Just to be reminded, the certificate of membership [of the Mountain Trails Club] stated: 'You were not the first over the trail; leave the

> pleasant places along the way just as pleasant for those who will follow you.'
>
> The men of the National Parks and Primitive Areas Council were that type. All thought of other people, maybe 100 or 200 years hence. When cities and towns were more numerous bushland wilderness would become more valuable.

In support of their campaign in the Blue Mountains, the bushwalkers took out a four-page supplement in the now defunct *Katoomba Daily* on 24 August 1934. Much of this supplement was written by Myles Dunphy himself. As Peter Meredith later put it: 'In the more than sixty years since the supplement appeared, nothing quite like it has been seen in Australia. It was a fitting curtain-raiser to the Age of Conservation.'

Even so, it wasn't until 1959 that the Blue Mountains National Park was formally declared. The Blue Gum Forest was absorbed into it in 1961, with additional sections such as the Kanangra-Boyd and Wollemi National Parks being added over subsequent decades. In May 2001 the Greater Blue Mountains World Heritage Area was formally dedicated.

By the time he died, on 30 January 1985, Dunphy was considered by many to be the father of conservation in New South Wales. There were, of course, many others involved in campaigns before and since, who were just as crucial. And his son Milo was every bit as active. Yet many national parks in New South Wales owe their genesis to campaigns in which Dunphy was involved. And many other national parks in other states owe their existence and wildlife conservation organisations to the model developed in New South Wales by Dunphy and his colleagues.

As his obituary in the *Sydney Morning Herald* put it on 2 February 1985, 'In his lifetime, Mr Dunphy saw his dream of a system of national parks throughout the State come true.' In doing so, he preserved the environment that makes it possible for people to develop their bush skills and an appreciation for the bush for generations to come. City people can still become bushies. For example, all it takes is a two-hour train trip west of Sydney to walk in the footsteps of Myles Dunphy.

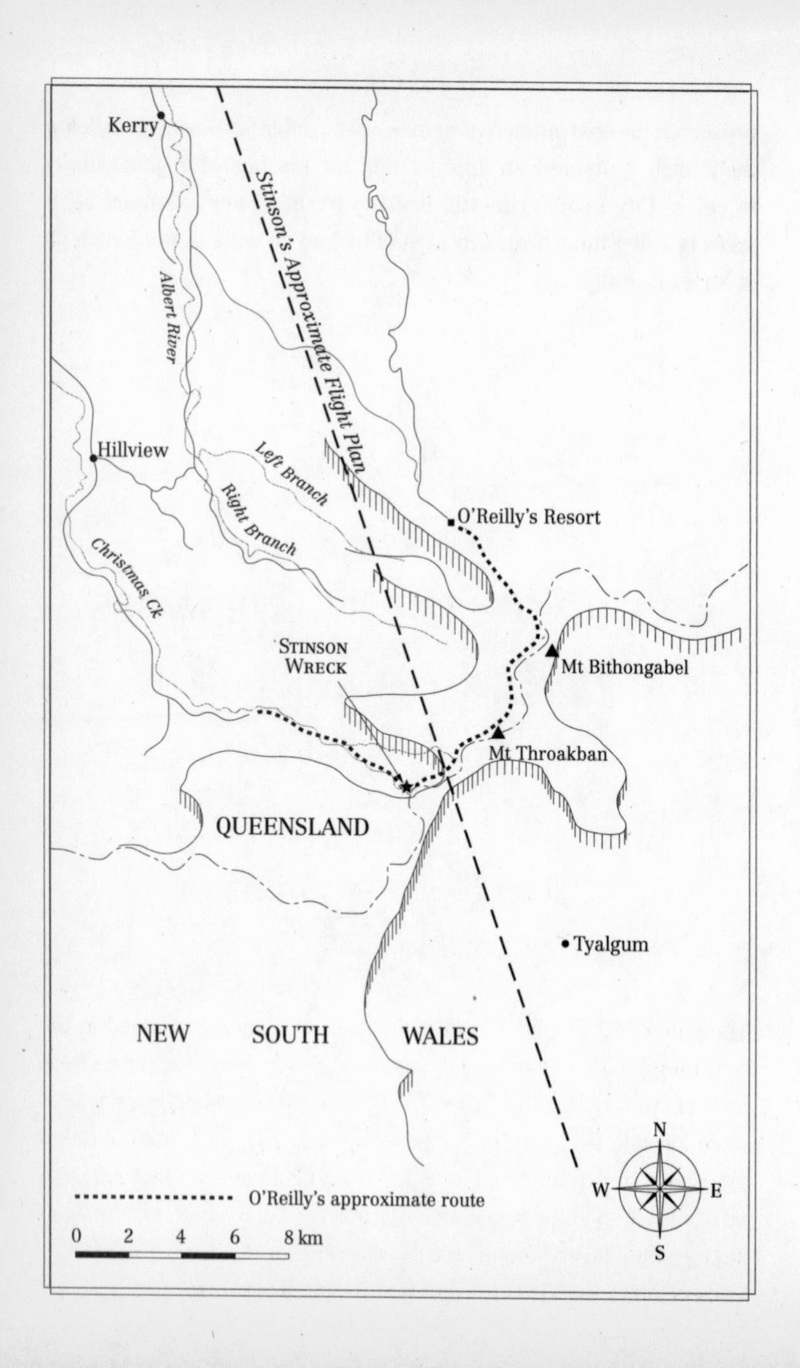
Kerry
Stinson's Approximate Flight Plan
Albert River
Hillview
Left Branch
Right Branch
Christmas Ck
O'Reilly's Resort
Mt Bithongabel
Stinson Wreck
Mt Throakban
QUEENSLAND
Tyalgum
NEW SOUTH WALES
N
W
E
S
O'Reilly's approximate route
0 2 4 6 8 km

Bernard O'Reilly, 1937
(Photo courtesy the O'Reilly family)

11

A VOICE IN THE WILDERNESS, 1937: Bernard O'Reilly (1903–1975)

The wife of Sydney wool broker Joe Binstead always worried at the very thought of her husband flying in an aeroplane whenever he went on his numerous business trips. Yet Binstead was one of the many who were already reaping the benefits of a fledgling Australian aviation industry that was rapidly taming the vast distances of the Australian bush, and in so doing transforming it forever. So, to keep Mrs Binstead happy, when he arrived to board the Airlines of Australia's eight-seat Stinson 'airliner', VH-UHH, on Friday, 19 February 1937, he gave his name as Barnett, thinking that what his wife didn't know wouldn't hurt her.

At 1.05 p.m. the plane carrying five passengers and two crew taxied to the end of the runway of Archerfield, on the then southern fringe of Brisbane. The hum of the aircraft's twin-engines rose to a roar as the aircraft picked up speed. The take-off was smooth, and the plane climbed into skies that were cloudy, although there was no rain. The aircraft was bound for Sydney, via the northern New South Wales town of Lismore, the aircraft in the capable hands of pilot Rex Boyden and co-pilot Beverley Shepherd.

Boyden had considerable experience as a pilot. A World War I veteran, in 1915 he'd been badly wounded while serving with the 18th Battalion Infantry at Gallipoli, discharged as unfit for service and returned to Australia. However, he was so determined to get back into the fight that he got himself to England where he joined the Air Force, was drafted into the Royal Naval Air Service and saw action in the North Sea and France. After the war he'd spent time as a bush pilot in New Guinea, on one occasion successfully bringing a stricken aircraft down in the jungle by 'pancaking' the plane on top of the trees. When it then fell to the ground, he got out unscathed.

Now, as his Stinson aircraft headed south, less than 100 kilometres ahead of it lay the northern flanks of the Mount Warning Caldera, a gigantic extinct volcano, the 1000-metre-high rim of which today measures some 30 kilometres across. There, a bushie who had no confidence in or experience with airplanes was tending his dairy cattle. As the *Courier Mail* was to report on 4 March, Bernard O'Reilly had once commented to a visitor when the Sydney mail plane passed over:

> 'I've never wanted to travel in an aeroplane. I'd rather have a horse.'
>
> 'Oh you can't beat flying,' his city-bred visitor replied. 'I've flown thousands of miles. I feel safer in a plane than on a horse.'

'I've seen lots of people on horses who would be safer in aeroplanes,' O'Reilly said with a smile.

On 19 February, though, O'Reilly didn't have time to think about aircraft. As he later wrote in his book *Green Mountains*:

> Before dawn on Friday, I awoke to find my little house shivering from the hammer blows of a raging cyclone, and at dawn I went out to find the air full of flying leaves, and with every gust a crash from the jungle told of the destruction being wrought . . . The cows were huddled in sheltered windbreaks, and nothing on earth would induce them to leave . . . A conservative estimate of the wind velocity over the McPhersons [the giant volcano's northern range] all that day would be 80 miles [130 kilometres] per hour. After one o'clock I went up to our tiny dairy cottage, and while it rocked in the wind like a ship at sea, I cooked my lunch, every gust blowing the smoke back down the chimney . . .
>
> – All O'Reilly extracts reproduced by kind permission of Bernard O'Reilly's Estate

About twenty minutes later, the Stinson was approaching the McPherson Range, and the weather was turning bad. When the plane flew into a squall, the wind became severe. At 1.30 p.m. the aircraft was jolted several times before plunging downwards in an air pocket.

The turbulence was so violent that passenger Binstead looked at the pilots to see how they were reacting. Reassuringly, Shepherd was talking, even laughing, to Boyden who was at the controls. Then he noticed the passenger in front of him, Jim Westray, wasn't enjoying his flight at all. Looking back to the pilots, Binstead realised Shepherd's expression had changed. He was making some kind of adjustment to the controls, after which the plane started to bank. It was trying to climb.

Tense minutes followed as the aircraft circled. Binstead could clearly see the trees below. Then, looking out of his window, another passenger, John Proud, saw tree-clad slopes only 15 metres from the starboard wing. The plane was banking sharply towards them. Then, as Binstead was to recall:

> The Stinson broke over the top of one tree, and crashed against a second tree about 18 inches [46 centimetres] thick. The machine struck the tree about 30 feet [9 metres] from the ground, and crashed through somehow to the ground. One wing was torn off and fell about a chain [20 metres] away from the main body of the plane. One propeller was smashed off, and, in falling through the branches, the rudder was carried away. A branch of the tree came through the metal side and struck [passenger] Roland Graham, killing him instantly. It hit me across the knee, and I believe that had it not struck Graham first it would have killed me.

Binstead was knocked out when his head struck the plane's bulkhead. John Proud later wrote in a diary: 'Got to the ground somehow or other and burst into flames. Cabin filled with black smoke.' He started trying to escape. Moments later, Binstead recovered consciousness:

> As I picked myself up I saw Proud, who had been sitting two seats away from me, smash a port window, and attempt to scramble through. He had his head and shoulders out, when I started to push him through from behind. 'Oh my leg,' he cried out. 'I think it must be broken.' Somehow I pushed him out, and then he seized me by the hand and started to drag me through. By this time the plane had burst into flames. Proud told me afterwards that the fire started two seconds after the crash. It could not have been very much more than that.
>
> Luckily I had taken my coat off – the first time I think I have ever done this when travelling in an aeroplane. Even without it getting through was a tight squeeze and nearly all my clothes were ripped off me before I was safely through the narrow window.

> The two of us saw Westray in the cabin. We called him, and between us got him through the window. The plane was then enveloped in flames, and before he got clear Westray was badly burnt on the back and on the right hand. We crawled to a safe distance from the fearful heat as the plane was reduced to a heap of twisted and charred wreckage.

Inside the aircraft the two pilots and two of the passengers, Roland Graham and William Fountain, if they weren't already dead, were trapped and burned to death before they could get free. The plane burnt for half an hour, setting alight several trees around it that continued to burn for some hours afterwards. Having seen farms not long before the crash, the survivors felt sure that help couldn't be far away, and someone would appear at the crash site before long.

When the plane did not land at Lismore, its first stop, it was assumed that the weather had prevented a landing and the plane had continued to Sydney, possibly taking the coast route. Even after the plane was overdue in Sydney, there was no great alarm. If it had struck trouble, Boyden had the experience to deal with it. Yet as time went on, and inquiries turned up no sign of the plane, fears for its safety mounted. Finally, the Stinson was listed as missing.

As word spread, reports of sightings started coming in all along the route the plane was supposed to have taken, all of them consistent with the journey the plane should have made. A resident of Coffs Harbour said he saw the Stinson circling over Boambee, a few miles down the coast from Coffs Harbour, about 3 p.m. It was raining heavily at the time, but the red and blue plane could be plainly seen through the clouds. It then headed away southward. Other people reportedly heard it over Coffs Harbour and Nambucca Heads at around the same time.

It was then heard over the Macleay River, 100 kilometres further south. Mrs Donald Anderson of Gladstone, near Kempsey, reported at 11 p.m. on the 19th that she'd heard the machine at 3.30 p.m. over nearby Crescent Head. Mrs Mulholland, postmistress at James Island, 8 kilometres from Manning Heads, near Taree, 100 kilometres south of Kempsey, said that she heard a plane at 4 p.m., the time when the Stinson usually passed over. It was seen by three persons in three different locations passing between Taree and Wingham, centres about 15 kilometres apart, a few minutes after 4 p.m. Mr A. Setree, postmaster at Davistown, 50 kilometres north of Sydney, said the plane passed over at 5 p.m. Three residents of nearby Patonga, on the Hawkesbury River, also said the plane passed over at 5 p.m., heading for Cowan (towards Sydney).

People in Bernard O'Reilly's district had seen the plane, too. As he told the *Courier Mail* of 1 March:

> Residents of Lamington and Hillview, on the main air route between Sydney and Brisbane, heard the mail plane about 2 p.m. on Friday, 19 February, flying low and circling over Mr Gordon Stephen's home at Darlington at the foot of the range. The plane seemed in heavy weather and thick rain. When it headed towards the range observers thought it did not have sufficient height to clear the range.

As a search was started, due to the number of sightings along the route, it naturally focused on the rugged bushland area just north of Sydney. Meanwhile, as the fires burned down at the crash site, darkness enveloped Jim Westray, an athletic Englishman who had not long before moved to Australia; John Proud, a young mining engineer; and the wool broker, Joe Binstead. As Binstead described it, 'Proud, although in great pain from his injured leg, was cool, but Westray was unnerved by the crash.'

None of them knew that they were lost deep in some of the wildest country in Australia, the almost impenetrable jungle and impassable mountains and gorges of the New South Wales–Queensland Border Ranges. At night, for those who aren't used to it, the rainforest can be a terrifying place. However, the darkness and thick vegetation did have one plus. It hid from the survivors just how desperate their situation really was.

Not far away, as the crow flies, were people who weren't daunted by the rainforest. Yet as Bernard O'Reilly, his wife Viola and tiny daughter Rhelma battened down in the storm-tossed night, they were oblivious to the disaster that had taken place some 10 kilometres and several ranges away.

O'Reillys had been on their properties at Green Mountains since before World War I. Before that, they'd battled to make their farms pay in the equally rugged Blue Mountains west of Sydney. Bernard O'Reilly had been born there in 1903, in a slab house on Long Swamp Creek, far from any hospital or doctor. He gave credit to his mother's courage in his book, *Green Mountains*: 'Let me here pay tribute to the wonderful pluck and spirit of the women of Australia's bushland, who, as in the case of my own birth, far away from any medical or nursing assistance, went through such critical periods with no help but a neighbour's, giving a like service in return.'

O'Reilly had an idyllic childhood, despite being dirt-poor. When World War I brought rationing it made little difference to a family that was used to having so little:

> We had always been very poor so to us added hardship meant little or nothing; who would bother with butter when they could have Mother's bread spread thickly with dripping and sprinkled with pepper and salt or perhaps spread thickly with moist sugar. Show me the bare-footed

> bush lad who isn't sorry for the poor boy who has to wear boots! We did not know we were poor. The most precious thing of all to a child is freedom, and in that we were millionaires; all that was best in Australia was ours, the bush land and our imagination made us kings of the world.

Despite having so little, his father instilled the value of literature in his children. O'Reilly recalled two dog-eared books, by the poets Byron and Thomas Moore, which his father had treasured. Whenever O'Reilly Senior left the property to work as a stockman, the poets travelled across the outback in his packsaddle.

Part of the reason for the family's straitened circumstances was the losing battle they were fighting with rabbits. As rabbit numbers increased, the farm's viability diminished to the point where the family was eventually forced to leave. In 1910, they sold up. While most of the family temporarily settled in the Megalong Valley, west of Katoomba, five of O'Reilly's older brothers and three of his cousins moved to the Queensland border to carve their selections out of the virgin country of Green Mountains. They little knew what they were getting themselves into, wrote O'Reilly:

> The blocks were sprawled across the rugged top of a high volcanic plateau, the soil was bright red, deep and rich enough to support a lavish rainforest; giant trees stood together thicker than the pillars in a cathedral with an undergrowth of tangled vine where every step had to be won by the chop of a brush hook. The plateau, like Conan Doyle's Lost World, was ringed by great cliffs and accessible only at one point by a bridle path over which only the hardiest of mountain horses could travel. The nearest vehicular road was 16 miles [26 kilometres] distant; it was of bottomless black soil, trafficable only in dry weather. The nearest railway terminus was Beaudesert, 26 miles [42 kilometres] away . . .
>
> We know now that it was a task which should never have been

> attempted, that it was hard enough finally to break the spirit of those iron men, but we know just as surely that it was the very colossal nature of the task, which made it an irresistible challenge to young men whose veins ran rich with pioneering blood – men who were bred in difficult times and whose lives had been just a succession of obstacles to be overcome.

Just a few years later, though, O'Reilly's father died, and the Megalong branch of the family moved to Queensland in 1917. O'Reilly, only fourteen, often found himself alone on the mountain for months on end, tending the cattle while his brothers and cousins ranged across Queensland looking for work and money to support the ongoing effort of trying to clear their border selections to the point where they could support them.

It was during the night that the terrible storm that had brought down the Stinson blew itself out, and Saturday, 20 February 1937, dawned calm. Out on the range, the three injured men had endured a horrible time in the open. While the fire had burned, they had been warm, but as the flames died down the rain soaked their ragged clothing, chilling them to the bone. According to Binstead:

> Early next morning [Westray] said he would try to make his way to the nearest habitation. Proud and I urged calmer counsels, but he would not listen. The last we saw of him was when he disappeared behind a thick brush about 60 yards [55 metres] away. I thought it risky for him to attempt it, for he was a young Englishman and certainly not a bushman. Still, he was game, and so confident of bringing help that for a time it gave us both fresh heart.

The only supplies Jim Westray took with him were cigarettes. The men had divided up what they had, Proud pressing his cigarette case on the Englishman. Then he was gone. As Proud recorded in his diary: 'Saturday 20th. Morning. Weather clear. Englishman left seeking assistance. He sang out he could see a farmhouse, but did not return.'

Despite the rain, Proud needed water. Binstead, though his hands had been badly burned, raked through the cold coals of the charred aircraft, looking for some kind of container. It was a grisly business, surrounded by the remains of the unfortunate pilots and passengers, at least one of whom appeared to have been trying to struggle out of the plane when he was engulfed in flame.

Finally, Binstead had some luck. He found a large metal coffee flask that had survived the fire and was perfect for carrying water. The difficulty, though, was finding a stream. Although not a young man and unaccustomed to physical exertion, Binstead descended the steep side of the range until he found a small creek that flowed down the cleft of the valley. Then it was a 300-metre, almost-vertical climb through thick jungle and vines, some of which were armed with vicious thorns. Despite his injuries, he succeeded in getting down and back with the vital water for Proud.

At the O'Reilly farm, they still had no idea of the fate of the Stinson airliner. In fact they had lost all direct contact with the outside world, as fallen trees had brought down 6 kilometres of the telephone line that they had laid themselves. As O'Reilly set about repairing the phone line, he found the track thick with leaves that had been stripped from the trees, countless broken branches, even trunks of healthy trees snapped off by the tremendous winds.

The phone line was just one of the hard-won luxuries of the

O'Reillys' mountain. When his brothers had first arrived, they'd been forced to carry everything up the mountain on their backs. They couldn't use packhorses because there was nothing in the rainforest for them to feed on. The ancient rainforest resisted their efforts from day one. O'Reilly recalled his brothers' first camp:

> Before blankets were rolled out, six tiger snakes had to be killed and two bulldog ants' nests burnt out. Herb had been sitting on the brink of the cliff watching the opalescent spray of the falls leaping into the twilight. On getting up to go back to the camp site, he found two hissing reptiles blocking his path; there was no stick handy and no retreat. 'Bring a stick!' he yelled to the others. 'Two snakes here!'
>
> 'You can have my stick,' Norb called out, a bit out of breath, 'as soon as I've finished killing these beggars over here.'

Acquiring the conveniences most people took for granted (like the telephone) had required an inordinate amount of O'Reilly invention, as when, in 1920, they'd finally bought a stove. Initially, they'd planned for several men to carry it slung between poles using fencing wire, the theory being: 'There's nothing a selector cannot accomplish given abundant wire and greenhide.' They were eventually forced to bring it up in pieces, on a packhorse, only to find that putting it back together required a factory vice. O'Reilly wrote:

> Things looked blue for a while, then Tom [a brother] had a brainwave; he went up to the dairy and returned with all the hemp rope we had. This was tightly bound and twitched around the stove; a few kerosene tins of water were then poured over the rope and the resultant shrinkage of the wet rope forced the warped metal into line so that the top could be bolted on.

Yet even as the O'Reillys laid the axe to the forest, and threw themselves into the backbreaking task of gaining even a toehold on their mountain, the pristine beauty of their environment was entering their hearts:

> Here tower bright green soft woods smothered in all manner of living parasites, orchids and ferns; looped and twisted with hundreds of feet of great vines, thick as the upper arm. The jungle teems with exotic birds who never cross the dark threshold into the sunny warmth of the eucalyptus country. Here, too, are colourful outlandish flowers which bloom only in the green twilight.

Despite all their efforts, the dairy farms always struggled, and eventually the family realised they'd be better off supplementing their income with a guesthouse that would allow visitors to share the spectacular beauty of their home. However, without a road, that meant more years of backbreaking effort, hauling equipment and supplies for their guests.

Meanwhile, as Bernard O'Reilly went about the major task of repairing the phone line, the news of the Stinson's loss finally arrived at another family member's nearby home via radio. However, the ten o'clock morning broadcast said that the plane had last been seen south of Coffs Harbour. So, as the search intensified far from the McPherson Range, no-one saw any need to look for the missing men that far north.

Though Binstead had reservations, Jim Westray's chances of making it out of the mountains were quite good. Despite the severe burns to his back and hands, he was a fit twenty-five-year-old with considerable experience of walking and climbing in Europe. However, nothing in his experience could have prepared him for the treacherous rainforests and ravines of the McPherson Range.

Westray soon found himself negotiating one of the steepest gorges in the region. It was so narrow that trees that had fallen in the storm couldn't crash into the stream – they were stuck, wedged across the top of the gorge. Where the stream tumbled down the valley, huge boulders were covered in moss, and the spray made them slippery and treacherous. In places there were cliffs or near-vertical slopes of loose earth, studded with tree ferns and palms. It was incredibly difficult and dangerous, yet Westray knew enough to keep following the creek down. It would eventually reach the valley floor and lead to the open country around the nearby farms.

Westray faced some descents that left him in no doubt about the risks he was taking. Yet as he pushed himself onwards, it also became obvious just how inaccessible the crash site really was, how unlikely it was that anyone would stumble on it. Binstead and Proud had been adamant they should wait for rescue, but Westray realised the chances of that were slim – so he kept going.

Only a kilometre from the wreck site, Westray came to a 10-metre waterfall with cliffs on both sides. It was almost impassable, but he'd already negotiated worse. The best way down appeared to be to the right, where the vegetation still grew thickly and might give him handholds and footholds to the bottom. As he started down, he soon discovered to his cost that the plants – *Helmholtzia* lilies – were brittle and snapped off easily. When one broke, he slipped, grabbed for another, but it was already too late. Gaining momentum, he grabbed at anything he could, slid faster, then lost all control and fell almost all the way to the bottom of the cliff.

Incredibly, the fall didn't kill him – at least, not right away. One ankle was a shattered, broken mess, and Westray had sustained severe head injuries. He was now unable to walk, but when he'd recovered as much as he was able, he started to crawl. Slowly, agonisingly, he dragged himself over the rocks and pools along the creek bed, for kilometre after kilometre.

By Sunday, 21 February 1937, news of the loss of the Stinson was beginning to grip the country. Saturday's search had found nothing, and the disappearance of the plane somewhere in a coastal strip that was well populated, despite having areas of rugged terrain, was deepening into mystery. It wasn't helped by the fact that the search area was concentrated far from the actual crash site, as the *Sunday Mail* indicated in banner headlines: 'IS MISSING STINSON DOWN IN SEA? FRUITLESS SEARCH BY PLANES. MAY HAVE GONE DOWN BETWEEN TERRIGAL AND SYDNEY. WAS WITHIN 15 MINUTES OF JOURNEY'S END.'

As the days passed, the search area grew ever wider, until it was the largest aerial search ever undertaken. The Australian Air Force and civilian aircraft criss-crossed the entire route the plane had taken. In the days that followed, the O'Reillys frequently saw planes flying over. Yet none of these planes saw any sign of the downed aircraft in the thick jungle below.

After several days, Proud scratched on the fuselage of the plane, beneath which he was attempting to shelter: 'Long time; nothing done. Do not know why search is not made.' And Binstead recalled:

> There was never any panic. Jack and I talked it over, and decided to reserve our strength as much as possible. We would each take it in turns to cooee at half-hour intervals. We kept this up for days, but never got any response.
>
> Proud's injured leg became steadily worse as the days passed. I did all I possibly could for him. I cut what remained of my shirt into bandages, but as we were out in the rain all the time, the bandages were of little use to keep the wound clean and dry. Jack never complained, but

several times the pain sent him a little delirious and he would call for me. All I could do was to make him more comfortable.

Often he urged me to go and leave him, as he believed he was done for, but he had saved my life, and I told him I would stick to him, whichever way things came out. It was an utterly unselfish act on his part to try to persuade me to go, although he tried to make me believe that he wanted me to seek help as he feared mortification would set in if his injured leg was left unattended. I realised that his only chance was in my staying with him, and looking after him as best I could until help came – if it ever did come. He had to have water.

By Wednesday, the 24th, five days after the crash, searches of isolated areas were being conducted up and down the coast in response to reports from people who were sure they'd heard the plane. An area near the New South Wales–Queensland border was searched – this after a report from a farmer near Tuntable Creek, north of the town of Nimbin, who said he'd heard a plane flying low over treetops, followed by 'a loud report'. His four children were also sure they'd heard something. However, the area searched was on the southern side of the Mount Warning caldera, more than 30 kilometres south of the wreck site. Meanwhile, just a few kilometres north of Sydney, a report came in that, on the Saturday after the crash, Hawkesbury residents had heard cries and cooees coming from the area around Coal and Candle Creek. By then, too, it was realised that passenger Barnett didn't exist, and the fears of Binstead's wife about flying had become reality. Binstead was listed among the missing.

In the McPhersons, common sense told the O'Reillys that after so many days the plane was almost certainly lost forever. And common sense was a quality they had in abundance:

Anxiously we stood by the radio during news sessions hoping for word. Little hope was left to us when we heard that the liner was missing over the wild Hawkesbury country near Sydney, and then, when the wreckage was 'seen' out to sea off Palm Beach, we regretfully said goodbye to Captain Boyden and his gallant company, and considered the sad chapter closed. It had been established beyond all doubt that the Stinson had been lost south of the Hawkesbury. Not only had it been 'seen' and 'heard' by casual observers, but its appearance had been recorded in the log of a steamer off Barrenjoey Heads.

As the days wore on, Binstead's strength started to fail him. The journey to the creek through the scrub was taking a terrible toll. His hands and feet were full of thorns from the vines, and between them and his burns, infection had set in. He could no longer walk. He was dragging himself through the scrub, every day, to get water. He said of the experience:

> While my strength lasted our water supply was assured. For food, all I could get was a few small berries [from midginbil palms, refreshing but not particularly nourishing]. I did not know whether they were poisonous or not, but they tasted sweet, so we took the risk. After a few days my hands became so numb and powerless from the thorn scratches that I was forced to carry these berries back to Proud in my mouth. I would say to him: 'Here comes momma bird with the eats.' I don't think they did us much good, but they did us no harm.
>
> During the days we spent together we talked of many things. Cricket, I know, was one of the chief topics. Jack busied himself with a rough sort of diary, but I mostly kept a lookout for searching planes. I was unable to light any signal fires, as our matches were soaked. I am afraid I am not much good at rubbing two sticks together.

Eventually, Binstead was too weak to both fetch water and gather berries. He decided to conserve his energy for the vital water. By Thursday, 25 February, even that was getting to be too much. He said of that day: 'I so doubted my strength to get back to the plane from the creek that I scratched on a piece of the fuselage a message to let searchers who might come too late know that I was down at the creek and that Proud was lying near the plane with a broken leg.'

The message read: 'Binstead at creek – water. Proud lying at plane with broken leg. Rapidly tiring.'

By then, too, Proud's leg had begun to putrefy and was crawling with maggots. Around the plane, which now contained four rapidly decomposing bodies, the stench of death was overwhelming.

It was a full week after the crash, on Friday, 26 February, that Bernard O'Reilly and his wife, Viola, left their mountain to visit his brother Herb, who by 1937 had a little farm at nearby Kerry, a beautiful locality at the foot of the mountains, named after the equally beautiful and almost as rugged district of Ireland. While O'Reilly helped his brother with the chores, the two bushmen talked about the missing plane. Herb was one of many who had seen it flying towards the McPhersons the previous week. He thought it was heading for Lismore, battling a strong headwind before disappearing into a cloudbank.

When they went back to Herb's for lunch, O'Reilly got a chance to catch up on all the theories that the newspapers had been discussing during the previous days. One thing struck him as odd. Most thought that the pilot, Boyden, must have decided to bypass Lismore and had therefore flown down the coast, rather than inland. However, talking to Herb, he realised that wasn't the case. The Stinson had been trying to reach Lismore, and had never got there.

The next morning, having returned to his mountain home, O'Reilly's curiosity got the better of him. He decided to go for a bit of a walk through the rainforest and have a look around. First though, he phoned a friend, Bob Stephens, who lived on a farm at the head of the Albert River, the last place where anyone in the local area had seen the plane. To the best of his ability, Stephens gave him the plane's last known position.

After hanging up the phone, O'Reilly got out an aerial survey map of the mountains, and plotted the position Stephens had given him. Then, with a ruler, he drew a straight line from there to Lismore. As he later wrote: 'This plotted line contacted four high mountain ranges, and I reasoned that, if the missing airliner was to be found in this locality, it would necessarily be on the northern slopes of any of these four.'

He started making preparations for a two- or three-day journey: two loaves of bread, some butter and half a dozen onions, tea, sugar, a billy can and a cup. Before he left he treated an injury where he'd stepped on a rusty nail. While he was pouring iodine on it, his four-year-old daughter, Rhelma, came up to him.

'Daddy, where are you going?' she asked, and was told.

'Can I go, too?' she asked, and was told why she couldn't.

'Well, will you bring the aeroplane home with you?' she then asked, sure her father would find it.

Unknown to O'Reilly and his family, time had run out for Joe Binstead and John Proud. Binstead's last trip down to the water had taken him five hours. He was too exhausted to go again. 'I was too weak to move from the plane,' Binstead said, 'we both lay there, hoping against hope. At the finish my job was to try to keep the flies from getting to his injured limb. Finally, I ripped away a piece of the charred fuselage and bent it over it into the form of a shield, which I placed over his leg.'

Some 10 kilometres but several impassable valleys away, the route

O'Reilly planned to take required extraordinary courage, especially in attempting it alone. It was mostly through wild jungle, much of it precipitous, and there was little hope of finding anything except sudden disaster. First, O'Reilly followed a riding track from the guesthouse up to Mount Bithongabel, from which there are spectacular views across the entire Mount Warning caldera and surrounding district. He took one of the farm horses to the lookout, then, to its astonishment, sent it on its way home. That alone says something about the country he was entering. As the Man from Snowy River might tell you, sure-footed horses can pick their way through some incredibly rough places, but this was beyond O'Reilly's mount.

O'Reilly started along the cliffs at the rim of the caldera, heading west towards the first of the high mountain ranges. He first followed a 3-kilometre track that ended at the scenic Valley of Echoes, and then: 'From here on it was trackless, lawyer-vine jungle.' (Lawyer-vine is so called because, like a lawyer, once it gets its hooks into you, it's almost impossible to get free.) He was now so deep in the rainforest that he needed all of his experience not to become lost himself. In an interview in 2003, his daughter Rhelma explained some of the bush skills he used, and imparted to her and other children:

> He had two rules for the children: always tell someone where you're going, and be home by sunset. He also taught them to notice significant features, like a conspicuous tree, and to look back at it so you'll recognise it on your return trip. He taught us to turn all around at key places so we'd remember them again. If you've been there before, you'll never forget a place.

It's a technique similar to the Aboriginal method of creating a songline – a way of remembering features along a route from one place to another.

By dusk, O'Reilly still hadn't reached the first of the possible ranges for the wreck site. He dropped down from the ridge to make camp on one of the many creeks that stream away from the volcano's rim. Of that night's camp O'Reilly wrote:

> With wet wood, damp ground and no blanket, sleep was just about impossible, but Nature kept me entertained. First, some black phalangers [possums] fought and screamed horribly in the vines overhead. I suppose they only lost some fur, but it sounded as though there would not be an animal left alive by morning. Later, as the moon struggled out of a cloud mass, a large pack of dingoes commenced to howl away down the gorge. The tones of their howlings were spread over an octave, and I thought of a chorus of banshees. I thought, too, that dingoes howl in packs about dead bodies, and a nasty cold feeling got hold of me. Down in that gorge, there might have been what?

Rhelma O'Reilly also spoke of the way the rainforest can unnerve even the experienced: 'There are places that really do make you feel fear, a shiver up the spine that makes you want to run for home.' Even Aboriginal people in the district preferred to camp in the open eucalypt forest rather than the haunting rainforest. When Charles Chauvel filmed part of *Sons of Matthew* (1949, based on *Green Mountains*) at O'Reilly's, an Aboriginal horse wrangler took sick and later died. Aboriginal elders said it was because he knew he shouldn't have been near the rainforest at night.

On Sunday, 28 February, John Proud scratched on the fuselage of the plane: 'Eleventh day today. Hope dwindling.' He and Binstead had lost track of how long they'd been in the rainforest. It was in fact ten days. Not that it made any difference. They were now sure rescue wasn't coming. They were only waiting for death.

Not many kilometres away, though, O'Reilly had been up before dawn and was already climbing towards the first ridge that his estimated flight path crossed. He was making for the highest point on the ridge, 1140-metre Mount Throakban. From there, he hoped to get a view of all the ridges. Unfortunately, at around 8 a.m., when he reached the top, it was wrapped in early morning cloud. All he could do was wait and hope for the sun to burn off the mist and give him a glimpse of the surrounding jungle. He later wrote:

> For fifteen minutes I stood in cool moist wind, looking into a grey blank, and then suddenly the racing clouds split, and a vast green sea of ranges and gorges came into view to the west. It gave a good view of the three remaining ranges in the plotted line of flight. Here and there were creamy white splashes which I knew to be trees in bloom, and then suddenly I saw something which made me jump. Eight miles [13 kilometres] away by the map, on the third range, Lamington Plateau, just where it swelled up to join the border range, was a treetop which was light brown.

To an untrained eye it would have meant nothing. It might have been a tree flushed with new growth. But O'Reilly knew it was the wrong season for that. Was it a dying tree? O'Reilly knew that in his rainforest trees only died a branch at a time. Was it a lightning strike? He consulted his map. The tree was right near the line he'd plotted. What were the chances of lightning striking in exactly that area? Fire? There hadn't been a natural fire in that rainforest for thousands of years.

O'Reilly realised he was on to something, but reaching the tree was no simple matter. Between him lay a wild and rugged valley, a steep climb to the second ridge, and another wild valley. Maintaining his bearings accurately enough to reach the spot was going to require incredible skill and care. Nevertheless, he set off from Throakban, heading for the one burnt tree.

It took five hours to reach the top of the next ridge. By then, O'Reilly was starting to tire, having pushed himself hard for over a day, and spent a restless night in the jungle. With his exhaustion came a slump in morale. It was too much to expect to find anything in such a deep, dark forest. Up on the ridge he also found himself back in cloud, trying in vain to get a closer view of the burnt tree and another bearing to ensure that he was on the right course. He waited for a break that never came.

And then: 'From the direction of Lamington Plateau – about 3 miles [5 kilometres] away by the map – came a short, clear human call, and then another. A human voice in that green wilderness.'

'Coooooo-ee!'

It came from across the gorge.

'I cooeed back and moved on as quickly as I could. I could still hear cooees, but could not be certain they were answering mine. Then the cooeeing stopped, but I went on in the direction I thought it had come from.'

However, O'Reilly couldn't bring himself to believe the calls came from the survivors of the Stinson. More likely, it was someone else foolish enough to be out searching the rainforest. O'Reilly may even have been hoping it wasn't anyone from the Stinson, knowing that after so many days they could only be in a terrible condition.

Three hours later he finally reached the Lamington Plateau. He couldn't be sure his dead reckoning had got him close to the burnt tree, or the voice in the wilderness. Still, he thought he was close.

He took a deep breath. 'Coooooo-ee!'

Then he waited.

'Cooo-ee!'

The reply may have been weak but there was no mistaking the fact that it was very close. O'Reilly estimated it was only 200 metres away, down through the trees. He called again, already moving towards the voice, and was answered. Another voice joined in. They kept calling as he pushed through the jungle:

> A numbness shot through my limbs, a sort of coldness that was worse than fear and worse than pain or shock. I knew that I would see a mass of smashed and charred metal. It was more than that; it was a horrible, unclean thing, which held the trapped remains of what once were men – a repulsive thing which I could not go near.
>
> Proud, I saw first, his eyes far back in his head like those of a corpse, lying as he had lain for ten days on that wet ground with a broken leg that was green and swelling and maggoty. 'My God!' I thought, 'You have lain all these days in hell, and now I'm too late to save you.'
>
> Then I turned to Binstead – he tried to shake hands, a poor hand that was like raw meat. His legs, too, were like that, and the legs of his trousers were worn away in crawling over the rocks to bring water.

Binstead recalled O'Reilly's arrival: 'When Mr O'Reilly walked in on us, I could have kissed him, but Mr O'Reilly was more overcome than we were. His first greeting was: "Oh you poor bastards." He did not seem to be able to grasp the full significance of his discovery.'

O'Reilly later told the *Courier Mail*: 'Then there was silence for seconds; we were all too excited to speak. One of them broke the silence, saying to the other, "We will be able to have that drink at the Australia after all." "What's the score?" was one of the first questions. I told them that Bradman was 165 not out.'

In *Green Mountains*, O'Reilly wrote: 'There was some talk, lots of talk; but who remembers what was said? The first sane remark I remember was Binstead's, "How about boiling the billy?"

O'Reilly quietly set about making the men a cup of tea, and gave them the little food he had left, wishing he'd had the good sense to bring more. He was being a bit hard on himself. After an extraordinary piece of deductive reasoning, followed by one of the greatest feats of bushmanship in Australia's history, he had found the wreck of the Stinson.

It wasn't over yet. As it turned out, the plane had actually managed to clear two higher ridges before being literally swatted out of the sky by the ferocious turbulence. It had almost reached the rim of the caldera when a downdraft slammed it into the Lamington Plateau. Now, seeing the condition of the men, and with a clear idea of how inaccessible the wreck site was, O'Reilly knew it was going to take a miracle to save them, especially the horribly afflicted John Proud. First, though, he had to reach help.

O'Reilly guessed, and later found he was correct, that he was on the southern branch of Christmas Creek and that if he followed it down he'd be close to the settlements of Hillview and Lamington, about 15 kilometres away. Binstead and Proud told him that Jim Westray had followed the creek down, but they had heard nothing of him since.

It was about 4.30 p.m. when O'Reilly took the wool jacket his wife had knitted him the previous winter and gave it to Binstead. He gave him the aerial survey map too, to spread over his legs to keep off the rain. Then, despite knowing that he'd be journeying through treacherous country in the approaching darkness, and risking his life in the process, he reassured the men: 'I'll bring back a doctor and a hundred men.'

He descended to the creek following Binstead's track, noticing the scattered remnants of the man's deteriorating condition – scraps of torn clothing, a shoe that had come off and been left when Binstead was too weak to put it back on. Then he picked up Westray's tracks and started to think he might be lucky enough to find another man alive. The further he went, the more his hopes grew, as the tracks successfully negotiated several difficult descents. Then, O'Reilly came to the cliff and saw the broken vegetation where Westray had fallen.

With the benefit of a lifetime in the steep terrain of the Border Ranges, O'Reilly started to descend, expecting to find Westray's broken body at the bottom. He was surprised when he found nothing, but appalled to see the signs that the man had gone on, crawling down the creek bed. As he followed the terribly injured Westray, O'Reilly was sure he couldn't have got far. Yet as he kept on through the twists and descents of the gorge, his admiration for Westray grew. Finally, he saw a man just ahead, resting with his back against a big boulder.

'Hullo,' O'Reilly shouted, 'hoy there.'

Westray didn't move. O'Reilly walked around to the front of the rock. Westray had taken off his right shoe and sock to bathe the mangled remains of his ankle. There was a cigarette between his fingers. It had burned all the way down to the butt. His eyes were gazing down the gorge, towards the safety that was now forever beyond him. O'Reilly later rightly praised Westray's attempt to reach help as 'a feat of endurance beyond human conception'.

For the already emotionally raw dairy farmer, though, this last shock was too much. He later wrote:

> It must have been just after the place where Westray fell, that I lost my head and began to run and leap across the gaps between the slimy lava blocks – if I'd slipped, I too would have been smashed up and help would never have got to the men, but, I thought, as far as I was capable of thinking, that they would die, anyhow, if I didn't get help that night.
>
> It is like a dream now, that wild run. I was quite mad – my heart had been wrung out with horror and with pity – no one who looked upon those poor survivors could help praying as I did that God would let me live long enough to help these men. I knew that I was sobbing and that I only paused when tears blinded me. I remember too, that the shock

> and jar of leaping and landing on these rocks at top speed was telling on me, even though I was in splendid condition, but I was given strength to complete the task.

As he ran, he fell over and over again, landing heavily on the rocks of the creek bed, plunging through deep pools. Yet every time he fell, he rose to his feet and drove himself onwards. It was a run down the mountain every bit as dangerous and inspiring as the Man from Snowy River's ride, only Bernard O'Reilly was doing it on foot and, once night fell, in darkness. 'All track of time went,' he wrote, 'and all feeling from my body. I seemed to be running an obstacle race in the bed of a black underground river, miles down in the earth. One sharp thought only in all the chaos: "Hurry! Proud is dying."' The word he used afterwards to describe his state of mind was 'hell-driven'.

Finally, three hours after leaving Proud and Binstead, O'Reilly broke out of the rainforest and into the open eucalypt country. Soon he was running through grazing land. It was just after he'd found a track that he heard a gunshot, and located a young farmhand out shooting. The vision that appeared in the shooter's lamplight was a shock – a man soaking wet, with torn clothing, covered in cuts, bruises and blood.

'I've found that missing aeroplane,' O'Reilly gasped, 'and there are two men still alive.'

Still there was no chance for rest. The farmhand, a young member of the Buchanan family from Christmas Creek, was soon saddling horses to get O'Reilly to a road and a phone. Once at the Lamington property of John Buchanan, Airlines of Australia was alerted and authorised O'Reilly to do whatever was necessary to effect the rescue.

The news was already spreading like wildfire. The phone system, with a manual exchange and many farms sharing lines, was soon buzzing. The operation that was rapidly being organised was helped by the fact that some of the bushmen were former army officers, well able to deal calmly with the logistics involved in a rescue. Others were bushies like O'Reilly who, living closer to the Lamington Plateau, knew the terrain in detail.

When O'Reilly had told Binstead and Proud that he'd be back with a doctor and a hundred men, he had no way of knowing he'd underestimated the people of the Australian bush. By midnight, the entire district was on the move, men and women answering the call regardless of the hour, establishing where they had to be, what had to be done and setting about doing it.

The plan was straightforward. One party, including a doctor, would assemble by 2.30 a.m. near where O'Reilly had met the young Buchanan, and guided by O'Reilly they'd head back up Christmas Creek with enough medical supplies to treat the injured men. Given that, in 1937, the helicopter was only just moving into production from inventor Igor Sikorsky's prototypes, the survivors weren't about to be winched to safety. So a second, larger party would begin to cut an access track up one of the plateau's less-steep ridges, then along the rim of the caldera, from where the injured men would be able to be evacuated by stretcher. Making a track over the 22 kilometres involved would normally have taken days or even weeks. The track-cutting party was given little more than twenty-four hours, starting in the small hours of the morning. O'Reilly provides glimpses of the operation:

> To postmistress Gracie Silcox must go most of the credit for getting together the volunteers. She stuck to her telephone all night, calling numbers, explaining where to go and what to take, and all this in between floods of incoming press and radio calls and 'long distances' from incredulous relatives and friends. I rushed to the store and

> ordered incredible amounts of bread, butter, tea and sugar and tinned food – a final thought was a large quantity of flat files for sharpening brush hooks.

In a press interview he explained: 'Altogether I had walked 18 miles [29 kilometres] since I left my hostel. I then set out to walk the 12 miles [19 kilometres] to Hillview to organise the relief party, and now at 11 o'clock, after a little more than a quarter of an hour, getting the party together, we are ready to set out.'

In fact, organising men and materials meant O'Reilly didn't get away from Lamington until 1.30 a.m., rushing by car then horseback to meet the doctor at the appointed hour. When they reached the rendezvous it was raining, but the men already there had a fire going. There was a chance for a cup of tea while the last of the men and supplies arrived, enough time to think of Binstead and Proud up there on the mountain enduring yet another night of cold, rain, darkness and pain.

At the campsite, Doctor Lawler also tried to treat a man who already looked to be a casualty: Bernard O'Reilly. As Rhelma explained: 'Running out of the creek, my father suffered numerous falls while he was running over the rocks. He'd actually damaged his eardrums and had some severe injuries. When the doctor met him he wanted to put him to bed, but he refused. He had to guide the men back to the wreck.'

The medical and track parties were soon on the way, long lines of lanterns snaking up the creek and the ridge. Dawn saw both parties pressing deep into the rainforest, while behind them ambulances had arrived and were waiting, and the district's women had set up a canteen and were preparing hot food to be sent to the men hacking their way up the narrow jungle-clad ridge. More and more people arrived and moved up to help cut the track. The media had descended in droves. Local businesses were sending vehicles with anything needed or that might be useful, often free of charge.

Unknown to O'Reilly, his wife, Viola, and sister Rose, a trained nurse, had saddled their horses and were riding down their mountain, aiming to ride across country to be by his side. When they got to the farms at the foot of the mountains, they found them all deserted. Cows were left unmilked, tools lay idle. Everyone had joined the rescue.

As O'Reilly recorded and Rhelma further detailed, even the 'Hermit of Lamington' joined the effort. Charles Burgess was a digger who had been badly wounded in World War I. Deeply affected by the horrors he had experienced, he had retreated to a cave on another branch of Christmas Creek and lived by one commandment: Thou shalt not kill. He grew corn for sustenance and even went so far as to refuse to wear leather boots. A figure not unlike William Buckley from Chapter 1, he helped the track-cutting party to establish the shortest, safest route through what was effectively his backyard.

Some indication of O'Reilly's extraordinary feat in coming down Christmas Creek comes from the fact that, where he had taken three hours to descend, the rescue party took eight to make their way up. The doctor finally reached the injured men at 11 a.m. on Monday, 1 March. O'Reilly recorded:

> The doctor, wan and exhausted, did not pause a moment to rest, but went straight to work on Proud's leg. Less than an hour later he told me confidently that Proud's life and limb would be saved. The very maggots which seemed to make the case so hopeless had eaten away the gangrenous flesh and checked the spread of fatal infection. Nature, with her own antiseptic, had protected a man beyond the reach of medical aid. I was to find out later that during the Great War many a Digger's life had been saved by flies.

There was no rest for the rescue party. A route to the ridge was cut, where it would meet the main track-cutting party. Stretchers were fashioned from branches, sacks and clothesline rope. Up on the ridge a shelter was erected to protect Binstead and Proud from the elements and they were carefully carried to it. Well-fed and warm, they were soon sleeping with the aid of sedatives.

Then the bushmen, who had not slept at all the night before, started cutting a track along the ridge, towards the one coming up from below. During the day there was one disaster, when a packhorse carrying supplies slipped on a steep slope. It slid downwards, out of control, until it reached the edge of a cliff, where it then fell 45 metres to its death.

At sunset, the two parties made contact. The track was cut, and some of the men headed back down to the large support camp that had sprung up around the ambulances and the canteen. Others pressed through to the plateau camp. In the darkness more and more men straggled in, exhausted from their phenomenal efforts, but ready to help bear the stretchers down the new track as soon as it was light. O'Reilly vividly described the scene:

> I can say, without hesitation, that that night was the worst in my life. Two smoky sodden fires for thirty worn-out men, no shelter from the wind and rain which redoubled as night fell; it seemed years since I had felt warmth, or had dry clothes on my body. Nobody made any pretence of trying to sleep. Most of the men stood up all night.

In the darkness before the dawn of Tuesday, 2 March, the men began to rouse themselves. They built up the fires and soon billies were boiled and breakfast prepared. Then, as soon as it was light enough to see, the stretcher parties lifted their frail burdens and started the delicate task of carrying them out of that forbidding terrain.

'There was no stopping for a rest,' O'Reilly wrote. 'When a man tired, another took his place; the cavalcade kept moving. Around the bend ahead came a number of rain-sodden men; the leader, a tall chap with a drooping hat and a wet cornsack over his shoulders. He strode forward and grabbed my hand.'

O'Reilly's brother Herb and his group had also stayed in the mountains that night. They'd slashed at the jungle until it was too dark to leave safely, and spent a night sheltering beneath a large beech tree. When he met his brother, Herb, O'Reilly was so stricken with emotion he was unable to speak.

The stretcher-bearers kept on, often in heavy rain, sometimes through what were effectively tunnels through the undergrowth. Eventually they were met by sodden reporters from the *Courier Mail* who had climbed the range. When they interviewed Joe Binstead, he said of O'Reilly, 'Now that I know the kind of country we were in I am amazed that we were ever found at all. He is certainly a wonderful bushman. Jack and I owe him our lives, and we will be eternally grateful.'

As the stretcher parties struggled on, two women on horseback came up to them – O'Reilly's wife and sister Rose. 'Although I was hatless,' O'Reilly wrote, 'Viola would have passed me without recognition, such was the change that the few days had made.'

His daughter, Rhelma, explained: 'Finding the Stinson was a nightmare to him. He was a very sensitive person and suffered with the men. He lost 16 kilograms from the Saturday to the Tuesday.'

In all that time, he had gone almost entirely without sleep, and had fought his way through some of the most difficult terrain imaginable. It was a phenomenal feat of endurance, but even O'Reilly had his limits:

> About mid-morning, while carrying Proud's stretcher, I stumbled badly twice. I was relieved at once. Only willpower had been keeping me together, and now with extra help arriving every moment, and the end of the job in sight, the old legs refused duty. Quickly we were joined by

other groups of wet and worn men from the previous day's cutting party, their faces and hands and arms torn with lawyer and wild raspberry.

At one point where the mountain broke away sharply, a stout rope was put around an entire stretcher party and anchored to another group of men, who steadied them down the declivity. Slowly and resolutely, the carriers tramped down the last long slope; down at last to where the creek swelled up to meet the ridge. And then, eleven hours after that start in the grey of dawn, Binstead and Proud were put into the ambulance cars; the big job was done.

Bernard O'Reilly was a hero. He was mobbed by reporters, interviewed on radio and movie newsreels. Subscriptions were opened and generous donations poured in. There were official functions to thank O'Reilly and all the people involved in the rescue.

In a souvenir program for a benefit night at Brisbane City Hall for Beaudesert Hospital (where the rescued men were treated), Joe Binstead and John Proud gave their thanks:

> Alone, unaided, relying on his own sound judgment and his splendid knowledge of bushcraft, he climbed gorges; he hacked his way through primitive scrub; he followed his plan; and he found us . . . And then they came, from near and far, uncaring for their own comfort, bearing no thought for themselves, they hurried to our aid. In blinding rain, from far off places they assembled, those wiry bushmen, those heroes, true Australians all . . . Powerful hands, supple as steel, were childishly gentle as they lifted us on to litters and carried us on their backs once more into a living world.

The bodies of the men who had not survived the crash, and of Westray, who had died seeking help, were buried on the Lamington Plateau. It was considered hard enough to bring out Proud and Binstead. Their graves, and monuments to the crash, remain there still. Proud and Binstead recovered and returned to their lives. John Proud went on to become Sir John Proud, one of the leading figures in the Australian mining industry, chairman of Peko-Wallsend. He also helped establish the environmental organisation Earthwatch Australia. He died in 1997, at the age of ninety.

As for the many well-meaning people who were sure they'd 'seen' the Stinson all along its usual flight path on Friday, 19 February, and in so doing threw confusion into the search effort, the Coroner commented: 'Those fanciful people with fertile imaginations who saw and heard things that did not exist must now have troubled consciences.'

Meanwhile, the man at the centre of all the attention was still recovering. On a trip into Beaudesert to shop, he was mobbed by well-wishers. Some wanted autographs, others wanted to shake his hand despite the fact he had, as the *Courier Mail* reported:

> a few dozen thorns which, embedded in every finger of both hands, are now beginning to get rather painful . . . Mr O'Reilly confessed that he was very weary. Since Friday night he had had only an occasional hour's sleep – one in the drenching rain when propped against a tree, and on Tuesday night when he dropped into bed at midnight, but awoke almost every hour with the thought that there was still something to be done.

Not long after, O'Reilly went bush. He and his immediate family took the train to Sydney, where they were again mobbed and pressed into several official engagements. Then they headed for a relative's property deep in the Blue Mountains of his childhood.

His daughter says he was forever haunted by his experiences with the Stinson, and those he subsequently had in World War II. He joined the Light Horse, a corporal with the 2/15th Battalion, and saw action in North Africa, before being wounded in New Guinea. He suffered a shrapnel wound and contracted scrub typhus.

During the war he worked in intelligence mapping. Remarkably, when he joined the army, he had to be taught how to use a compass. When he'd searched for the Stinson, he hadn't used or needed one. As Rhelma put it, 'He had a built-in compass.' In the army, his unerring sense of direction was sometimes overruled by his commanding officers, but he was later proved to be right.

Rhelma remembers her father as a well-read man with an inquiring mind and a keen interest in natural history, his intellect balanced by a bushman's sense of humour. 'It was in his character to laugh at disaster, all the family had it. The worse the disaster, the louder they laughed.'

One of the consequences of the Stinson rescue was that O'Reilly also learned that he could speak in public and that he had a talent for writing. Three of his books are still in print, *Green Mountains* having been part of the Queensland school curriculum for many years. As Rhelma explains: 'The book was written while waiting for the [often delayed] supply car in a sack chair slung beneath a stinging tree. In later years the tree was dying but Bernard loved it and hoped it would outlive him. The night following his burial [in 1975], the tree fell.'

The O'Reilly Rainforest Guesthouse is now one of the treasures of Queensland tourism. It sits in the heart of the Lamington National Park and is still owned and run by several generations of the extended O'Reilly family. It is frequented by people from around the world who appreciate the beauty of the rainforest and its stunning wildlife. The guesthouse also has monuments to O'Reilly's extraordinary feat of bushmanship.

And it has a Stinson plane. In 1937, a four-year-old Rhelma O'Reilly had asked her father 'Will you bring the aeroplane home with you?' In 2003, the remarkably young seventy-year-old got her wish. A replica of the Stinson, used in the filming of the 1988 movie *The Riddle of the Stinson*, was obtained by O'Reilly's guesthouse. Like their first stove's transportation in the 1920s, the Stinson was trucked up the mountain in pieces, along the spectacular sealed road that now extends all the way. The assembled plane will be the centrepiece of a Lamington region heritage centre that will detail both the natural history of the area and the history of the remarkable people who live there.

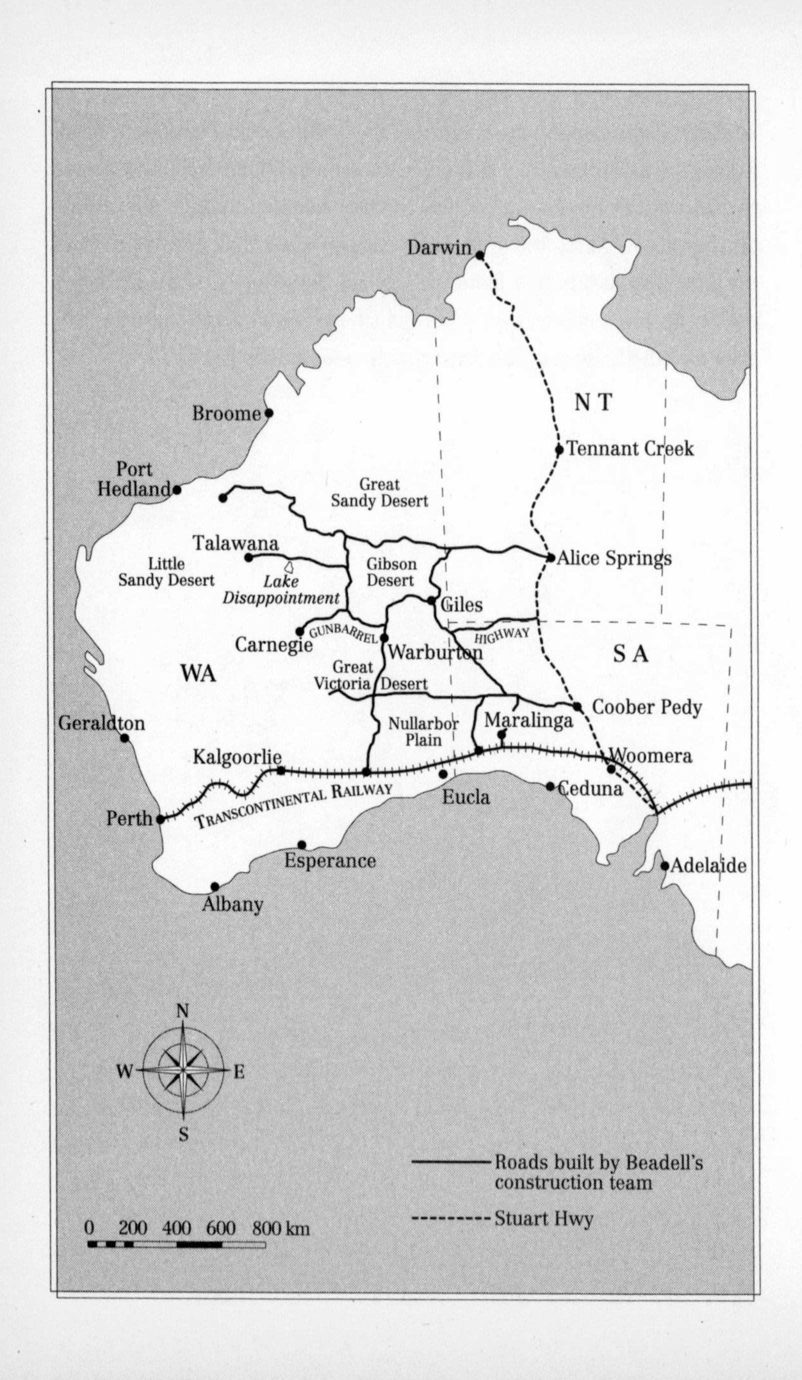
Darwin
N T
Broome
Tennant Creek
Port Hedland
Great Sandy Desert
Talawana
Alice Springs
Little Sandy Desert
Lake Disappointment
Gibson Desert
Giles
Carnegie
GUNBARREL
HIGHWAY
Warburton
S A
WA
Great Victoria Desert
Coober Pedy
Geraldton
Nullarbor Plain
Maralinga
Kalgoorlie
Woomera
TRANSCONTINENTAL RAILWAY
Eucla
Ceduna
Perth
Esperance
Adelaide
Albany
N
W
E
S
Roads built by Beadell's construction team
Stuart Hwy
0 200 400 600 800 km

Len Beadell, date unknown
(Photo courtesy the Beadell family)

12

THE GUNBARREL, 1958: Len Beadell (1923–1995)

In the years after World War II the world started reaching for the stars. Space was widely regarded as the final frontier as nations scrambled for supremacy in rocketry and missile technology, driven by defence concerns and the potential for international prestige. Yet among the heroic achievements and scientific advances on the edge of the heavens, there was to be found an unassuming Australian bushie whose concerns were much more down to earth. They included dealing with a frontier that had defied man's best efforts to tame it for over a century.

From 1947 until the 1960s, Len Beadell was responsible for the reconnaissance work and subsequent road building associated with central Australia's Woomera Rocket Range. From the launch facility just north of Port Augusta in South Australia, across the continent to Eighty Mile Beach near Broome in Western Australia, the range's 1.6 million square kilometres of sand dunes, spinifex and mulga included some of the most formidable desert regions on earth. There was almost no water to be found anywhere; there were no roads or settlements of any kind. The area was seldom visited, even by Aboriginal people, who today still dwell in settlements mostly on its fringes.

Yet it was Beadell's job to survey and provide access to what was to become one of the biggest science labs on the face of the earth. It included the construction and mapping of a network of nearly 7000 kilometres of roads over a ten-year period from 1953 to 1963. It was a monumental achievement that called on bush skills few could hope to match. Often leading a construction party, but also conducting long-range reconnaissance trips on his own, the project was not without considerable risk, as Beadell was to discover when building one of the network's most famous roads, The Gunbarrel Highway. The 'highway', an irony-laden description of what is essentially a graded dirt track, runs right through the Gibson Desert, named in memory of Alfred Gibson, the first white man it killed.

Alfred Gibson was a member of Ernest Giles's expedition into the western deserts in 1874. In April of that year the two men took four horses and 140 litres of water with them, and set out to explore to the west of the expedition's base in the Rawlinson Range, on what is now the South Australian–Northern Territory border. At first traversing sand dunes and spinifex, after two days in oppressive heat they let two of the horses return to base on their own, cached some water at a spot they called The Kegs, then continued on with rapidly dwindling water supplies. On the third day out, Gibson's horse died and the pair were forced to turn back, taking turns riding the remaining horse. Some 50 kilometres from The Kegs, Giles realised their situation was becoming desperate:

> We were both excessively thirsty, for walking had made us so, and we had scarcely a pint of water left between us. However, of what we had we each took a mouthful, which finished the supply, and I then said – for I couldn't speak before – 'Look here, Gibson, you see we are in a most terrible fix with only one horse, therefore only one can ride, and one must remain behind. I shall remain: and now listen to me. If the mare does not get water soon she will die; therefore ride right on; get to the Kegs if possible tonight, and give her water.

It was the last anyone saw of Gibson. Giles, incredibly, made it back to his base. He reached the Kegs and saw that Gibson had, too:

> After I had thoroughly digested all points of my situation, I concluded that if I did not help myself providence wouldn't help me. I started, bent double by [a keg weighing 20 kilograms], and could only travel so slowly that I thought it scarcely worth while to travel at all. I became so thirsty at each step I took that I longed to drink up every drop of water I had in the keg, but it was the elixir of death I was burdened with, and to drink it was to die, so I restrained myself. By next morning I had only got about 3 miles [5 kilometres] away from the Kegs, and to do that I travelled mostly in the moonlight. The next few days I can only pass over as they seemed to pass with me, for I was quite unconscious half the time, and I only got over about 5 miles [8 kilometres] a day.
>
> To people who cannot comprehend such a region it may seem absurd that a man could not travel faster than that. All I can say is,

> there may be men who could do so, but most men in the position I was in would simply have died of hunger and thirst, for by the third or fourth day – I couldn't tell which – my horse meat was all gone. I had to remain in what scanty shade I could find during the day, and I could only travel by night.

Not far from The Kegs, within sight of the Rawlinson Range, Giles saw where the less experienced Gibson had followed the two horses that had been let go when they had deviated from the main tracks, probably losing their way while maddened with thirst. Giles followed a little way hoping Gibson would have realised his mistake and turned aside, but his tracks continued on into the wilderness. Giles was forced to return to the main track.

Barely able to keep going at night, finding any shade thronged with bull ants during the day, Giles's march became a nightmare:

> On what I thought was the 27th I almost gave up the thought of walking any farther, for the exertion in this dreadful region, where the triodia [spinifex] was almost as high as myself, and as thick as it could grow, was quite overpowering and, being starved, I felt quite light-headed. After sitting down, on every occasion when I tried to get up again, my head would swim round, and I would fall down oblivious for some time. Being in a chronic state of burning thirst, my general plight was dreadful in the extreme. A bare and level sandy waste would have been paradise to walk over compared to this. My arms, legs, thighs, both before and behind, were so punctured with spines, it was agony only to exist; the slightest movement and in went more spines, where they broke off in the clothes and flesh, causing the whole of the body that was punctured to gather into minute pustules, which were continually growing and bursting. My clothes, especially inside my trousers, were a perfect mass of prickly points.

And this was the territory through which the missile men wanted Len Beadell to build their roads.

There's hope for all of us in the way Len Beadell became a bushie. Born in 1923, he was raised in and around Sydney, where his first experiences of the bush were like those of many other city kids. Through its organised hikes in the bush, camping trips, and experiences of boiling the billy on a campfire, the Scouts organisation has given several generations their first taste of bush life, and the impression that they possess a subset of survival skills that could sustain them in an emergency. Most of us are kidding ourselves, but Beadell was exceptional.

His first taste of the bush was to develop into a passion, nurtured by his scoutmaster, who happened to be a surveyor. John Richmond had served in World War I as a lieutenant in Intelligence, subsequently joining the Sydney Water Board where he started taking groups of scouts with him on weekend surveying trips that would establish routes for the Water Board's pipelines. From 1931 to 1941, Beadell and Richmond spent nearly every weekend out bush south of Sydney or in the Blue Mountains. Inspired and helped by Richmond, Beadell became a surveyor himself, first with the Water Board, and then, after the outbreak of war, with the Army Survey Corps. As the much-older bushie Bernard O'Reilly was to do (see Chapter 11), eighteen-year-old Beadell soon found himself mapping in the mud and tropical heat of Papua and New Guinea, which in 1942 was the last ragged line of defence against the advancing Japanese.

After the war, Sergeant Beadell worked on mapping projects in the Northern Territory until, in 1946 at the age of just twenty-three, he was asked to assist in determining the site for Woomera (the local Aboriginal word for 'a spear-thrower'). Arriving early in 1947, he found the area was still recovering from a rare event in such an arid region: floods. The water turned the fine red dust to mud and Beadell got around by zigzagging his jeep from rocky spot to rocky spot, not realising his tracks would later become the base's accepted routes. 'As people came and a town appeared on the prairies,' he wrote for the October–December 1960 issue of Woomera's *Missile* magazine:

> they all followed my exceptionally twisting wheel tracks instead of going anywhere, as was possible when things dried out. You can see a bull ant for 10 miles [16 kilometres] in that country, but still the same tracks were used. I heard many remarks about people being able to see their own tail lights, snakes unable to negotiate the turns, good job differentials were invented, and so on. I repeated the reason [for the winding tracks] so many times that I have been going dead straight ever since. Later, when we came to actually build all these roads in the Centre, I made them perfectly straight wherever possible, some 30 miles [48 kilometres] at a time without a curve. Straight as a gunbarrel.
>
> – Beadell extracts reproduced by kind permission of Len Beadell's Estate

To build the roads, Beadell put together a team that was to become known as the Gunbarrel Road Construction Party. Although road building had been going on since 1953, and the construction of airstrips and other facilities for some years before that, the team first formed in 1955 when it began work on the then 1347-kilometre Gunbarrel Highway, from near Kulgera in the Northern Territory to Carnegie in Western Australia. For many years it comprised bulldozer-driver Doug Stoneham, grader-driver Scott Boord, mechanic Rex Flatman, cherry picker Willy Appleton (the cherry picker followed the big machines, pulling out by hand anything that might puncture a normal vehicle's tyres), cook Paul Christensen and supply-driver Bill Lloyd. The latter was later replaced by Frank Quinn, a genius among bush mechanics. Shorty Williams eventually replaced Boord and Eric Graefling replaced Appleton.

Leading the charge was Beadell. Some idea of the extent of his responsibilities comes from the list of supplies he carried, listed in his book *Too Long in the Bush*:

> We then had two Land Rovers, one fitted out as a mobile workshop carrying oxy welding equipment, vice, and tools, and the other I'd had especially made up as a survey wagon. To mention a few of the items on it – a theodolite and tripod with stopwatches and calculation books for astronomical fixations, a radio transceiver also capable of receiving time signals needed for star observations, axe, shovel, mechanical spares and tools, a comprehensive outfit for emergency dental work and first aid, rifle, revolver, and hair clippers. One becomes quite good at packing in the bush, whether loading a vehicle or pack camel. The modifications on this survey wagon were the result of experience gained after many years of what is known as bushbashing, or pushing a vehicle through scrub.

Beadell's dentistry was the product of a crash course from Woomera's dentist, and a willingness to have a go. Not surprisingly, the same attitude prevailed when members of the crew got toothaches. Rather than face months of pain until they returned to civilisation, they put themselves in the hands of the resourceful bushie Beadell.

Building the Gunbarrel was a well-organised procedure. Having devised the general route from previous reconnoitring missions, Beadell would forge through virgin bush ahead of the construction machinery in his Land Rover, along the required course. He would then signal the dozer driver with a hand-mirror, or a flare if the bush was too high for him to be seen. The dozer-driver pushed the route through the scrub, followed by the grader and cherry picker. The support and supply vehicles could then follow on the newly constructed road, setting up the night's camp at a site selected during the afternoon.

While Beadell intended the roads to be straight, there were many reasons for deviations as he explained in *Too Long in the Bush*:

> Emu tracks are also around but, as is the case with many birds, we rarely see the emu itself. I did see one once, however, in thick scrub, after firing a flare pistol in lieu of the mirror flash on the bulldozer. It suddenly sprang up in a flurry of feathers and raced off into the bush as if pursued by demons. I went to where it had been sitting and found seven still warm eggs. Not having the heart to disturb them, I put a bend in the road especially to by-pass the nest. This is known as Emu Egg Bend, but from an inspection of the eggs next morning I could have saved myself the trouble. They were still there, but had not been revisited by the mother [Beadell later learned the male emu tends the eggs] and were white with frost and just as cold . . . We had better luck with another mother bird and her nest of eggs. They had been in a small bush complete with the little bird still sitting, but when the noise of the bulldozer grew louder she became frightened and flew away. Her particular selection for a home was in a sand saddle narrow enough for only the road, so we carefully dug up the whole bush, nest and all, and replanted it half-way up the sandhill. As we passed along the road next day, we noticed, to our delight and satisfaction at our house-removal system, that the mother was chirping from her nest as if nothing had happened.

Deviations were also necessary in order to preserve Aboriginal sites, which could be found in the most unexpected places. In open country the road ran as straight as possible, in hilly country or among dunes it followed the easiest terrain. Where possible, Beadell also deviated slightly to take in sites of interest along the way, to provide some relief for motorists during what could be hours of driving through monotonous sandhill country.

The first leg of the Gunbarrel, completed in 1956, ran 600 kilometres from the cattle station Victory Downs, near Kulgera (on the main road to Alice Springs), to the site of the meteorological station that was to be established in the Rawlinsons once the road was built. Appropriately, the station was named Giles. Writing in 1967, when Aboriginal people were only just being formally recognised as Australian citizens, Beadell reflected on what had been achieved and what had been lost:

> It had taken months to make the road, and now the same trip could be done in hours . . . For the first time I had some misgivings about being involved – a fleeting insight into the feelings the Aboriginals must have had when they saw the first white settlers arriving in ships they were powerless to stop, trespassing on waters that had been theirs for centuries. Projects such as this, however, must keep abreast of progress, and many share in the ultimate benefits. Even the Aboriginals, as in a case when a Flying Doctor plane, on a mercy trip to a member of a tribe, flew around instead of through a storm, which was located and radioed through by the Giles Meteorological Station.

Beadell also had misgivings about the second leg of the road, built in 1958, for here the Gunbarrel traversed the feared desert that had claimed the life of Alfred Gibson eighty-four years earlier. In March 1958 Beadell was involved in a solo reconnaissance trip of nearly 300 kilometres. He was searching for trig station (survey marker) sites along the centreline of this part of the Woomera Range, from Giles to an Aboriginal mission at Warburton, well to the south-west. It may have been the end of the summer, but as Giles and Gibson had found when they travelled in the area during April 1874, the heat could still be murderous. However, the space race and the arms race weren't going to wait a month or more just so Beadell could travel in cooler weather.

Beadell was already well aware of the hazards of reconnaissance trips through the trackless regions of Central Australia. On a previous expedition, having broken an axle, even his skills as a bush mechanic couldn't help him. Fortunately, he'd been able to summon help on the radio, though it took three weeks for the rescue party to reach him, in the middle of an area without human habitation for 500 kilometres in any direction. By the time the rescue party arrived, they'd thought up a greeting to rival Stanley's 'Dr Livingstone, I presume'. They asked, 'Excuse us, but do you know of anyone around here who needs help?'

For his 1958 reconnaissance trip, Beadell's route started by following that taken by Giles and Gibson, along the edge of the Rawlinsons to the west, then skirting Lake Christopher (a salt lake) before pushing on into the seemingly endless dunes and spinifex. Forced to close the windows of his Land Rover to keep the scrub out of the vehicle, by noon on his first day he found the mercury in his temperature gauge was pinned to the top of the tube, which meant he was driving in temperatures over 53 degrees Centigrade. He was already feeling parched with thirst, but knew (as Giles had done) that he had to remain disciplined about his water consumption or it wouldn't last throughout the journey. Then he got a flat tyre.

> The sun was unbearable and the scrub offered no shade at all, but it was almost a relief to be temporarily out of that inferno of a cabin. Although the tools were under the vehicle, they were soon too hot to handle, as the ground temperature was even worse than that inside the cabin. After one of the spare wheels was in place and the tools were put away, I had to make a big effort to lift the wheel with the flat tyre on it into the vacant rack, for it had been made hot almost to the point of burning by long, slow contact with the fiery sand. Covered in spinifex

> dust clinging to soaking sweat, and trying to ease the burns from the tyre, I sat on my heels in the small shade cast by the Rover, and thirst finally took over.

From a tin cup he drank water that was almost boiling, before forcing himself back into the vehicle to continue over the dunes. No sooner did he get going than the engine stopped. The petrol in the fuel lines had become so hot that vapour locks in the line were starving the engine of fuel. Beadell had to use some of his precious water to cool the fuel lines – water he would have preferred to drink himself. To do so he had to spray the water from his mouth onto a particular area of the engine. While he was doing that, he received burns to his chest from leaning on the vehicle's mudguard. 'I tried the engine. It fired and I was on my way. Grudgingly taking a doctor's advice, I was wearing a hat on this trip, and I think I would have perished there and then without it.'

By day's end, he had covered some 70 kilometres, less than a quarter of the distance to the mission. Significantly, he hadn't got as far in a day as Giles and Gibson had managed on horseback, their mounts being far better suited to bush-bashing through trackless desert. First, he had to mend his punctured tyres. To save petrol, the tyre was then pumped up by hand. When the work was finished, the heat was still so intense that he had no appetite and fell straight into bed.

The sun rose the next day at around 5 a.m. and Beadell was quickly on his way, taking advantage of the first few hours of the day which were cooler and therefore more bearable. During the morning, he came to the end of the Rawlinsons and the beginning of the Gibson Desert. As he turned south, all he could see ahead were red sand dunes covered in spinifex rolling towards a low range of hills. He wrote of the area:

> As I changed my course towards the hills my thoughts were very much with Gibson who had done the same thing, only he had mistaken these

> hills for the Rawlinson Range. I was within a radius of perhaps 10 miles [16 kilometres] of where he had ultimately lost his life, and I wondered what remains were left after the years of weathering. There would be a compass, revolver, and the metal parts of a horse's harness buried under the sand drifts, but even with the information about the tragedy extracted from Giles's diary they would be impossible to find.

Into the afternoon's furious heat he drove, parched with thirst, vaguely aware of not having eaten for two days. The vehicle fought its way over the dunes until it reached the low hills, one of which Beadell climbed to search for more high ground that might be suitable for a trig station. There was nothing but endless sandhills and mulga stretching to the horizon. The only hope was an area far to the south-west, his direction of travel, that looked like open spinifex without the sand dunes that were so punishing for his vehicle.

He took a compass bearing to the area and started down from the hill. When he returned to the vehicle, 'I noticed that the iron nails in my boots had loosened with the intense heat and the steel heels had fallen off.'

He also had another flat. After he'd repaired it he continued on, only to find the sandhills even bigger than before. Some required up to a dozen attempts before he was able to cross them. Others forced him into long detours. The engine failed repeatedly as the fuel vaporised. Worse, he realised that there was no turning back as he'd slid down the backs of some of the dunes with no hope of return. And then:

> During one enforced spell I opened the [radio] transmitter box and found to my dismay that in the intense heat of the cabin some plastic parts on the instrument panel had withered to half their size and dropped out of their sockets. The packing around other dials had melted, causing the glass covering to drop on to the needles so that they couldn't be tuned, and I began to wonder what havoc would be found

> behind the instrument panel and if the transmitter could still operate at all. I decided not even to try until it was needed.

Weakened from lack of food and suffering dehydration in the unrelenting heat, he drove into the second afternoon, and had yet another flat tyre. Then the engine lost power. In the middle of the desert, a major fault could be fatal, especially if the molten remains of the radio couldn't be used to call for help. As dusk fell, Beadell peered into the engine bay hoping to trace the fault. Suddenly, there was a shower of sparks. It was spectacular, but it gave away where the problem lay. It was a simple matter, a cracked spark plug that he easily fixed.

Having battled sand dunes all day, Beadell suspected he'd been driven off his course towards the open spinifex, and decided to get a fix on his position using the stars. He set up his theodolite, only to find that he was so weak that he couldn't stand at the instrument for more than short periods at a time. Nevertheless, he persisted until the job was done. What he found was depressing. His speedometer indicated he had travelled some 40 kilometres that day, yet his astrofix showed he'd covered a mere 25 kilometres in the direction he wanted to go. At that rate there was a good chance he was going to run out of water or fuel before he reached the mission. Yet there was no turning back. He managed to eat a small tin of meat and drink a mug of water before falling asleep.

Dawn of the third day. 'When I opened my eyes next morning I saw without even having to move my head the dismal sight of a tyre that had gradually gone down overnight.' For a moment he thought it was a bad dream, then the realisation of where he was came back to him and he knew his first job of the day was to change a tyre. Then he ate a 'pelican's breakfast' (a drink and a look around) and set off to take advantage of the cool morning air.

All morning he flogged over the sandhills, but in the afternoon he finally reached the open spinifex. For the first time he was able to travel more easily, in the direction of the mission, still over 100 kilometres distant. By late afternoon he had made about 60 kilometres for the day. However, now he found himself having to force his way through the narrow belts of extremely thick mulga that sprang up in every slight depression that ran through the parched country. He was sometimes forced to hack his way through – the mulga retaliating by puncturing tyres with sharp stakes broken off by his passage. The temperature was around 48 degrees Celsius, but there was some relief in being able to open the vehicle's windows between mulga belts.

Then, another flat: 'I got my third flat tyre for the day after coming out of a hundred-yard wall of scrub, far enough away to be unable to return to the shade of a tree and not near enough to the next. This necessitated mending the whole three on a completely barren flat with no protection at all from the blistering sun.'

A sip of water did little to help his condition and 'by nightfall the violent ache across my eyes and a feverish feeling of weakness prevented me from being able to stand up unaided; after pulling up for the night I fell asleep over the steering wheel. When I woke just before midnight, the temperature had dropped to 100 degrees [38 degrees Celsius].'

Day four saw Beadell making good ground, although the vehicle was using a lot of water. He had to deal with vapour locks, and the radiator was overheating as it became clogged with pieces of spinifex. In an effort to keep the engine's temperature down, he frequently used a length of wire to clean out the core. He was also going through spark plugs, and the fanbelt looked like it was on its last legs. The wear and tear bore testament to the punishing terrain and heat.

Then came disaster. During the afternoon, when he opened the tap on his vehicle's water tank, there was only a thin trickle. He needed water to cure a vapour lock, but there wasn't enough even for that. To get what little water was left, he had to jack up the front of the vehicle to send the remaining water in the tank towards the tap. He got what he needed, but now his situation was desperate. If he didn't reach the mission soon, he'd never reach it at all.

Beadell decided his best chance was to keep going after nightfall, when the cooler air would be easier on the vehicle. He'd steer by the stars. But that plan was thwarted when he got caught in a large patch of boulders and could go no further. He stopped for the night, but was up again before dawn, preparing to set out once more. Survey work was no longer in his mind. It was now just a matter of getting out alive. Moreover, he was down to his last tank of petrol.

Beadell battled on, now stalked by thirst and the falling petrol gauge. It was while negotiating a tricky gully that his bush skills gave him the hint of a chance for survival:

> As the vehicle laboured over the boulders towards the water-worn gutters in the folds of the hill, I was increasingly aware of some freshly made marks in the red clay between the rocks that could have been cut by trickling water. At this stage the vehicle was straddling a narrow water-worn gully where one slip would have put one pair of wheels into the gutter for good, so I couldn't relax for a moment.
>
> It was not until I had cleared the worst part that I was able to examine the story written in the ground of a quite recent fall of rain. Determined to follow this evidence to its conclusion, even if it meant going on foot, I managed to persuade the vehicle to clear the last of the rocks and allow me to follow the logical course of the water. It was at the extreme point of a sharp angle, where the creek bed almost doubled back on itself a quarter of a mile [400 metres] further on, that I eventually came upon one of the most valuable finds I had ever made. The evidence of water had been strong, but it was not until I discovered this pool of water, which was several feet in diameter and a few inches deep, that I dared allow myself to grow too elated.
>
> I had been tempted to cut across the sharp corner instead of following the creek bed around, but previous experiences again came to

> the rescue. I have usually found that water mills about at the bends, cutting a hole for itself, and the sharper the bend, the larger the hole. It was fortunate that I did investigate this bend, for it turned out that there was not another drop of water throughout the length of the watercourse. I felt sure that some unseen hand had guided me to this place.

There was enough for him to drink deeply, and to replenish his vehicle. He filled the water tank, the radiator and the battery. He washed out the cabin and washed himself. He took photographs of the site, and then reluctantly drove away, though he also hoped he would never see the place again.

Beadell camped early that night, mended his tyres and went to bed. The next day would decide his immediate fate, as he had only enough fuel to last the day. He had to find the mission. At midday he decided to do a sun observation to check his position and the bearing to the mission. He estimated he was within 30 kilometres, provided it was where he thought it was. Then:

> As I drove to the top of a rise, a small mountain range came into view with flat country covered by dense mulga scrub sweeping away to the western horizon. Making now for the foothills of the range as the only possible site for a settlement of any kind, I came upon native footprints, and when I saw wheel tracks I knew this nightmare was over.

When he arrived, he had just 27 litres of fuel left. He had travelled a total of 480 kilometres in order to cover 320 kilometres as the extremely thirsty crow flies. Now all that was needed was to build the road itself, then tackle the remaining 500 kilometres of the Gunbarrel.

Despite the difficult terrain and often life-sapping heat, all this was eventually done. Along the way, one of the trig sites was named in Beadell's honour. Its namesake wrote of 527-metre Mount Beadell:

> Under one red rocky bluff we decided to use as a survey station we found some small caves, on the walls of which were Aboriginal ochre finger painting, consisting of crude circles and zigzag lines, giving us definite proof that this region had once been inhabited. When we climbed the short distance to the summit further proof was to be found. A small rock hole contained about a gallon [4.5 litres] of water from some recent shower; not unusual in itself, but the aperture of the hole had been 'stoppered' against evaporation, and use by animals, with a well-fitting round boulder uncommon to the geological pattern at the top of the hill. This was certainly remote country, so remote in fact that it was in the Zone A taxation concession area, but nomad natives had known about it first.

By 1958, with the completion of the Gunbarrel Highway, the Gunbarrel Road Construction Party had developed into a highly efficient unit that was capable of building a phenomenal 8 to 10 kilometres of road a day, six days a week, on two five-month expeditions a year, through heat, flies and the ubiquitous sand dunes. They were able to handle breakdowns in the bush with extraordinary ingenuity, as when the transmission fell out of the supply truck, and Frank Quinn simply unbolted the front bumper, bolted it under the chassis to hold the transmission in place, and kept going. On other occasion a mulga stake punctured the radiator, so he used a couple of hoses to reroute the coolant through a large water tank in the back of his truck, and kept going.

Remote as the areas where the roads were built were, and though well able to snatch away human life (as Beadell had almost found), this harsh country didn't stop him taking his family along on occasion. Beadell and wife Anne's discussion of an outback trip (quoted in his biography, *A Lifetime in the Bush* – extract reproduced by kind permission of Mark Shephard) mirrors John Ross's interview with Overland Telegraph expedition member Alfred Giles in Chapter 3. Anne recalled that during their courtship: 'I became fascinated with his life and asked if I could go on a trip with him. He said, "Wee-yall, can you make an apple pie?" I assured him I could. When, in my naivety, I asked him what he did in the evenings in those long months away from civilisation, he replied: "Oh, I do my tapestry!"'

The couple were married in 1961; the first of three children was born later the same year. Beadell ended up taking them all outback on his trips. Rather than perish, his family look back on their trips as being among the greatest experiences of their lives. They weren't alone. In *A Lifetime in the Bush* dozer-driver Doug Stoneham said of his many five-month trips 'to nowhere': 'I loved every minute of it . . . As Len always told us, we were making the maps obsolete on a daily basis, and creating our own piece of history. And when we were finished, everyone would follow in the tracks which we had made.'

They continue to do so today, some on tours assisted by Anne Beadell and daughter Connie. Some of the roads have fallen into disuse, or been bypassed by shorter routes, or have restricted access as they cross what is now designated Aboriginal land, but their legacy remains considerable. Aboriginal communities, in particular, find it much easier to travel the Central Deserts, accessing services and other remote communities, thanks to Beadell and his men.

In recognition of Beadell's achievement, he was awarded the British Empire Medal in 1959. In 1989 he received the Order of Australia. In 1987, Beadell's Asteroid was named in his honour by American astronomers Eugene and Carolyn Shoemaker, both having used his roads to gain access to meteorite craters in Central Australia. In 1997, Beadell's Mallee was named in his honour, in recognition of the fact that it was first located near one of his roads.

After the road building ended in 1963, Beadell continued working for the Woomera defence establishment, despite repeated bouts of ill-health that may have been exacerbated by the punishment he had endured over decades in a variety of harsh climates. And like many of the bushies in this volume, he started to write. His seven books, mostly about his road-building adventures, were hugely successful and remain in print today. He was also a brilliant illustrator whose sketches fill his books, and have since become collector's items. He also lectured widely over many years until his death, from a heart condition, in 1995. Typically, those lectures were both highly informative and full of humour, as he recounted the details of what was to him the adventure of a lifetime. From *A Lifetime in the Bush*:

> I was standing around a campfire 30 years ago on a freezing July night in the desert. I casually asked the fellow alongside me if there was anything wrong or whether something was troubling him.
>
> He said: 'No, why should you think that?'
>
> I replied: 'It's just that you haven't said anything to anyone since February.'
>
> He stated: 'Well I haven't got anything to say, have you?'
>
> I said: 'Oh no, I don't suppose so.' And I left it at that until October and then I asked him: 'Are you sure there's nothing wrong?'
>
> He said: 'You're always picking on me!'

Steve Jefferys on Ammo
(Photo courtesy Nicole Emanuel)

EPILOGUE:
AND THE WINNER IS . . .,
2000: Steve Jefferys
(1956–)

First impressions are everything. Experts on public performance are fond of noting that most audiences pass judgement within the first seven seconds. So there was a lot riding on the first few seconds of the Sydney 2000 Olympic Games' Opening Ceremony. The whole world would be watching, and that crucial first impression would set the tone for everything that would follow that night and for the ensuing days of the Olympics.

What could possibly convey a uniquely Australian image that would be instantly recognisable in all of the countries of the world, where an audience of millions was tuning in? Was such an image even possible? It was one of the toughest calls in show business, and there were no second chances. It had to be big. It had to grab the world's attention. It had to be perfect.

Unfortunately, just one month before that pivotal moment, amid final preparations for an event that was costing millions of dollars and drawing thousands of athletes and spectators from around the globe, the Olympic Opening Ceremony organisers didn't have a thing. Yet the show had to go on. So, on 15 September 2000, Sydney Olympic Stadium darkened as giant screens around the packed arena started the final countdown . . .

Of course, there'd been a plan. For more than two years prior to the Opening Ceremony, the organisers had been assembling a cast of thousands, supported by hundreds of technicians, to stage half a dozen distinct segments that conveyed the heritage and identity of host nation Australia.

One segment was a tribute to our bush heroes, the horses and riders, stockmen and women, whose courage, resourcefulness and endurance have been amply demonstrated in the preceding chapters of this book. Helping bring that segment together was a down-to-earth horse trainer named Steve Jefferys.

Born in 1956, Jefferys grew up in the semi-rural Sydney district around Terrey Hills, where he'd developed an interest in horses from the age of twelve. On a trip to a relative's property near Guyra, in central-western New South Wales, he'd found he could get on a horse and get it to do what he wanted. Back home, he was soon visiting the 'ranch' run by singer and bushman Smokey Dawson, learning to ride on weekends and doing odd jobs.

When he left school, he worked for a short time for the great horseman John Pinnell, who taught him how to break in horses. Then he went to work at Randwick, for horseman John Drennan, breaking horses for trainer Tommy Smith. Eventually, his horsemanship took him around the world, transporting racehorses. It was a great life, and one that required plenty of skill, especially in loading nervous thoroughbreds on cargo planes.

'You put them in a square box with an open lid,' Jefferys said in an interview with the author:

> They go up in a giant forklift, you've got nothing to stop them from jumping out except you standing on the front of this crate talking them out of getting excited. You do it by taking their focus off what's happening. You literally get a hold of him and say, 'Now listen, you know. You're okay.' While he's worried about things, he focuses on you. Horses pick up the emotion and the control or psych from the human. If you're calm and very settled about the way you deal with a situation, the horse feels that.

Jefferys eventually went to the United States to work with Ron Kellum, who'd come to Australia demonstrating American methods of horse training:

> I didn't realise when I went to work for him that he was working for Sam Wilson. Sam was a great American horseman – typical Texan, short hair, tall, big hat. Very powerful man. And I learnt a lot off Sam. He was actually the president of the United States Cutting Horse Association and a great horse trainer. I was learning to train cutting horses. They work like a sheepdog, where they basically are trained to work a cow without seemingly visual control of the rider. We put a cow up one end of a yard, all his mates are down the other, and the horse is in the middle. So the cow is trying to get back and the horse blocks it, basically blocks the cow from getting back and the rider sits with a loose rein. They're unbelievable athletes.

Jefferys worked in the USA for three years before returning to Australia in the early 1980s, still only in his twenties. He next went to work for News Limited's Rupert Murdoch and Ken Cowley, at Murdoch's property near Yass. He broke in horses that were part of a breeding program the two men were trying to establish. Unfortunately, Jefferys knew more about horses than he did about business. One day Murdoch asked when they'd start making money. Jefferys replied: 'Well, I don't think we're going to make a lot.'

He felt things change almost immediately. Jefferys regards as the biggest mistake of his life his mishandling of the opportunity with News Limited and Rupert Murdoch. 'They were people that recognised talent, and that's why I suppose I was there. They could have made me or broken me, and I broke myself in that I was honest with the man.'

Jefferys returned to Sydney, where he eventually married and got a job in, of all things, dry-cleaning. He'd found that the results he was getting in the horse business weren't reflecting the effort involved. He was putting in a lot of time and not achieving what he wanted to achieve. He eventually bought one of the longest established dry-cleaning businesses in Sydney's northern beaches. He hung up his reins, seemingly for good.

In his spare time he also started refereeing touch football, eventually officiating touch football test matches and the first 'State of Origin', and conducting training clinics for referees. He may have been attracted to horses because it was something he was good at, but it was becoming clear that, in many things he did, he wasn't satisfied with second best. However, it was the end of his marriage in 1994, when he was thirty-eight, that left him questioning his future and set him on course for the greatest test of his life.

'Almost instantly I felt like going back to horses,' he recalls. 'Divorce is a very emotional and traumatic situation and I suddenly was on my own and horses were something I was good at. I felt a need to do it again. I don't know if it was that I knew through horses

I could impress people with what I did. I don't know the complete logic behind it.'

He also rang one of the girls he'd known at Smokey Dawson's ranch, Sandy Langsford, who'd gone on to become one of the first women in the New South Wales Mounted Police, breaking in horses and training them for police work, and teaching other constables how to ride.

'I'm interested in getting back into the horse business,' he told her.

She said, 'I've got this horse I want broken in.'

When he'd turned his back on horses, Jefferys had kept all his gear. Soon he and Langsford had set up in the horse business together, teaching and attending competitions in dressage and stockhorse events, especially with a smart young stallion named Jamieson. It was at an event in Grafton that Jefferys bumped into another old friend from his Smokey Dawson days, horse master Tony Jablonski. Jefferys recalls:

> I said, 'I'm back into the horses,' and he said, 'Well, I'd like you to help me do this project.' And that was two years out from the Olympics. And it was all confidential in those days, it was almost just an idea, it wasn't even really going to happen. He wanted me to help him find the horses, horsemen. I was the Sydney person and he was in Queensland, so I did all the work with SOCOG (the Games organisers) at the stadium.

While maintaining close secrecy about exactly what they were doing, they started advertising for riders who wanted to be in 'Olympic celebrations'. When people turned up for trials, they were asked to sign a secrecy agreement. Then they were told that the celebration was actually a segment in the Opening Ceremony, based on that icon of the bush: The Man from Snowy River. Says Jefferys, 'We had to find people who were not necessarily great riders; what was more important was that they were calm and able to methodically handle situations to give their horse confidence. The pressure we were going to put those horses under, the environment we were putting them into, was certainly not one for the average horse or horseman.'

The initial plan devised by Opening Ceremony artistic director David Atkins and segment designer Ignatius Jones called for 200 horses and riders. However, when the horsemen measured the space available, they realised this was far too many. Gradually the number was reduced until they settled on 120 horses and riders who would perform a number of choreographed moves en masse.

By this time, Jefferys and Langsford had moved in together, and were building a home around their stables up in Ingleside, a suburb adjoining Terrey Hills:

> As this place was actually being built, we sat up there with Ignatius Jones on some gyprock and drew up some diagrams of what we thought would be the choreographing. We came up with a pattern that we thought would work and then that was given to [the troop's drill leader, Senior Sergeant] Don Eyb who was from the Mounted Police and had done a lot of musical choreographing of rides. He finetuned what we had done to make it work.

As the plan was refined, so were the riders:

> We were rehearsing them to ride in military sections, where a lot of these guys were cow cockies that came from the bush, never ridden with another horse alongside them in their life. Others were dressage riders that were very used to that sort of thing. We had pony club kids, we had people seventy years old, and from all walks of life, and they all had to learn to ride and work these formations.

At this point, Jefferys was training one of the five groups of riders who were going to form their mounts into the Olympic rings. They included his partner, Sandy Langsford. Meanwhile, the night of the Opening Ceremony was fast approaching.

Two months before the ceremony, two 'boot camps' were held for the riders, at Scone, north-west of Sydney. It was at these three-day-weekend sessions that the finishing touches were put on the segment. It was also at the second boot camp, in July 2000, that the stakes were raised considerably. As Jefferys recalls:

> There'd been talk of different things at the very opening. At the July boot camp the guys from SOCOG were there. They said, 'You guys are going to open the Olympic Games.'
>
> That was the first that we knew it was actually the opening segment. It was exciting. At that stage, I wasn't even riding. I wasn't really fussed about riding. I was just happy to help pull it together and make it happen.

The organisers realised that the horsemen were perfect for the image of Australia they wanted to convey. The Australian bush hero, the stockman, was a figure all Australians could identify with, and the rest of the world recognised it as well. Yet they still needed that initial impact. Says Jefferys, 'They had ideas of several horses coming in fast, and they canned all those. They wanted something out there that was going to take everyone's attention while all these horses suddenly appeared. They decided they were gonna have a rearing horse.'

The organisers even had the horse that was going to do it. Tony Jablonski had a horse and rider up in Queensland that he'd used in various movies. The notion, however, interested Jefferys. 'I thought at the time, "Gee, I wouldn't mind riding that horse. That'd be all right".'

It was when the Opening Ceremony organisers flew to Queensland to check on their rearing horse that things started to go wrong. They commented that when the horse reared 'he had stretch marks on his belly'. It was nothing like what they wanted. Worse still, it left them with a terrible gaping hole at the head of their program. So, a month before the Opening Ceremony was due to take place, Ignatius Jones rang Steve Jefferys.

'Have you got a horse that can do this job?' he asked.

The organisers assumed that Jefferys would put forward his magnificent stallion, Jamieson. He was the kind of animal they had in mind, 'black and wild looking'. He'd also been taught to rear on command, but not with Jefferys in the saddle. However, Jamieson was already committed. He was in quarantine because he was going to be part of the entertainment at the Olympic Equestrian Centre, mixing with horses from all over the world.

Jefferys was as honest with Jones as he'd been with Rupert Murdoch. 'It's too risky,' he told the man who, at the time, had no attention-grabbing opening for the greatest show on earth. 'The risk of getting a horse to rear up under that sort of pressure at that instant is pie in the sky. The chances of it happening are so remote, it's not worth having.'

Once again, Jefferys was being offered a chance of a lifetime. Once again, he was talking himself out of it. 'I was afraid of failure,' he explains. 'That's why I said to them, don't do it. I didn't want to be involved in something where other horsemen would say: "Did you see Steve Jefferys trying to get that horse to rear up and it didn't work?"'

He had a point, and Jones accepted it. However, Jefferys soon heard that Jones was asking around, trying to find anyone who had a horse that could rear. With three weeks to go, things had reached the stage where what was needed was someone who could show some of that legendary bush spirit and resourcefulness, someone who was prepared to step forward in a tight situation. Or as Jefferys said to his partner, 'Well, if they're going to do it, I may as well do it.'

He rang Jones and said, 'We've got a horse here that has never reared, but I think he probably could. Give me a week and I'll let you know how he's going.'

Then he and Langsford went down to the arena where they had a horse named Ammo. 'An obnoxious character,' is how Jefferys describes him:

> He's what you call a rig, which means he's never been castrated properly. So he thinks he's a stallion even though he's classified as a gelding.
>
> He didn't care about anyone. He was easily distracted; you'd go out somewhere and he'd look over here and look over there. But because he was strong and didn't like being bossed around, I just thought, 'Well, let's see what happens.'
>
> So we went down here and I said to Sandy, 'You just tap him on the feet.' That's one way to put them under pressure, which is maintained until they give you the correct answer, and you reward them when they do. He went up a little bit and we shoved a carrot in his mouth. And he thought, 'Oh, this is all right.' So he said, 'If that gets me a carrot, try this!' And he almost instantly started rearing.

The two horse trainers were delighted, but Jefferys was still cautious. It was one thing to get a horse to rear in his own arena, quite another to get it to happen in an Olympic Stadium before 100 000 people. So it wasn't until two days later that he rang Ignatius Jones and said, 'Things are going okay. This horse might make it.'

Three days later, he rang again and said, 'Iggy, you can come and have a look at him. He's going all right.'

Jefferys recalls the visit of the folk from SOCOG: 'I set out a video and we ran him at the video camera and reared him up, and they were ecstatic. They were saying, "This is fantastic! He's the horse!"'

After they'd left, Jefferys confided in Langsford. 'That's a lot of crap. They've got other horses that they've got in mind for this.'

Meanwhile, he continued working with Ammo. Jefferys, the perfectionist, knew the horse had a long way to go: 'He would come in and rear four times out of five, and that wasn't good enough. If number five came up on the day, I'd be in big trouble.'

He also needed the rear to be spectacular, wild and big. That was part of the reason the Queensland horse had been excluded. So the schooling continued. And all too soon there were only ten days before the Opening Ceremony.

Then came another boot camp. Was there another horse? Or were Jefferys and Ammo going to open the Olympics? Of more concern to Jefferys was the fact that Ammo was tiring. He wasn't used to all the work and his rears were becoming intermittent. Jefferys was so concerned he turned to one of the other riders at boot camp, John Pinnell, the man who'd taught him to break in horses more than twenty years earlier. The Olympics were such a big thing for Pinnell that he'd come out of retirement just to ride.

'I've got a problem,' Jefferys told him. 'This horse is starting to back off a bit.'

Pinnell worked with Jefferys to get the horse rearing again, but he also worked on giving Jefferys confidence. He kept telling him it was going to be okay.

'And the big thing was there was no other horse there,' Jefferys recalls. 'There was no backup. I still hadn't seen the other horse and I said to Sandy, "These guys are mad. There's no other horse here and he should be here because if they're going to call him in at the last minute his horse won't be used to what's happening".'

By then, though, they were going into the stadium every night for rehearsals. A convoy of vehicles would leave Castle Hill Showground at 7 p.m., pass slowly through the enormous security operation screening the ceremony's preparations, and then, around midnight, the rehearsals would begin. Jefferys recalls:

> I'd go in each night and he was going pretty good. He did some good stuff and one night he got up, and he stood there, and it felt like an eternity. And the SOCOG people go, 'That's it! That's what we want!'
>
> They were so excited, they wanted it all the time. They'd make him run out and I said, 'Look if you keep doing this, it's not going to work. He's going to get sick of it; he's going to get tired. You can't do this to a horse.'
>
> And they said, 'But we need it for the timing.'
>
> So we compromised. We didn't run him every time and the unique thing with horses is they're very quick to work out repetition. They know what you're doing and they get faster and harder and they anticipate things. So I wanted to take him to different places on the arena and not let him know that that was the only place that he was going. I wanted to mix it up. Sometimes rear him, sometimes not. So we started doing that.

Jefferys still wasn't confident that he was going to launch the Opening Ceremony, even as they rehearsed doing that very thing. He was convinced that, if it wasn't working, his entry would be dropped at the last minute. They couldn't have a horse ride out before a world audience of millions and look stupid.

'I wasn't convinced until the first dress rehearsal,' he recalls. 'The first dress rehearsal we went out and I said to Sandy, "We're going to do this. We're going to open the Olympic Games."'

Throughout those tense days, Jefferys lost a lot of weight. While in boot camp with several hundred people, all of them living on top of each other, he'd also caught the flu. It got to the stage where most of the riders were sick, exhausted by the 9 a.m. starts and 3 a.m. finishes.

One night the horsemen said to the organisers, 'We don't have enough healthy riders to do this. We can't rehearse tonight.'

'They can ride sick,' was the answer. 'It's gotta happen. We need the timing.'

The horsemen said, 'We'll send eighty horses.'

The organisers said, 'No, we've gotta have 120 horses.'

Adding to the pressure for Jefferys was the tension created by having 140 people (including twenty reserves) of whom only 120 would get to ride. Whenever anything went wrong, people became afraid they would be dropped. Not surprisingly, Jefferys started losing sleep:

> I'd wake up at night and I'd have nightmares. One was the horse standing on the whip. Simply that he wouldn't go up. Things like not stopping square. How to hold the whip. How would I hold the reins so there was no chance of not stopping him? And then my hat blowing off. How would I stick the hat on so it wouldn't come off?
>
> Originally I was just going to rear the horse up. Then they said, 'You're going to crack the whip.'
>
> And I just thought they'll have a mechanical sound and they'll cue it. 'No, you can't do that because it won't look right. You've got to do it.'
>
> So they microphoned up the horse. All these blokes, all cow cockies, they all came around giving me their whips to try. I'm standing up on this 44-gallon drum, trying all these whips because I wanted to get the whip that would sound the best. So we came down with this whip, a young boy's whip it was. Little things that normally you wouldn't care about, but you only had one shot at this and everything had to be right.

Finally, the moment arrived. Weak from the flu, sleep-deprived and considerably thinner than he'd been ten days earlier, Jefferys mounted Ammo and prepared to open the 2000 Olympic Games:

> I'd done quite a bit of public performance and worked horses under pressure, so I wasn't really nervous as such. The whole time it was a job and I didn't really get nervous until I heard John Williamson start 'Waltzing Matilda' and I heard the crowd. Up till then I had time to talk myself out of it. I'm quite controlled in doing that, to overcome that through

mind over matter. I was sick on the night, but it's funny how adrenalin gives you the power to do something that you think you can't do. Because by then I was concerned about stopping Ammo. He was getting so powerful it was going to take a lot of strength to control him.

I really thought, 'We're getting close.' That was the start of the real thing. I was thinking, 'This is really going to happen.' And the horse gets excited if you get excited. I must have started to transmit some sort of excitement. He was agitated. He knew, because he'd done it so many times, he was going out and he was getting excited and started to run backwards in the entrance. And I'm thinking, 'The countdown's going to start and there's horses piled up behind me waiting to come out.' And I'm trying to settle him down and get him under control because I'm waiting for this girl to give me the signal. It was a lot happening in a short space of time.

I had some people to feed him, to keep his mind off what was happening, and I'm on the horse and I kept shuffling the whip around. I had all this stuff. 'Okay, that's right, that's right, the hand's in the right place on the reins.' This is the way I was thinking the whole time.

[Then came the signal.]

I blanked out from looking at anything. It was an image of noise and flashes and all I was focusing on was what I had to do. There could have been a kangaroo sat beside me; I wouldn't have seen it. I was that focused on doing the job. He was unbelievably strong. He was just so on fire, which was the look they wanted, they wanted this wild image coming out. He came out at a million miles an hour, jumped up because there was a lip up onto the arena. He flew up and I'm thinking, 'This thing's not going to stop', and I'm really working overtime at making it get to the middle. It was an immense amount of energy going into making this few seconds happen. I'm talking to myself as I went out, 'Stop, drop the whip, crack the whip', and I was really oblivious to anything.

And he knew once he'd stopped that the next thing was to rear; he'd done it so many times. He had so much energy coming out that the

> chances of him not rearing at that stage weren't real high. He was pretty pumped up, like I was. And he ran in, I cued him for the rear. He went up once. Then he went up again, and the second one was a good one.

As the television images and thousands of photos taken at that moment still show, the rear was huge. The massive black animal was power incarnate, an expression of the ultimate in horsemanship. And on his back The Man from Snowy River had come alive to welcome the world to Sydney. The stadium was filled with camera flash, the world's attention was gripped by the Olympics from that moment, and it was held until the Closing Ceremony sixteen days later.

The organisers had done it – they'd found the image that identified Australia to the world. They'd brought Australia's bush legend to life. While attention was focused on Steve Jefferys and Ammo, the stadium filled with 120 other riders, and the Olympics had begun.

Back in the tunnel leading into the arena, Jefferys somehow managed to get the mighty Ammo to stop without trampling the countless other performers waiting to go out for their segments. Appropriately, those segments included strong indigenous elements that recognised and honoured, as many of the bushies in this book have done, the traditional owners of the country. Meanwhile, Jefferys was coming back down to earth:

> The minute I was inside that tunnel I thought, 'I've done it.' And I could hear the music going and everyone coming in and I tried to get back so I could see into the stadium and watch what they were doing as they came in. I remember the music playing as the other horses were coming in, the sense of pride at that time and the emotion of what these guys were doing. I can feel it now, it was incredible.
>
> The honour wasn't something I was thinking about at that time. It was a great relief. We all realised what we'd done afterwards. We went back and you could see the crowds of people and the excitement that the

> whole Olympics Opening had lit and that we'd started. Lots of people were so taken with that opening segment that when they realised that you were the person that did it, you were an instant celebrity wherever you went. That still happens to some degree today. A lot of elderly people that saw it were extremely emotional; people who were overseas at the time told me later how it made them proud to be Australian.

Jefferys now runs horse-riding clinics around the country. He was also involved in the national tour of 'The Man from Snowy River Arena Spectacular', as were some of his horses. And, as with The Man from Snowy River, people are still telling the story of his ride:

> Even today, we'll be somewhere doing something and they'll say 'You're the guy from the Olympic Games. Mate, when you came out, I was so proud.' And they must have been to come up this much after the event and have that sort of feeling, and want to talk about it. You can imagine how it made those people feel.

Australia has come a long way since the first days of European settlement. Today, it's one of the most urbanised populations on earth, and the reality of existence for most Australians is far removed from the bush. Yet many of us still identify with the world beyond the urban fringe. Walk into a fashionable shopping mall and, among the Italian suits and French couture, you'll find bush outfitters R.M. Williams, the clothing chain established by Sidney Kidman's saddler. Drive down the street and you'll lose count of the four-wheel-drive vehicles that are ready to head down roads surveyed by Len Beadell, on tours led by his wife or children. Go to the horse-riding schools dotted among the hobby farms circling our cities, and people like Steve Jefferys will teach you to ride.

When Jefferys rode out to open the Sydney Olympics in September 2000, it was anything but a solo effort. He carried with him the memories and heritage of every bushie from William Buckley to Harry Redford, from Alfred Canning to Bernard O'Reilly, from Myles Dunphy to Steve Jefferys himself. Before he made his entrance the crowd were united in singing 'Waltzing Matilda', and the character he embodied was The Man from Snowy River. Every one of those people rode with Jefferys that night, and millions more besides. Anyone identifying with the skills, courage and resourcefulness of the people of the Australian bush was in the saddle that night. And Ammo, who now enjoys celebrity status while travelling the country with Jefferys and Langsford, was strong enough to carry us all.

'We still like to have a bit of that wild colonial boy in us,' says Jefferys:

> We think we still are the convict country. Much as we like to think we're sophisticated on the one hand, we like that image, that Man from Snowy River. We like to know those mountains are still there, the wilderness is still there, we've still got people living like that. And we're not that far gone from it. It's still here.

SOURCES

Chapter 1: William Buckley

Anon., 'The Life and Adventures of William Buckley,' *Hobart Town Almanack and Van Diemen's Land Annual*, 1837, pp. 119–20.

Bonwick, James, *William Buckley, the Wild White Man, and His Port Phillip Black Friends*, George Nichols, Melbourne, 1856.

Clarke, Marcus, *For the Term of His Natural Life*, R. Bentley, London, 1875.

Langhorne, G., *Reminiscences of William Buckley . . .*, c. 1838, Manuscripts Collection of the State Library of Victoria (also Newspaper Cuttings, Volume 96, Mitchell Library, pp. 252–4).

Morgan, John and Buckley, William, *The Life and Adventures of William Buckley*, Archibald MacDougall, Hobart, 1852.

Wedge, J.H., 'On the Country around Port Phillip,' *Royal Geographical Society Journal*, Volume 6, London, 1836, pp. 419–20.

Chapter 2: Joseph Hawdon and Charles Bonney

Atkinson, Alan and Aveling, Marian (eds) *Australians 1838*, Fairfax, Syme & Weldon Associates, Sydney, 1987.

Bull, John Wrathall, *Early Experiences of Life in South Australia*, E.S. Wigg & Son, Adelaide, 1884 (facsimile edition, Libraries Board of South Australia – source of Bonney's account).

Carter, Jeff, *In the Tracks of the Cattle*, Angus & Robertson, Sydney, 1968.

Kain, Kevin, *The First Overlanders*, Gould Books, Ridgehaven, South Australia, 1991 (includes transcripts of Joseph Hawdon's 'Journal of a Journey from New South Wales to Adelaide' and Charles Bonney's 'Account of the Hawdon and Bonney Trek with Cattle from New South Wales to Adelaide 1838').

Loyau, George E., *Notable South Australians*, G.E. Loyau, Adelaide, 1885.

www.southaustralianhistory.com.au/royalflying.htm

Chapter 3: John Ross

Anon., 'Obituary', *Adelaide Observer*, 7 February 1903.

Giles, Alfred, *Exploring in the Seventies and Construction of the Overland Telegraph Line*, W.K. Thomas, Adelaide, 1926 (facsimile edition, Friends of the South Australian Library, 1995).

Symes, Major-General G.W., *The Exploration and Development of the Northern Part of South Australia between 1850 and 1869 and the Early Life of John Ross*, Proceedings of Royal Geographical Society, South Australian Branch, 1956–57.

——, *John Ross – a Refutation and a Chronology*, Proceedings of Royal Geographical Society, South Australian Branch, 1957–58.

——, *Exploring in the MacDonnell Ranges, 1870–1872*, Proceedings of Royal Geographical Society, South Australian Branch, 1959–60 (includes references from John Ross's diary).

Taylor, P., *An End to Silence*, Methuen, Sydney, 1980.

Chapter 4: Harry Redford

Adelaide Advertiser, 6 April 1957.

Brisbane Courier, 18 February 1870, 28 February 1870 and undated issues.

Flannery, Tim, *The Explorers*, Text, Melbourne, 1998.
Holthouse, Hector, *Up Rode the Squatter*, Angus & Robertson, Sydney, 1970.
McCarthy, Patrick, *The Man Who Was Starlight*, Allen & Unwin, Sydney, 1987.
Matthews, Rachel, *Queensland v. Henry Redford, 11 February 1873, Trial Re-enactment*, self-published, Roma, 2002.
Walkabout, 1 May 1936.
Warren Herald, 1 June 1901.
Whittaker, Mark and Willessee, Amy, *The Road to Mount Buggery*, Macmillan, Sydney, 2001.

Chapter 5: Jack Riley

Argus, 17 July 1914.
Bulletin, Sydney, 26 April 1890.
Carmody, J., *Early Days of the Upper Murray*, Shoestring Press, Wangaratta, 1981.
Catholic Weekly, 15 May 1952.
Corryong Courier, 23 July 1914, 20 January 1949 and undated issues.
Gough, Noel, *The Man from Snowy River*, Centenary Celebrations Booklet, 1995.
Mitchell, T.W., *Corryong and the Man from Snowy River District*, Wilkinson Printers for R. Boyes, Albury, 1981.
Paterson, A.B., *The Man from Snowy River: Collected Verse of A.B. Paterson*, Angus & Robertson, Sydney, 1921.
——, *Singer of the Bush*, Lansdowne Press, Sydney, 1983.
Riverlander, September 1956, pp. 21–2.
www.manfromsnowyriverbushfestival.com.au

Chapter 6: Samuel Hoffmeister

Bulletin, 1 and 8 September 1894.
Jeffreys, Max, *Australian Shipwrecks: Murder, Mayhem, Fire and Storm*, New Holland, Sydney, 1999.
Magoffin, Richard, *Fair Dinkum Matilda*, Mimosa Press, Charters Towers, 1973.
May, Sydney, *The Story of Waltzing Matilda*, W.R. Smith & Paterson, Brisbane, 1955.
Paterson, A.B., *Three Elephant Power and Other Stories*, Sydney, 1917.
Sydney Morning Herald, 11 February 1939.
Worker, May 1891 and September–December 1894.
www.nla.gov.au/epubs/waltzingmatilda

Chapter 7: Sir Sidney Kidman

Adelaide Observer, 5 September 1903.
All about Australians, Yewen Publishing, Sydney, 1904.
Anon., 'Sackville Kidman Obituary', *Critic*, 8 July 1899.
Anon., 'Sir Sidney Kidman', *Sydney Mail*, 11 September 1935, pp. 10–11.
Anon., 'With the Cattle King: Overland to Norley', *Observer*, various issues, June–August 1928.
Argus, 2, 3 and 5 September 1935.
Bowen, J., *Kidman: The Forgotten King*, Angus & Robertson, Pymble, 1987.
Carter, Jeff, *In the Tracks of the Cattle*, Angus & Robertson, Sydney, 1968.
Idriess, Ion, *The Cattle King*, Angus & Robertson, Sydney, 1936.
Peck, Harry H., *Memoirs of a Stockman*, Stockland Press, North Melbourne, 1942.

Chapter 8: Alfred Canning

Canning, Alfred, *Report to WA Mines Department*, 10 January 1907.
Fyfe, W.T., 'Surveying the Rabbit-Proof Fence: Outline of Explorations and Surveys by the Late Mr A.W. Canning', *Early Days: Journal and Proceedings*, Western Australian Historical Society, Volume 2, October 1939.
Hewitt, David (ed.) *Australian Geographic Book of the Canning Stock Route*, Australian Geographic, Sydney, 1998.
Smith, Eleanor, *The Beckoning West: The Story of H.S. Trotman and the Canning Stock Route*, St George Books, Perth, 1966 (reprinted 1985).

Chapter 9: Daisy Bates

Bates, Daisy, 'From Port Hedland to Carnarvon by Buggy', *Journal of the Department of Agriculture in Western Australia*, July–December 1901, pp. 183–202.

——, 'Ooldea Water', *Royal Geographic Society of Australia – SA Branch Proceedings*, Volume 21, 1919–20, pp. 73–8.
——, 'Quaint Legends', *Argus*, 29 September 1923.
——, 'Our Aborigines: Can They Be Preserved?' *Adelaide Register*, 13 May 1924.
——, *The Passing of the Aborigines: A Lifetime Spent among the Natives of Australia*, London, Murray, 1938.
Hill, Ernestine, *Kabbarli: A Personal Memoir of Daisy Bates*, Angus & Robertson, Sydney, 1973.

Chapter 10: Myles Dunphy

Anon., 'Obituary: Myles Dunphy, Conservationist', *Sydney Morning Herald*, 2 February 1985.
Dunphy, Professor Dexter, 'Occasional Address', 25 September 2001.
Dunphy, Myles, 'First Perambulator to Kanangra Tops', *The Sydney Bushwalker*, No. 334, October 1962, pp. 15–18, and No. 335, November 1962, pp. 10–11.
——, 'The Blue Gum Conservation Campaign', *The Bushwalker*, Volume 2, No. 3, c. 1963, pp. 15–20.
——, 'The Bushwalking Conservation Movement 1914–1965', *Australia's 100 Years of National Parks*, Wendy Goldstein (ed.), National Parks and Wildlife Service, 1979, pp. 54–64.
——, *Selected Writings*, compiled by Patrick Thompson, Ballagrin, Sydney, 1986.
Macqueen, Andrew, *Back from the Brink: Blue Gum Forest and the Grose Wilderness*, self-published, Springwood, NSW, 1997.
Meredith, Peter, *Myles and Milo*, Allen & Unwin, Sydney, 1999.
Redgum (J.C. Lockley), 'A Hundred Acres: Blue Gum Forest', *Sydney Morning Herald*, 19 November 1931.

Chapter 11: Bernard O'Reilly

Anon., '5 Die in Air Crash', *Sydney Mirror*, 3 March 1937, p. 1.
Anon., 'Plane Survivors Taken to Hospital', *Sydney Morning Herald*, 3 March 1937, p. 15.
Anon., 'The Stinson Airliner Tragedy', *Sydney Mail*, 5 March 1937, p. 24.
Anon., 'Stinson Inquest, 27 March 1937', *Daily Telegraph*, 28 March 1937.
Anon., 'Obituary: Sir John Proud', *Sydney Morning Herald*, 15 October 1997, p. 33.
Binstead, Joe and Proud, John, writing in 'Binstead–Proud Entertainment, City Hall, Brisbane, Souvenir Programme', April 1937.
Courier Mail, 24 February, 1, 3 and 4 March 1937.
McDonald, Bruce, *Once Upon a Mountain*, Boolarong Publications, Brisbane, 1988.
——, *Once Again Upon the Mountain: The Story of the Rescue of the Stinson Survivors*, McBenny, Brisbane, 1991.
——, www.stinson-plane-crash.com
O'Reilly, Bernard, *Green Mountains*, Envirobook, Sydney, 1996 (first published 1940).
Proud, John, 'Diary', written on the Stinson's fuselage at Lamington Plateau, 1937.

Chapter 12: Len Beadell

Beadell, L., *Too Long in the Bush*, New Holland, Sydney, 2000 (first published 1965).
Giles, E., *Australia Twice Traversed*, Volume II, London, 1889 (facsimile edition, Libraries Board of South Australia, Adelaide, 1964).
Shephard, M., *A Lifetime in the Bush: The Biography of Len Beadell*, Corkwood Press, North Adelaide, 2000.

ALSO AVAILABLE FROM PENGUIN

SHIPWRECKS

Australia's Greatest Maritime Disasters

Evan McHugh

From the first wreck in 1622 off Western Australia to the tragedy of the 1998 Sydney to Hobart Yacht Race, Evan McHugh captures all the drama of Australia's maritime history. There are swashbuckling mutineers, violent storms, uncharted reefs, enemy warships, as well as ripping yarns about Dutchmen and lascars, Aborigines and escaped convicts.

Shipwrecks is a white-knuckle voyage through chaos and tragedy that proclaims the courage and strength of the human spirit. It is a powerful reminder that even in the twenty-first century the sea remains a great, unconquered frontier.

'A work of considerable research. McHugh has a feel for crashing waves and filthy weather. His re-creation of the 1988 Sydney–Hobart race is fast-paced and gripping.'

THE AUSTRALIAN

'Writer and sailor Evan McHugh presents 13 episodes of maritime disaster and bravery. He does a grand job capturing the drama.'

AGE

'What is surprising is how few wrecks, with all the human tragedy and drama they entailed, have been absorbed into the folk memory of the nation. McHugh attempts to correct our ignorance by telling the stories of each of these misadventures.'

SYDNEY MORNING HERALD

'There are tales of mutineers, warships and escaped convicts. Plenty of reasons not to go down to the sea again.'

DAILY TELEGRAPH

ALSO AVAILABLE FROM PENGUIN

PIECES OF BLUE

Kerry McGinnis

At the age of six, Kerry McGinnis loses her mother. Her father, left with four young children to raise, gathers up the family and leaves the city to go droving. For the next fifteen years, the McGinnis clan travels the continent, droving, horse breaking and living off the land. Kerry grows up in the harsh outback, and the animals that inhabit the land are her closest friends.

With the memory of her absent mother ever present, Kerry begins her difficult journey to young womanhood.

'This is a beautifully written collection of fragments, vivid but tantalising snapshots of McGinnis's life.'

SYDNEY MORNING HERALD

'McGinnis relates the saga of her childhood and her growing up years with verve.'

TOWNSVILLE BULLETIN

'Kerry McGinnis's personal – and personable – story offers insights into an Australia unknown by urbanites. And into the human values and verities that underwrite life there.'

THE AUSTRALIAN

'It is the author's word pictures of the sights, smells and sounds of the bush, and her perceptive rendering of the characters along the way, that make Pieces of Blue *a book to be treasured.'*

SUNSHINE COAST SUNDAY

ALSO AVAILABLE FROM PENGUIN

WISDOM MAN

Banjo Clarke, as told to Camilla Chance

'Life should be looked upon as a sacred thing, to be handled carefully. If something terrible happens, you stop for a while and have a think, and then you work around the next big problem coming up. Like water around a rock. And you still help people when you can, even your worst enemy.'

Some lives, like that of Banjo Clarke, are so special they touch countless others without trying. Banjo was born in the early 1920s in the Framlingham Forest near Warrnambool, Victoria, and by the time he passed away he was known and loved by thousands for his wisdom and kindness. He carried a swag during the Great Depression, fought with Jimmy Sharman's famous boxing troupe, built roads for the army in World War II, and had 67 great-grandchildren. Despite the great hardships he faced in his life, Banjo was renowned for espousing love and forgiveness, sustained by his deep connection to his land, his ancient culture and its spiritual beliefs. His conviction that these could prove the saving of the world was his motivation for telling his story.

'I've met Nelson Mandela, and Banjo Clarke was the same quality of person.'

Keith Hamilton, FORMER VICTORIAN MINISTER FOR ABORIGINAL AFFAIRS

'Banjo Clarke was extraordinary . . . his life was one of forgiving; a life of kindness and a life of love.'

Malcolm Fraser